THE GREEK WAY OF DEATH

THE GREEK WAY
OF DEATH

Robert Garland

Cornell University Press
Ithaca, New York

© 1985 by Robert Garland

First published in 1985 by Cornell University Press.

Library of Congress Cataloging in Publication Data

Garland, Robert.
  The Greek way of death.

  Bibliography: p.
  Includes index.
  1. Greece—Religion. 2. Death—Religious aspects.
I. Title.
BL795.D4G37 1985   292'.23   85-470
ISBN 0-8014-1823-2

Printed in Great Britain

For my parents

Contents

Preface

Freud in his essay 'Das Unheimliche' published in 1919 wrote (p. 241f.): 'There is scarcely any other matter ... upon which our thoughts and feelings have changed so little since the very earliest times, and in which discarded forms have been so completely preserved under a thin disguise, as our relation to death. Two things account for our conservatism: the strength of our original emotional reaction to death and the insufficiency of our scientific knowledge to it.' The opposite view, that in the face of the universal impact of death there exists a diversity of cultural reactions, has lately been emphasised by Huntington and Metcalf (1979, 2), who write: 'In all societies ... the issue of death throws into relief the most important cultural values by which people live their lives and evaluate their experiences. Life becomes transparent against the background of death, and fundamental social and cultural issues are revealed.' If the study of death has undergone a more sensitive appraisal in the sixty odd years since 'Das Unheimliche' was written, Freud is not yet completely ripe for burial. Undeniably there is much in man's reaction to death that is universal and timeless: it is the business of the ethnographer and the historian, more than of the psychologist, to isolate from the subject what is idiosyncratic and unique.

The study of Graeco-Roman burial practices has itself an extensive history which stretches back to the seventeenth century with the publication in 1658 of Sir Thomas Browne's *Hydriotaphia, or Urne-Buriall*. As Humphreys (1980) has recently demonstrated, the preoccupations of researchers over the centuries have constantly mirrored 'the practices, practical concerns and fantasies of the period in which they were written' (p. 97). Hence in the eighteenth century attention was centred on the treatment of the corpse and on the subject of reunion in the afterlife, whereas in the nineteenth century interest came to be focused on the cult of ancestral tombs – a shift of emphasis which reflects modern society's continuously evolving relationship with its own dead. The current fascination with death in

the newly evolving field of thanatology is by no means restricted to
scholarly treatments of the subject by classicists, historians,
ethnographers and social anthropologists. Over the last twenty years
in particular considerable research has gone into the study of the
phenomenology of near-death experiences. The ethics of abortion
have continued to remain a live issue in both medical and
non-medical circles. There is much current controversy about the
definition of death and the use of life-support systems for patients who
have been diagnosed as having undergone brain-stem death. In
addition, modern western society's attitudes to death have come
under close scrutiny in recent years and the not-altogether surprising
conclusion reached that 'the majority of the population lack patterns
or ritual to deal with the crisis inherent in man's biological nature'
(Gorer 1965, 111).

As much as possible this book is about what ordinary Greeks felt
about death and the dead. It is much less to do with what
philosophers and theologians thought and taught about the subject.
The period of study extends from the Geometric to the Classical age,
concentrating primarily on Attika. In a different temporal sense it
covers the period from moribund to cadaver to ossified or calcified
remains. The sources for such a survey are not without their
difficulties, the interpretation of the archaeological data being
especially problematic. *Prima facie*, for instance, we might expect
burial gifts to exhibit a close correlation with conceptions of the
needs of the deceased in the afterlife. So they undoubtedly do – but
not in all cases. To take only a single example: how are we to
interpret the common Greek practice of placing a scraper (*strigil*) in a
young man's grave? Were the dead conceived of as exercising in
some great underworld wrestling-school or *palaistra*? Was a *strigil*
such a personal item, like a woman's mirror and comb, that for this
reason alone it was regarded as best buried with the dead? Or,
finally, was it deposited in the grave in recognition of the deceased's
athletic prowess? Our own mortuary practices are likely to prove
equally baffling to future archaeologists. What, for instance, will
they deduce about twentieth-century beliefs in the afterlife from the
discovery of 'a teddy bear, coats and blankets, collars, favourite toys
and foods in the shape of rubber bones and actual chocolate' which
have been deposited with the dearly departed at Woodlands Private
Animal Cemetery at Burwash in Sussex (Ucko 1969, 265)? Nor can
we assume that the richness or paucity of grave-goods is an accurate
index either of the general level of prosperity in that society or of its

involvement and interest in its own dead, since, as Ucko (p. 266) notes, 'as society becomes richer, so also it becomes more reluctant to "waste" its riches'.

But it is not only the archaeological data that presents difficulties. This study depends largely upon statements made by Homer and the tragedians, whose evidence must be treated with particular caution. Homer, because the ritual cannot be securely dated to any single historical period; and tragedy, because it draws more from hero-cult than from the cult of the ordinary dead. Further on the contentious issue of Homer's usefulness for the study of funerary ritual and belief, though agreeing in principle with Snodgrass' statement that 'no Greek ever witnessed in real life the precise sequence of events narrated in Patroklos' funeral', I am firmly of the opinion that his testimony cannot be ignored. If scholars are unable to agree as to whether it mainly evokes the practices of Geometric, Dark Age or even Bronze Age Greece, this in itself does not invalidate the fact that many of the practices which the poet describes, as well as the basic structure into which they fit, were still current in the Classical and Hellenistic period. In addition, it is worth pointing out that Archaic and Classical epitaphs relied heavily on Homeric eschatological phraseology, a circumstance which indicates that the poems continued to exercise a profound influence and control over popular speculation about the afterlife.

Epitaphs are in fact of limited value to this study since, with some signal exceptions, the majority record little more than the achievements and virtues of the deceased and the sense of loss which he has bequeathed to his relatives. A useful source of information for our understanding of post-burial rites is provided by the large series of fifth-century Attic white-ground *lêkythoi* or oil-flasks. The continuing importance of tomb-cult in the fourth century is indicated by references in the Attic orators suggesting that it was an essential duty of the close kin of the deceased. *Stêlai* (gravestones) tell us next-to-nothing about the world of the dead. Such is our state of ignorance about the climactic moment of a Greek funeral that we do not even know whether the disposal of the body was accompanied by a regular liturgy.

It is the progress of the departed, together with the accompanying reactions of the survivors, that forms the structural basis of this book, as we follow the process by which the deceased finally achieves separation from the world of the living and full integration in the world of the dead. Not only has the deceased to undergo re-habilitation in another society, however; so, also, must the bereaved re-establish group-identity. Separation is a bilateral process requiring vigorous and determined efforts on both sides: as the body must leave the group, so the group must leave the body. My approach is greatly indebted to van Gennep's identification (1909) of the tertiary structure inherent in all rites of passage whose aim is to achieve separation from one status and re-integration in the next by an intervening period of liminality. I also owe much to Hertz's study of secondary burial, and in particular to his insight that the pollution of death is not a reflection of a hygienic rationale, but 'has to do with the gradual elimination of the social status of the deceased and the effect that that has on the status and self-conception of the living' (1907, 65).

A list of all the works of classical scholarship on the subject that have been produced in the last hundred years would be very long indeed, and I can name only a few. By far the greatest in my view is Erwin Rohde's *Psyche* (1897), which, as its title indicates, is primarily concerned with the beliefs held by the Greeks about the fate of the soul after death. Not only does it contain a wealth of important detail on a wide variety of subjects, but, more important, it represents an early attempt to incorporate the researches of anthropologists such as Tylor. Bruck in *Totenteil und Seelgerät im griechischen Recht* (1926) made a study of the property rights cf the Greek dead from Minoan to Christian times and drew attention to the fact that limitation of the amount which goes into a tomb increases the amount which can be inherited by the heirs. A comprehensive survey of the archaeological data from the Bronze Age to the Hellenistic period appeared in 1971 with the publication of Kurtz and Boardman's *Greek Burial Customs*. Vermeule's admirably illustrated *Aspects of Death in Early Greek Art and Poetry* (1979) conveys much new information in an engaging belles-lettres style.

In addition to wide-ranging treatments of death, there also exists a number of important monographs which give detailed consideration to individual themes. Of these I would single out Brückner's study of family tombs in the Kerameikos (1909), Boardman's study of black-figure funerary plaques (1955), Bradeen's work on Athenian casualty lists (1964, 1967 and 1969), Alexiou's study of the themes and formulae of the ritual lament as they have evolved in the Greek tradition from Homer to the present day (1974), Kurtz's dissertation (1975) on Attic white *lêkythoi* (oil-flasks), together with those of Kokula on marble *loutrophoroi* (water-jars) (1974) and Stupperich

(1977) on public and private grave-monuments in Attika, and finally Humphreys' revision of Fustel's seminal work on tomb-cult (1980). In addition, our knowledge of the Kerameikos continues to be advanced by the work of the German Archaeological Institute and the Greek Archaeological Service: it was in the belief that the time was ripe for a systematised collection and analysis of some of the mass of information that is normally only available in scattered archaeological reports that I prepared *A First Catalogue of Attic Peribolos Tombs* (1982).

This book is an attempt to revive and re-live the complex texture of feelings provoked in the living by the dead as moment by moment the two shift their ground in relation to one another. Hence, where possible, I have tried to concern myself not merely with the facts about Greek death (i.e. the observances), but also with the psychological context of the facts (i.e. the attitudes behind the observances). Where this is not possible I hope that detailed description may help to build up a representation of the visual and aural effect of Greek burial rites, which in itself is significant to the understanding of attitude. Thus the questions which lie at the heart of this book are as follows: the extent to which death was a preoccupying concern among the Greeks; the kind of feelings with which the ordinary Greek anticipated his own death; the nature and quality of the bonds affiliating the living to the dead; and, finally, the kind of light shed by Greek burial practices upon characteristic elements in Greek society.

I would like to express my warm thanks to the following: to Mrs S.C. Humphreys, who supervised this work when it was a thesis and whose exacting standards of scholarship have been an inspiration to me at all stages; to the British School at Athens, under the direction of Dr H.W. Catling, which provided me with its excellent research facilities while I studied in Greece; to my colleagues in Keele who have supported and encouraged me in the final stages; and finally to my wife Roberta for everything that cannot be said in words.

University of Keele   R.G.
May 1984

Illustrations

1

The Power and Status of the Dead

By way of prologue, it will be useful to provide an outline of the physical and mental condition of those who lived 'over there' (*ekei*), as Hades was obliquely termed: that is to say, the character, temperament and resourcefulness of the Greek dead together with some idea of their status and standing vis-à-vis the world of the living and the world of the gods.

Our earliest as well as our most complete picture of the Greek dead is provided by Homer. The Homeric dead are distinguished from their living counterparts in their lack of strength (*menos*), an attribute which they share with dreams. Their lack of *menos* is presumably the reason why they are unable to exert any influence over earthly affairs. A hero might die in a temper, as Sarpedon did beneath the spear of Patroklos, but his temper descended with him to the grave and incommoded no one but himself. Thus Ajax might rage against Odysseus for being awarded the arms of Achilles in preference to himself, yet his feelings are a matter of perfect indifference to the object of his hate. It is true that on one occasion the poet suggests that it is safer to respect the needs of the dead and accord them proper burial, which Odysseus has rashly neglected to do in the case of the wretched Elpenor, but even then the failure to do so arouses the vengeance (*nemesis*) of the gods, not that of the dead man himself.

The Homeric dead lack not only *menos*, but also the full command of their faculties. Achilles remarks that although there is soul (*psychê*) and image (*eidôlon*) in Hades 'the *phrenes* (wits) do not exist at all'. The single exception to this rule is the seer Teiresias, whose *phrenes* are said to be 'everlasting' (*empedoi*), and who retains in addition the gift of prophetic utterance. It is perhaps because the dead are witless that Agamemnon describes them as 'heedless' or 'uncaring' (*aphradeës*). Loss of personality at death is also implied by the use of the expression 'he himself' (*autos*) in contexts where it is contrasted with *psychê*, that portion of a man's being which departs to the world

below, as at the beginning of the *Iliad* when we are informed that the
psychai of many heroes have been hurled into Hades, 'but they
themselves (*autoi*) became a feast for dogs and birds'. It is also
instructive that when summoned from the lower world by means of
sacrifices performed on their behalf, the Homeric dead do not
immediately recognise their nearest and dearest, but must wait until
they have imbibed the sacrificial blood. Perhaps because they lacked
phrenes, the Greek dead could be cheated. Attic *lêkythoi* (oil-flasks)
manufactured specifically for the grave were sometimes provided
with an internal oil-container which sealed the bottom of the neck,
thus creating a vacuum beneath, so that only a minimal amount of
oil was required to fill them (fig. 27). In addition, re-used and even
repaired vases were requisitioned for funerary use.

The ignorance of the dead about affairs up on earth presented a
major obstacle in the way of those who wished to enlist their services
or advice. The difficulties of communication are most clearly
demonstrated by Atossa's invocation of the witless ghost of King
Dareios in Aeschylus' *Persai*. When the *eidôlon* appears, it is in total
ignorance of the disaster sustained by the Persian fleet off the island
of Salamis in 480 B.C., news of which has just reached the court at
Susa. On learning the full story of Persia's ruin, the ghost serves up a
pious homily on the folly of youth directed at its absent son Xerxes,
while at the same time preening itself on its own faultless record as
king. Asked what action Persia should take, its advice is unhelpfully
post eventum. Don't, it says, invade Greece. Predicting a further
disaster at the battle of Plataia shortly to be fought – though
ignorant of the past it can suddenly see into the future – it gives
utterance to the following piece of homespun wisdom: 'Let no man,
despising his present fortune and desiring more, waste great wealth'.
Thereafter, however, the ghost displays a more practical turn of
mind. Xerxes, it informs the queen, has torn his clothes up in his
grief. His mother should have another set ready to hand him on his
return. It would be a kindness as well if she didn't raise her voice to
him. Departing, the *eidôlon* has this insightful comment to offer to its
people in their hour of need: 'Enjoy life daily, even in the midst of
disaster. Wealth isn't much use down in Hades.'

Other instances of the dead being invoked in Greek literature
include Aristophanes' comic description in the *Birds* (1553ff.) of the
unwashed Sokrates holding a séance beside a lake inhabited by
the Shadowfoot tribe, a passage clearly modelled on *Odyssey* 11.
Sokrates is visited by the spirits of the politicians Peisander and

Chairephon, the latter in the form of a bat, who comes to drink the blood of a sacrificial victim described as a 'camel-lamb'. Necromancy seems to have flourished in Greece from the fourth century onwards. An oracle of the dead near Ephyre in Thesprotia in western Epiros was excavated by the Greek Archaeological Service between 1958 and 1964. A labyrinthine entrance led to the sanctuary proper, a square building with internal colonnade, resembling the Eleusinian Telesterion, constructed over a vaulted subterranean chamber where, presumably, the encounter with the dead would take place. Finds from the sanctuary mainly belong to the third or early second century B.C., though the earliest belong to the fourth. In distinction to the ordinary dead who could only be summoned forth from the underworld abode by rituals conducted by the living, the heroic dead upon occasion spontaneously make contact with the world above in order to signify their displeasure, as does Agamemnon in Aeschylus' *Choêphoroi* who exacts offerings from his murderess-wife Klytaimnestra, and Achilles in Euripides' *Hekabê* who demands the sacrifice of Polyxene at his tomb.

Since the dead could only be contacted with difficulty, a useful device was to charge the dying with a message to be conveyed to those below. Polyxene before being executed asks her mother what message she should take to Priam. The grim exchange later in the play between Hekabe and Polymestor who has murdered one of Hekabe's sons turns upon this same belief. To Polymestor's question, put with feigned ingenuousness, 'Am I to pass this advice on to your son?', the queen, who has already plotted his murder, replies: 'Yes, personally.' The process could also work in reverse. A *stêlê* erected to a dead woman bears the following message and instruction to her husband: 'Greetings, and kiss my family for me'. The distance between the two worlds is also indicated by the fact that objects destined for use in Hades were often 'cancelled' or 'killed', either by burning, breaking or bending.

As already noted (above, p. xi), Greek tragedy has more to tell us about the cult of heroes than that of the ordinary dead, but notwithstanding the greater status and power of the heroic dead we never learn anything very precise about their capabilities. Though the dead are frequently invoked in tragedy, it is not altogether clear what form their intervention took in practical terms. As we shall see, prayers addressed to the underworld were sometimes in the forms of requests and at others general pleas for 'good things' (*esthla*). We are not informed to what extent the spirit of Agamemnon is working behind the scenes in the *Choêphoroi* of Aeschylus, or in the *Orestês* or *Elektra* of Euripides. His spirit is frequently invoked before a dangerous enterprise, but is never actually thanked afterwards. Characteristically, it is Euripides of the dramatists who casts doubt upon the power of the dead. In the *Helen*, Menelaos says to the dead Proteos beside whose grave he happens to be standing, 'Return my wife whom Zeus sent here for you to protect, I beg you', and then adds a second later, 'I know you can't, being dead'; and Theseus in the *Suppliants* ridicules Adrastos' fear that his dead enemies might continue the fight from the grave. More explicit is a fragment from Euripides' lost play the *Kresphontes* which states: 'For if he dwells beneath the earth, among those who are no more, he would have no strength'.

Among the beneficent dead should be counted the *Tritopatores* (or *Tritopatres*), 'fathers to the third degree or third forefathers', whom Rohde (1897, ch. 5 n. 124) defined as 'the souls of ancestors who have become wind-spirits and travel in the wind like other *psychai....* From these as from real life-giving breezes (*pnoai zôogonai*) their descendants hope for aid where the entry into life of a new *psychê* is concerned' (see figs. 1, 2 and 22). Possibly connected with the generative properties of the dead is a statement by Hippokrates that 'from the dead come nourishment, increase and seed', but the context makes it ambiguous whether the physician imagines the departed to be agents of fecundity or merely symbols of generation when they appear in dreams.

It is perhaps because the power of the dead was most strongly experienced in the neighbourhood of the grave that a tomb afforded protection to those in distress. Certainly the dead retained the use of their senses enough to be able to perceive when a friendly or hostile presence approached their graves. This is the reason why Odysseus is warned not to participate in Ajax's funeral and why Alkmene is ordered not to pour libations or blood-offerings at the tomb of her enemy Eurystheus. Because of the touchiness of the dead one was advised to pass their graves in silence. Hence a hero might acquire the epithet Sigêlos, 'the Silent One'. At the same time cemeteries were not such awesome places that they could not be violated in times of emergency. On at least two occasions in Athenian history walls were hastily constructed out of grave monuments, first in 479 after the Persian sack and again in 338 after the Battle of Chaironeia (fig.2).

Judged overall, in fact, the Greek dead tend to be disagreeable and

Fig.1. Boundary marker of the *Tritopatreion* in the Kerameikos. The exact date of construction is uncertain, but it is possible that it was built around the middle of the fifth century in order to provide house room for the spirits of the dead who had been evicted from their graves by the construction of the Themistoklean Wall in 479. See also figs. 2 and 22.

irritable, rather than actively malevolent. Thus the drink-offerings or *choai* poured in honour of the murdered Agamemnon are described as 'appeasement for the dead' (*nerterois meiligmata*). According to the lexicographer Photios, it was advisable to chew buckthorn and smear the doors of one's house with pitch on the second day of the Anthesteria, when the dead were believed to leave their graves and wander abroad, though the practice was perhaps merely intended as a defence against their polluting presence rather than as a means of diverting their anger. Categories of the dead especially to be feared were murderers and their victims, discussion of whom is reserved for Chapter 6. Significantly, however, the power of the murdered dead did not inevitably extend to exacting vengeance on their murderers; it is Apollo who constrains Orestes to carry out a killing on Agamemnon's behalf, and the Furies who must be invoked to assist the murdered Klytaimnestra. Indicative of the superstitious dread attaching to the murderer is Plato's recommend-ation in the *Laws* (873b) that those guilty of the worst crimes should be buried outside the city at a crossroad with a stone over their head. In a malevolent class of its own is the ghost of Achilles in Euripides' *Hekabê* (94ff.) who demands as his prerogative (*geras*) the sacrifice of the virgin Polyxene before permitting the fleet to sail home.

The practice of placing in cemeteries, graves, pits or rivers the small folded lead plaques known as *katadesmoi* (curse-tablets) is not an indication that the dead themselves possessed awful powers, but rather that they were useful deliverers to chthonic deities. *Katadesmoi* are found in Attika, Boeotia, Cyprus, Epirus, Euboia, Magna Graecia and Sicily (Selinos), from the late fifth century to the Roman era, though they do not become common until the Hellenistic period. Especially favoured as 'pillar-boxes', as Kurtz and Boardman (*KB* 217) note, were those who came to a violent end or those who died young. Some contained merely the name or names of the persons to be cursed: in certain cases as many as ten or fifteen persons are cursed on a single tablet. Other tablets are more explicit, containing formulae which curse the tongue, the eyes, the mouth, the *psychê*, the sanity, the arms and the legs of the named person, and invoke the assistance of the underworld deities, Persephone and Hermes. Such tablets are often transfixed with a nail so as to cancel them and dispatch them to the dead. Often the reason for cursing appears to have been a lawcourt testimony. A further form of cursing in Athens in the late fifth century was to set a small lead figure with bound hands inside a lead coffin with an inscription on the inside lid.

Fig. 2. The Themistoklean Wall seen from the inside, looking west towards the Kerameikos. The bases for grave monuments shown on the left were used in the hasty reconstruction of the wall in 338 B.C.

As Zuntz (1971, 284) notes, leaden *katadesmoi* form a counterpart to the gold leaves which have been found in some graves, 'the dark, heavy lead' – as it becomes when buried in the earth – 'used to promote destruction and death'. From a reference in Plato (*Rep.* 364c) to the effect that 'if a man wishes to harm his enemy, for a trifling fee he can harm him, whether the man is just or wicked, by means of charms and binding spells' (*katadesmoi*), we gather that such items were professionally produced.

The general ineffectiveness, and indeed defencelessness, of the dead is further demonstrated by the clear impression received from literature that their interests need to be protected. Towards the end of his speech *Against Eratosthenes*, Lysias (12.99) declares that he has acted vigorously 'on behalf of the dead, to whom you, being unable to protect them when they were alive, render assistance when they are dead'. So, too, Antigone says somewhat obscurely to her sister: 'Cheer up. You're alive. My *psychê*, however, died long ago so that I could help the dead' (S. *Ant.* 599f.). Lawcourt speeches containing disputes over wills frequently conclude with an appeal to the jury to ensure that the deceased's interests are upheld. For instance, at the end of a speech by Isaios delivered in support of his claim to be the legal heir of Menekles' estate, the unknown defendant urges the jury to 'come to the assistance both of us and of him who is in Hades, and not allow (the dead) Menekles to be insulted by my opponents'. The idea that the dead continued to possess legal rights is a principle enshrined in Greek legal theory. Solon made it a criminal offence to speak ill of the dead. A more serious charge was that of telling lies about the dead. In such cases it fell to the heir to carry out the prosecution on the deceased's behalf. Denial of the rite of burial constituted an act of *hybris* against the dead. In addition, one could be charged with 'ill usage of parents' (*kakôsis goneôn*) for failing to perform the cult of the tomb on their behalf (and that of grandparents and great-grandparents), though, as Humphreys (1980, 101 n. 10) notes, it is difficult to imagine that those Athenians whose ancestral tombs were not all in one place can have been expected to visit them all. Finally, forensic oratory exploited the idea of the weakness of the murdered dead by exhorting the jury to ensure that the deceased obtained revenge by the judicial killing of the accused.

Greek tragedy repeatedly insists that one must revere (*sebein*) the dead. That is the reason why Admetos, following the self-sacrifice of his wife Alkestis, is reluctant to take the substitute bride offered him by Herakles. The reward for having exhibited reverence (*sebas*) towards the dead is a reputation among their ranks for piety (*eusebeia*), as Elektra informs Chrysothemis when seeking to enlist the latter's support in her plot to avenge their father's murder. One who failed to show proper respect towards the dead was not so much likely to invite reprisals directly at their hands, however, as to lay himself open to the vengeance of the gods. To deny Ajax burial, Teukros informs Menelaos, would be to dishonour the gods and invoke punishment. 'You wouldn't hurt Ajax,' Odysseus points out to Agamemnon. 'It would be the laws of the gods that would suffer.' It was unwise to display ingratitude to the dead for past services by denying them their prerogative (*geras*), not, we are told, because they themselves were all-powerful, but because they might go and tell tales to Persephone.

In order to determine the status of the Greek dead we need to consider the significance of the epithets by which they are characteristically denoted. Both *makarios* (blessed) and *makaritês* (blessed, or a blessed person) are commonly used to describe the dead. Aristophanes in his lost play the *Tagênistai* (Broilers or Fryers) writes: 'Everyone says that so-and-so is *makaritês*, he's passed away,

Fig. 3. Spartan *stêlê* showing the seated dead as heroized and magnified beings receiving gifts from diminutive worshippers.

gone to sleep. He's a *eudaimôn* (fortunate) fellow because he no longer feels any pain.' In early Greek *makarios* is an epithet which properly describes the condition of the gods in distinction to that of mortal man. It was Hesiod who extended the meaning to include those who were exempted from the normal dreary existence of the dead in

Hades, by referring to the men of the silver generation who live underground as *hypochthonioi makares* (blessed beneath the earth). In the fifth century *makarios* seems to have been used especially of the heroised dead. In later writers it commonly applies to a person who has recently died.

An epithet frequently applied to the dead on Attic grave-reliefs is *chrêstos* (excellent), presumably in recognition of the deceased's virtues when alive. In Thessalian and Boeotian funerary inscriptions the dead are commonly accorded the title *hêrôs* (hero), even in the case of persons of no consequence. In Athens this usage was regarded as sufficiently exotic to provoke from Plato Comicus the remark: 'Why don't you hang yourself and become a Theban hero?' Peculiar to Athens is the expression *Dêmêtrioi*, or 'people of Demeter', which Plutarch (*Mor.* 943b) informs us was applied to the dead in olden times, and which was perhaps reserved for those who had been initiated into the Eleusinian Mysteries. Especially interesting is a comment by Aristotle (Fr. 44*T*) to the effect that the reason why it was considered impious to say anything false or slanderous against the dead was because 'they are judged to have already become better and stronger'. However, in the light of our inquiry and in the absence of corroborative testimony, it would be more reasonable to apply such epithets to the condition of the heroic dead.

The conception of the dead as beings who have been raised to a higher state of dignity finds expression on Greek funerary monuments from Crete and Lakonia. An enhancement of their status is perhaps the intention behind the early Archaic Cretan practice of depicting the departed standing on a small pedestal. In support of this interpretation is a fragmentary *stêlê* from the same region on which a miniature worshipper is shown holding out a small offering to the enlarged dead. The exalted condition of the dead is more clearly evident in the case of the so-called Lakonian hero-reliefs which date from the middle of the sixth century and continue down to the Hellenistic period. The best known example is the so-called Chrysapha relief, where the dead, seated on elaborate thrones, are approached by two miniature worshippers holding a pomegranate, an egg, a flower and a cock (fig.3).

At the end of the Archaic period, a dramatic alteration is detectable in the relationship between survivors and the deceased: a fragmentary Lakonian relief dated *c.* 480 B.C. depicts a young woman who is pouring a libation to the dead on almost the same scale as the deceased. Johansen is surely right in interpreting this

Fig. 4. Stone *lêkythos* showing Hermes *Psychopompos* conducting Myrrhine to the underworld. On the left are the bereaved.

development as a diminution in the distance separating the living from the dead. Further evidence of the same trend is provided by a fragmentary grave-relief from Aegina on which the living and the dead now for the first time shake hands.

In the Classical period the dead on grave-reliefs generally enjoy exactly the same status as the living. A rare exception is the Athenian stone *lêkythos* of Myrrhine (*c.* 420) on which the dead woman, together with her escort Hermes, is depicted on a slightly larger scale than the survivors who watch her departure (fig.4). It is also instructive that the survivor who stands nearest to Myrrhine raises his right hand in what is evidently intended as either a gesture of salutation or perhaps even of homage. As we learn from both literature and vase-paintings, this gesture was performed in all ceremonies connected with the dead, and it is regrettable that its precise significance is unknown to us. Only once on an Athenian vase do we encounter a mourner kneeling beside a tomb in what is possibly to be interpreted as an act of homage (*proskynêsis*).

To conclude, the predominant image of the ordinary Greek dead is of beings which evoke pity rather than fear. Their pathetic status vis-à-vis the living is pictorially conveyed in scenes on Attic white-ground *lêkythoi* of the fifth century where the *psychê* of the deceased takes the form of a diminutive winged creature hovering plaintively and ineffectually in the vicinity of the grave. Linguistically their insubstantiality is suggested by such words as *eidôlon* (image) and *skia* (shadow), which unambiguously indicate that the dead as perceived by the living were in a very literal sense mere shadows of their former selves.

2

Dying

The business of passing 'from here to there' (*enthende ekeise*), as Sokrates (Pl. *Phd*. 117c) puts it, involves three distinct stages as follows:

(1) Dying
(2) Being dead but uninterred
(3) Being dead and interred.

Obviously each stage called for a different response on behalf of the survivors – what is desirable and appropriate for the moribund at stage 1 is hardly likely to be desirable and appropriate for the corpse at stage 2 – and so one should think of the business of passing from here to there as an undertaking in which the dying/dead and the living jointly participate.

It will be my contention that death in Greek belief was not conceived of as completely instantaneous. By that I mean that though the 'spirit' departed instantly from the body, it remained for some while in a state of transfer or flux. In modern Western society, until complicating distinctions between somatic and molecular death began to cloud the issue, the generally accepted view has been, as Hertz (1907, 28) noted, that death occurs in an instant. 'The only purpose of the two or three days' delay between the demise and the burial is to allow material preparations to be made and to summon relatives and friends. No interval separates the life ahead from the one that has just ceased: no sooner has the last breath been exhaled than the soul appears before its judge and prepares to reap the reward for its good deeds or to expiate its sins.' In ancient Greece, by contrast, death was not seen so much as an event as a process; a process, moreover, requiring strenuous action on the part of the survivors in order to be successfully terminated.

This investigation thus begins at the moment where death is imminent. Consideration must be paid to the condition not only of the very aged, the mortally wounded and the incurably sick, but also to persons in perfect health facing the immediate prospect of death. It is this last category of persons which sheds most light on our inquiry for it includes such figures as Sokrates about to drink hemlock, Oedipus about to be received in heaven, Ajax about to commit suicide, and Alkestis about to pawn her life in exchange for that of her husband Admetos.

In the case of Alkestis, her handmaid tells us (Eur. *Alk* 158ff.): 'When she knew that her appointed day (*hêmeran tên kyrian*) had come, she washed her white skin in river water, took out a dress and some jewels from her cedar chests, and adorned herself magnificently. Then standing before the altar of Hestia, the goddess of the hearth, she prayed, "Mistress, as I pass beneath the earth, I fall before you and pray for the last time. Look after my two children ... Let them not die before their time, as their mother died." Then she went up to all the altars in Admetos' house and adorned them with wreaths and prayed, plucking tresses of myrtles.' The last moments of Sokrates are reported in Plato's *Phaedo*. After dismissing the women so that there should be no weeping or display of violent emotion, Sokrates bathed and continued chatting with his friends. Upon receiving the cup of hemlock, he prayed that his 'change of residence' (*metoikêsis*) as he put it, might be blessed with good fortune. His famous last words were: 'Krito, we owe a cock to Asklepios. See that it's paid' (118a). The messenger in Sophokles' *Oedipus at Kolonos* tells us (1586ff.) that when Oedipus knew that his hour was at hand he called for running water, in order to wash himself and make a libation (*choai*). After he had bathed and dressed 'in the manner ordained by custom', Oedipus wept with his daughters. Then, being summoned by a mysterious voice, he committed them to the care of Theseus and ordered everyone, except Theseus, to depart so as not to witness the moment of his passing. Ajax in Sophokles' play of that name before taking his own life prays to Zeus that his brother Teukros may be the first to come across his body and give it a decent burial; to Hermes that his death may be swift; and finally to the Furies that the hated Atreidai may be made to pay for his death. Then, after bidding farewell to his homeland and hearth, to Athens, his relatives, and to Troy, he falls upon his sword (823ff.).

Admittedly these four cases can hardly be considered typical. The first is a substitute-sacrifice to Thanatos, the personification of

Fig. 5. *Stêlê* of Demokleides. The outline of the prow of a ship of war is probably intended to suggest that the deceased died in a naval battle.

Death, the second a condemned criminal and philosopher, the third a hero who gets spirited away, and the fourth a suicide elect. None the less, their preparations for death display certain features in common which, though doubtless compressed in time, may be judged to be canonical. These include:

(1) The ritual bath (Alkestis, Sokrates and Oedipus)
(2) The committal of one's children to the safe care of others (Alkestis and Oedipus)
(3) The settling of one's affairs (Sokrates; cf. Dem. 41.8)
(4) The prayer to Hestia (Alkestis and Ajax)
(5) The prayer for safe passage to Hades (Sokrates and Ajax)
(6) The farewell to family and friends (Alkestis, Oedipus and Ajax).

None it may be noted, chooses his last moments to make a will, a task which could be accomplished at any time in a person's life, though final instructions were perhaps given to trustees or heirs, as Sokrates' last words, ambiguous though they are, suggest. Other death scenes in both art and literature are extremely rare. On funerary *stêlai*, for instance, references to the manner in which a person died are allusive rather than explicit (fig.5).

This list of six duties to be performed by someone on the point of death lends support to Arnold Toynbee's contention (1968, 259) that all persons, whatever their beliefs about the sequel to death, have one wish in common: namely that at the moment of departing they may possess 'as clean a bill of spiritual health as it may be possible for a human being to earn'.* If this can be seen as a point of connection between the Greeks and other societies including our own, it is to be expected that there will be striking differences. In modern Britain, as Gorer (1965, 5) has noted, the majority of people die alone in a hospital bed with only medical attendants for company whereas 'if the evidence of nineteenth-century novelists is to be trusted, the presence of one's closest kin around a death-bed was then [i.e. in the

---

*It might, of course, be argued that in a largely atheistic, post-Christian society such as modern Britain or America, the desire for 'a clean bill of spiritual health' is not as keenly felt as it once was. None the less, the fact that burial (or more commonly cremation) is the one ceremony in a person's passage through life invariably attended by a minister indicates that scruples and uncertainties continue to exist regarding death itself. I know of no popular reform movement to challenge the church's undisputed authority in this area.

nineteenth century] general in all ranks of society'. Likewise Ariès (1974, 11), describing Medieval Europe, typifies the death-bed scene as 'a ritual organised by the dying person himself, who presided over it and knew its protocol' and as 'a public ceremony ... (at which) ... it was essential that parents, friends and neighbours be present'. In the case of ancient Greece, it is difficult, because we have so little evidence, to determine how formalised the last moments of a person's life would be. Doubtless anyway some degree of latitude was permitted. As we see from the *Phaedo*, Sokrates was certainly aware of the protocol which the situation called for, and his own last moments may be said to have been both consciously articulated and consumately executed.

Not everyone dies surrounded by family and friends, however. Herodotus (4.14) reports that when the poet Aristeas dropped dead in a fuller's shop, the fuller locked up and went in search of the relatives, who returned with the requisite items (*ta prosphora*) for burial. Evidently no death certificate was required. In Egypt under Roman domination death no less than life was a more complicated process. In order that the census could be implemented as efficiently as possible, the nearest relative of the deceased was either advised or obliged to submit a death certificate (*hypomnêma*) to his district official so that the name of the deceased could be struck off the list of those liable to the poll-tax and added to the *taxis tôn teleutêkotôn* or list of the dead.

What did the ordinary Greek feel at the moment of death? In a famous passage in Plato's *Republic* (1.330de) the aged Kephalos states that 'when a man gets near to the end of his life, he becomes subject to fear and anxiety about what lies ahead. The stories told about people in Hades – that if you commit crimes on earth you must pay for them down below – although they are ridiculed for a while, now begin to disturb a man's *psychê* with the possibility that they might be true.' The question is: how representative is the view here ascribed to Kephalos of non-philosophical Greeks? It must be borne in mind that Plato had reason to exploit any feeling of apprehensiveness about the next world, committed as he was to a belief in the immortality of the soul. But there is little evidence to support the claim that the majority of Greeks spent their declining years consumed with guilty foreboding at the prospect of making a reckoning in the hereafter (see below p. 60ff. for further discussion). Fear, combined with a healthy fatalism, seems to be the worst that the average Greek moribund had to cope with. As there was little sense of sin, so there was no need for the death-bed conversion so favoured by nineteenth-century Evangelicals whereby the sinful soul, even at the eleventh hour, could wrest itself from the toils of the Devil by a timely repentance. True, the prospect of an eternity in Hades for a Greek might not seem too rosy. True, as well, the Eleusinian Mystery religion, which gained such popularity in the fifth, and more particularly in the fourth century B.C., did hold out alternative prospects for the initiate and non-initiate (see below p. 61f.). But the condition of blessedness which it promised to initiates was, so far as we can judge, a consequence of purely external observances – the simple fact of having witnessed certain secret ceremonies – and in no way related to the spiritual state of the soul upon decease.

Characteristic of paganism, too, is the unconcern with – and indeed avoidance of – the dying by the Olympian deities, in marked contrast to the Christian God. Artemis' hasty exit at the end of Euripides' *Hippolytos* (1437f.) when her favourite is dying is made because it was not permitted by divine law (*themis*) for a god or goddess 'either to look at the dead or to sully their eyes with the expirations of the dying'. This avoidance of the dying by the Olympians may be contrasted with the appeal to Hades made by Herakles in the throes of death-agony to terminate his existence as soon as possible (S. *Trach.* 1040ff. and 1085).

A brief word about death as a biological event and the theories surrounding it. In Homer the most characteristic notion is that death is ushered in by the departure of the *psychê* 'lamenting its fate (*hon potmon goöôsa*)' either out of the mouth or from a gaping wound. This *psychê*, though denoting by its presence or absence in a man's body whether that man is alive, is certainly not synonymous with life, the life-instinct, consciousness or activity, and in fact only makes an appearance in the body when death is imminent. It is worth noting as well that of 240 deaths in the *Iliad*, only four are described in terms of the departure of the *psychê* and all four refer to persons of heroic status. For lesser personalities Homer has twenty different physiological ways of describing the onset of death, commonest of which are 'his *guia* (limbs) were loosed' and 'his *thymos* (heart) was taken away'. These expressions, however, seem to refer to symptoms of decease rather than to its actual cause. No subsequent Greek writer contributes anything new to the question why organisms die, with the single exception of Aristotle who advanced a notion that death is the result of a process of drying up or loss of vital heat (*auansis*). Whether popular opinion widely upheld these sorts of theories we cannot know.

The Greeks did not invariably view the onset of death as painful. In Homer death with a small 'd' might be heavy-handed and was capable of shattering the *thymos*, but it could also be shed around a person's head like a soft mist. Mythologically the idea of the painless onset of death was epitomised by the image of silver-bowed Apollo striking men down with his gentle arrows (*aganoisi belessin*).

At the beginning of the fourth century Plato introduced a note of morality later to be taken up and expanded by Christian eschatology into the *psychorrhagêma* or struggle on the part of the *psychê* to release itself from the body. Such would appear to be the view ascribed to Sokrates in the *Phaedo* where he paints a picture of the *psychê* which is desirous of the body being led away to the underworld 'only with violence and difficulty' (108f). The philosopher was blithely confident that his own *psychê* would put up no such resistance: when asked by his friends how he would like to be buried, Sokrates replied: 'Anyway you like, if you can grab me and I don't get away'(115c). It must be stressed that this notion of the *psychê* as capable of being corrupted by earthly desires is unlikely to have been shared by many Classical Greeks: the *psychorrhagêma* of Alkestis in Euripides' play is merely a wrenching apart of bodily constituents without any ethical overtones.

There exists a similarity between Medieval Christian and pagan Greek belief. Ariès (1974, 2f.) notes that the knights in the *Chansons de Geste* were usually warned about their approaching death, which enabled them to make suitable preparations. Similarly the Greeks believed that some time in the past men had been able to foresee the moment when they would die. It was Prometheus, the friend of man, who deprived them of this disconcerting gift by instilling 'blind hopes' in their minds. None the less there remained a strong conviction that each individual possessed an allotted span of life and that the day of one's departure (*peprômenon êmar*) was fixed in advance. In the *Iliad* this conviction finds expression in the concept of *kêr*, a word of varied application which in a general sense may best be translated as 'the fate of death'. Homer did not, however, apply the theory of a man's death-day being unalterably fixed with total consistency. Although references to fate determining the extent of a man's life abound in the *Iliad*, there are indications that death could be accelerated or impeded by both divine and human action. Zeus' debate with Hera as to whether to rescue his beloved son Sarpedon from death when struck by Patroklos demonstrates this proposition on the divine level, for the point of Hera's objection to such a course of action is not that as a god he cannot, but that he must not, interfere with the laws of nature, since if he does other gods will do likewise. Similarly Thetis' warning to Achilles that if he kills Hektor he is doomed to a speedy death 'because immediately your own *potmos* (fate) is at hand' (*Il.* 18.96) incontrovertibly indicates that human action may either expedite or delay the fulfilment of fate. Although there exist innumerable Homeric echoes in Greek epigrams to the effect that a man's death was fixed by fate, it is not improbable that a similarly judicious blending of individual will with impersonal destiny, the accidental with the pre-ordained, formed the basis of much ordinary Greek belief.

Finally, there seems to have been a belief that the soul, at the moment of departure, is elevated to a higher plane of consciousness, thereby enabling the dying person to prophesy with foreknowledge. Thus Patroklos in his dying breath predicts the death of Hektor at the hands of Achilles, and Hektor, as he in turn expires, predicts the death of Achilles at the hands of Paris. In addition, the Greeks had an expectation that the words of the dying would be memorable. Andromache, lamenting the fact that Hektor did not die in his bed, regrets that he failed to bequeathe her any word of wisdom (*pukinon epos*) 'on which I might have pondered night and day with shedding of tears' (Hom. *Il.* 24.744f.). The belief that a moribund has beautiful thoughts is common to many cultures and gave rise to this pathetic Hellenistic epigram: 'These were the last words which Gorgo spoke to her mother, as in tears she threw her arms around her neck: "Stay here beside Daddy and give birth to another daughter more lucky than I was who can look after you in your old age." ' (*AP* 7.647).

3

The Funeral

The Greek funeral, or *kêdeia*, was a three-act drama with precise regulations governing the most minute details of procedure. These three acts comprised the laying out of the body (*prothesis*), its conveyance to the place of interment (*ekphora*), and finally the deposition of its cremated or inhumed remains. It is evident from the most complete descriptions of a hero's funeral that we possess, namely those of Patroklos, Hektor and Achilles, that this ritual was already well-established by the time of Homer. In antiquity, no less than in the modern world, a funeral presented unrivalled opportunities for the conspicuous display of wealth, kin-solidarity and family pride. To appreciate that these opportunities were readily seized, we have only to consider the large body of funerary legislation which was passed in various places throughout Greek history. Indeed we learn a great deal about the character of Greek funerals in antiquity from examination of the abuses which the laws sought to check. While the maintenance of public order may have been an important consideration behind some of the legislation, this aim alone cannot account for it all. Other motives may have included the reduction of popular superstition, the transfer of funerary ritual from private hands to state control in order to weaken the power of kin groups, the prevention of disease, the curbing of needless expenditure, and finally, the ensuring that the claims of the dead were fully satisfied and their dispatch to the next world assured. While Athens provides us with the best evidence, funerary legislation is ascribed also to Delphi, Gambreion, Gortyn, Katana, Keos, Mytilene, Sparta and Syracuse. In the main, the legislation was enacted by law-givers, tyrants or the state. Only once, in the case of Delphi, is there evidence of a phratry or brotherhood, here the Labyadai, involving itself in funerary ordinances, which is perhaps curious in view of the leading role played by phatries in other rites of passage, namely registration of birth and the witnessing of betrothals. The laws with which we shall be chiefly concerned in this chapter were passed by Solon in Athens at the beginning of the sixth century B.C. Their principal aim as reported by Plutarch and Pseudo-Demosthenes would appear to have been to set a maximum limit on all forms of ostentation that could be practised in connection with the interment of one's dead kin. Their intended result would accordingly have been a thwarting of efforts to exploit such an event for political or propagandist effect.

It is, at any rate, reasonable to assume that the emphasis on the funeral itself was greatest in the aristocratic period, but with the rise of democracy in the sixth and fifth centuries, as efforts were made to curb this and other ostentatious displays of private wealth, its importance gradually dwindled away. The same tendency may perhaps be further traced in the reduction in the luxury permitted to private graves in the fifth century and the correspondingly increased emphasis on the public funeral celebrating those who gave their lives in the service of the state, developments judged by Stupperich (1977) to be closely allied. But we must be careful not to over-simplify the general picture. The notorious lack of grave-monuments datable to the first half of the fifth century is not necessarily a reliable indicator of the degree of licence permitted at the funeral. A popular view as quoted by Plato in the *Hippias Major* (291de) held that the best thing of all was 'to be rich, healthy, honoured by the Greeks, reach old age, and, after burying one's parents well, to be laid out well by one's own children and buried magnificently (*megaloprepôs*)'. Medea's sentiment would doubtless have found an echo in the audience when she says to her children, 'I once had high hopes in you that you would look after me in old age and lay me out well with your own hands, the envy of everyone' (Eur. *Med.* 1032ff.). Likewise the same audience was meant to be appalled at the spectacle of the toothless old Tithonos in Aristophanes' *Acharnians* (688ff.) deprived by sharpsters of the money he had set aside to buy his coffin.

Megaloprepeia (magnificence) is, of course, a relative criterion. It is not in dispute that a pre-Solonic funeral outdid anything that was seen in Athens subsequently. But whatever the political pressures of the age, and however exacting the legal restrictions, it seems clear that the desire for a better-than-average funeral persisted among the populace in the Classical period, presumably found some scope for satisfaction and is unlikely to have been confined merely to those who entertained hopes of being awarded the distinction of heroic burial by the state.

The prothesis

Upon a person's decease, the eyes and mouth were first closed, a practice known to Homer which was most appropriately discharged by the next-of-kin. The custom may originally have fulfilled a purely cosmetic function, but by the historical period at the latest it had acquired an eschatological significance as well. An inscription found at Smyrna possibly to be dated to the third century B.C. suggests that the closing of the eyes was believed to secure the release of the *psyché* from the body.

A late innovation by no means universally observed in Greece was the placing of an obol between the teeth of the deceased as payment to Charon for being ferried across the Styx. The earliest literary allusion to the belief that the dead must be provided with their boat-fare (*naulon* or *danaké*) occurs in Aristophanes' *Frogs* where it is spoken of as being two obols. Coins are not actually found in Athenian graves, however, before the Hellenistic period. They were not always inserted in the mouth, some being placed there, others randomly in the grave. The coin was normally of bronze, but examples of impressed gold-foil (bracteates) have also been discovered in the Kerameikos and elsewhere. Some of these 'Charon's pieces', so called, represent impressions taken from real coins, though an abbreviated version of a basic coin-type was occasionally manufactured specially. The custom of providing the dead with their boat-fare does not appear to be alluded to on *lékythoi*, a further indication that the practice is comparatively late.

Gold lip-bands, found in Mycenaean burials, are possibly to be identified as chin-straps, later known as *othônai*. Similar objects have been found in Geometric graves. In scenes of *prothesis* on Athenian vases of this period, however, there is normally only a cushion beneath the head to prevent the jaws from sagging open. Since nothing resembling a chin-strap has been found in Athenian graves of the Archaic or Classical period, such items in later times were probably made of linen. That they were certainly in use is indicated by a black-figure funerary plaque by the Sappho Painter which shows one being fitted around the jaw of the deceased, and by the red-figure *Nekyia* vase (*c.* 450) which depicts a young girl arriving down in Hades with her chin-strap still tied round her head. There are no representations of *othônai* on white *lêkythoi*, however, and it may be that in the fifth century pillows placed under the head often served instead.

The washing of the body was usually performed by the women of the household, although persons who knew that their death was imminent may have performed this duty for themselves. The ceremony may be compared with the ritual bathing of the bride before the marriage ceremony, and like the latter should perhaps be interpreted as denoting a barrier to be passed through in undergoing a rite of passage. Where available, sea-water was perhaps to be preferred. Particular attention was taken with the bodies of the war dead, whose wounds were washed and dressed at this stage.

After the corpse had been bathed, it was clothed and laid out on a bed (*klinê*). The feet were set facing towards the door, a practice recorded in Homer and indicated as well on black-figure funerary plaques. In Geometric art the bier is represented as a couch on high legs almost extending to shoulder height. On later vases it is often shown with delicately turned legs, though occasionally on white *lêkythoi* the legs are short and square, and may be raised up on blocks. One or more pillows were placed beneath the head of the deceased, and the *klinê* was draped in a bier-cloth (*strôma*). Scenes of *prothesis* on Geometric vases usually depict the bier-cloth decorated with a chequered pattern and suspended in the field above the deceased (fig.6). In later periods the bier is sometimes adorned with ribbons.

The funeral garment worn by the deceased in Geometric *prothesis* is represented as a long ankle-length robe. Later we hear of the corpse being wrapped in a shroud (*endyma*), supplemented by a looser covering known as an *epiblêma*. The custom of dressing the body for *prothesis* is frequently referred to in tragedy, indicated technically by the verb *peristellô*; of the funeral attire itself the noun *kosmos* is used. The usual, but by no means only colour of the shroud was white. The law code of Ioulis on Keos, dated to the second half of the fifth century B.C., stipulated 'white *himatia* (cloaks)' and Artemidoros refers to the custom of carrying out the dead in white garments. The funeral ordinance of the Labyad phratry, on the other hand, dated *c*. 400 B.C., decreed that the *chlainê* or mantle (i.e. *epiblêma*) should be *phaôtos*, a colour somewhere between white and black. Judging from representations on Attic *lêkythoi*, it is likely that in Athens a greater degree of variety was permitted than in some parts of Greece.

Fig. 6. Scene of Geometric *prothesis* decorating the handle zone of an Attic Dipylon *amphora c.* 760 B.C.

Certain categories of the dead were especially attired for the *prothesis*. For instance, the unmarried or recently married dead were laid out in wedding attire, and soldiers, particularly in the Geometric period, were buried in hoplite panoply. Certainly Homer knew of the practice of burial in armour, but few examples have been found which postdate 700 B.C. and these are confined to the remoter regions of Greece. A Spartan law ascribed to Lykourgos, which pared down funerary ritual to a minimum, ordained that the dead had to be laid out in a military cloak known as *phoinikis*.

Excavation, unfortunately, does not normally provide evidence of the body being clothed, though dress-pins are occasionally found in graves. It is to be noted that jewellery is generally less commonly found in Classical graves than in those of either the preceding or the following periods, an indication of the thrift in regard to the value of items placed in the grave during this epoch. The degree of ostentation permitted in clothing the deceased was something which legislators sought in particular to check. According to the Kean code, only a single *strôma*, *endyma* and *epiblêma* were to be used, their total cost not to exceed three hundred drachmas. The much meaner Labyad ordinance permitted only a single *strôma* and pillow. It also restricted a total expenditure on new items to a mere thirty-five drachmas.

It was a widespread custom in antiquity to place a crown on the head of the deceased (fig.7). The scholiast on Aristophanes' *Lysistratê* (601) says that crowns were given to the dead 'for having fought their contest with life', but I know of no evidence to suggest that the Greeks habitually viewed life in such dismal terms. Equally fanciful is Rohde's suggestion (1897, 164) that the custom was 'a sign of respect for the higher sanctity of the departed'. Pottier (1883, 19) perhaps provided the most plausible explanation when he suggested that it allowed a last chance to contemplate the deceased 'under a guise of tranquil and serene beauty', but a specific interpretation of their significance should not be insisted upon: crowns, as well as branches, served at most sacred occasions, as well as at symposia, their purpose perhaps being no more than to add dignity and lustre to the proceedings. According to Plutarch, celery seems to have been most commonly used for this purpose. In some fourth-century and Hellenistic Athenian burials, however, wreaths of gold have been found which were doubtless placed on the head of the dead during the *prothesis*. Women's hair was arranged as in life, and women are sometimes shown wearing earrings and a necklace.

Other objects connected with *prothesis* include branches, which were either placed under the bier or held over the feet or head of the corpse. On Geometric vases they are perhaps indicated by columns of M's and chevrons which commonly figure as 'filling-ornaments' between the legs of the bier. Small birds are also sometimes depicted under the bier, possibly to be interpreted as an offering to the dead. *Lêkythoi* of oil were placed around the bier and the walls were hung with sashes and ribbons of the kind commonly represented wound around *stêlai*.

In Homer the *prothesis* could apparently be extended indefinitely. Seventeen days are devoted to the obsequies for Achilles, nine for Hektor, and two for Patroklos, their duration being apparently determined either by the social standing of the deceased or by the grief felt by his survivors. In the historical period, however, the ceremony lasted a mere twenty-four hours and took place on the day after decease. A single day was expressly prescribed by Solonian law, implying that in the earlier period the *prothesis* was more extended. Neglecting to make preparations was considered a matter of reproach. In Gortyn on Crete relatives of the deceased were liable to prosecution if they failed to perform the ritual.

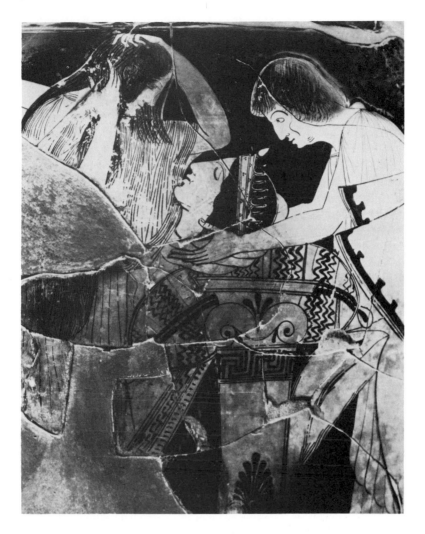

Fig. 7. Detail from a *loutrophoros* showing a scene of *prothesis*. The woman on the right fondling the corpse is perhaps a slave.

We cannot be sure exactly where the ceremony was held. Solon's stipulation that it should take place inside (*endon*) certainly implies that the tendency until then had been to hold it out of doors. From his study of black-figure funerary plaques depicting scenes of *prothesis* apparently taking place in the open, Boardman concludes that the law may have permitted the ceremony to be held in the courtyard within the house (*oikia*). As he himself points out, however, much must have depended on the size of the house and the time of year. Besides, if Solon's law permitted the *prothesis* to take place in the open courtyard, where exactly did it prescribe that it should not take place?

But whatever the answer, we can be certain that what Solon was seeking to discourage was *prothesis* 'on the scale implicit in the Geometric representations' (Boardman 1955, 56). *Prothesis* scenes occur on vases of various shapes from the eighth century to *c.* 400 B.C. In the Geometric period the subject is chiefly found in the handle zone of *amphorai* and less commonly on *kratêres* (mixing bowls) with high foot. Rarely is it depicted on *oinochoai* (wine-pourers) and other small vessels. In the black-figure period it appears chiefly on funerary plaques and *loutrophoroi* (vases for carrying sacred water). Red-figure representations occur only on *loutrophoroi*. *Prothesis* is an unpopular subject for painters of white-ground *lêkythoi* and is unknown on Attic grave-stones. But there are some interesting depictions on stone chests (*cippi*) from Chiusi (Clusium) in central Italy which were produced in the second half of the sixth century and first half of the fifth possibly copied from Attic vases. No portrayal can be dated much beyond 400 B.C. This decline in interest in the subject would at first sight clearly seem to suggest that although the ceremony did not fall into complete disuse, it occupied a less important role in funerary proceedings from the sixth century onwards but it might merely indicate that the subject failed to hold interest either for the artist or his client. At least in a formal sense, however, *prothesis* still retained its significance, as we know from references in the orators to undignified attempts to remove the corpse from the house in which the ceremony was being held by those claiming to be the deceased's legitimate heirs. From this we may infer that the holding of the *prothesis*, if unchallenged, signified that those conducting it had established their legal entitlement to inherit.

The iconographic structure of Geometric *prothesis*, which remained canonical for later periods as well, shows the deceased on a high bier with his head on the spectator's right. Mourners stand, kneel or sit on stools on either side of the bier as well as below it, some gesturing with their arms, others touching the bier or corpse. A special importance seems to have attached to the position at the head of the bier, which is usually occupied by women. They arrange the pillows, grasp the deceased by the shoulders, and occasionally hold something in front of him as if in the act of feeding. Rarely do they actually embrace the corpse. In a few cases a figure is represented standing on a footstool. Supporting the head of the deceased is an action performed by the nearest and dearest at Homeric funerals. Thus, Achilles cups the head of Patroklos, and Andromache and Hekabe that of Hektor.

There are two main gestures of mourning on Geometric vases: the female attitude of holding both hands to the head and tearing the hair, and the male attitude of holding one hand to the head, apparently beating it but not actually tearing the hair. The two-handed gesture, described as 'the traditional formula of lamentation in Geometric art' (Ahlberg 1971, 77), can be traced back to Mycenaean terracotta *larnakes* (chests) from Tanagra and is perhaps to be identified with the Homeric words *tillesthai* (tear one's hair) and *koptesthai* (beat one's breast), whereas the gesture of raising one hand to the head may have been intended not as a sign of grief but as a way of greeting the dead or leading the mourners in the dirge.

As at the *prothesis* of Patroklos, so in later times, women appear to have been in the majority, a fact indicated by their greater frequency in vase-representations. They are regularly shown in closer association with the deceased, often touching the bier or bier-cloth, whereas men process around it with one hand on the hilt of their sword or dagger. Children are also shown in attendance, sometimes in close proximity to the corpse. Occasionally slaves, too, are represented.

In black- and red-figure representations of *prothesis* the number of participants is generally much reduced and their gestures more restrained. To some extent this development simply reflects the changes in the vase-shapes themselves. The high, wide zone of a Geometric *kratêr* or *amphora* naturally lends itself to the depiction of large scenes with many participants, whereas a slender *lêkythos* clearly favours an intimate scene with only a few. At the same time we can hardly exclude the possibility that the change may to some extent indicate reforms brought about by Solon's legislative programme. Admittedly the law quoted by Pseudo-Demosthenes says that the law-giver permitted the *prothesis* to be held 'however you like', but both the restriction on the number of participants and the prohibition on lacerating the flesh may have had the practical consequence of reducing the level of emotional intensity at the *prothesis*, particularly since, as we have seen, it could no longer be held 'outside'.

The principal ceremony performed at the *prothesis* was the singing of the ritualised lament. Dirges took many forms, the most personal being the *goös* whose theme was 'the memory of the lives the two shared and the bitterness of loss' (Vermeule 1979, 15). The *goös*, which is commonly referred to by Homer, was an improvised lament sung by relatives or close friends of the deceased. In style and content it differed markedly from the *thrênos*, a formal lament sung by professional mourners called *thrênôn exarchoi* (leaders of the dirge). On Geometric vases hired mourners are perhaps to be identified with kneeling figures dressed in long robes. They are referred to obliquely by Aeschylus and probably existed throughout antiquity, despite possible efforts by Solon to abolish them by banning the singing of prepared dirges.

In Homer the singing of the ritual lament is antiphonal, the hired singers leading off with their formal dirge, and the kinswomen following with their *goös*. In accompaniment to both parts of the lament, a chorus of women utter a refrain of cries. In the Archaic period dirges appear to have been sung in chorus, whereas in the Classical period, judging from tragedy, antiphonal laments known as *kommoi* were sung in turn by the principals and the Chorus. Possibly a musical accompaniment attended the lament. The singing of the lament involved movement around the bier, as is perhaps indicated in those scenes of Geometric *prothesis* where figures at the side of the bier are occasionally represented in apparent movement.

What was the function of the *prothesis*? Later writers would have us believe that its aim was essentially a 'medical' or legal one. Plato in the *Laws* (12.959a) prescribes the rite for the prosaic reason of ascertaining that the deceased really is dead and not merely in a trance. Pollux (8.65) says that the *prothesis* served simply to confirm that the dead man had not died violently (*biaiôs*). As Zschietzschmann (1928, 36) rightly points out, however, vase-paintings totally contradict such rationalistic explanations by unambiguously demonstrating that the real purpose of the rite was to enable the mourners to sing a funeral dirge in honour of the dead in order to satisfy the claims of duty and to appease the soul of the departed. The importance of the ritual lament seems in fact to have rivalled, if not to have equalled, that of burial itself, as frequent passages in literature where the two actions are combined indicate. A study of surviving dirges suggests that they primarily afforded the bereaved an opportunity to indulge in shameless self-pity by bemoaning the effects upon their own lives occasioned by the loss of the beloved. 'You have dealt me a worse death than you have

Fig. 8. Scene of *ekphora* on the belly of a Geometric *kratêr c.* 750 B.C.

suffered', exclaims Theseus in Euripides' *Hippolytos* (839) on learning of the death of his wife, by no means alone in this kind of complaint. Such utterances should not, however, be regarded as totally spontaneous outbursts of purely-felt grief. In view of the fact that the *prothesis* was a stylised and carefully orchestrated proceeding, we should perhaps think of them as intended at least partly to satisfy the soul of the deceased, conceived at this time to be 'still invisibly present, and ... pleased at the most violent expressions of grief for its loss' (Rohde 1897, 164). The deceased's passage to the next world had yet to begin.

The ekphora

As compared with fifty-two representations of *prothesis* on Geometric vases, only three examples of the *ekphora* have survived. In each example the corpse is transported to the grave by a horse-drawn hearse (fig.8). Men carrying weapons lead the procession and women bring up the rear. The unpopularity of *ekphora* scenes with waggon or chariot may well reflect the rarity of the event in real life. If, on the other hand, the normal Geometric practice was to carry the body to the grave on a bier, we may speculate that the total absence of any surviving example in Geometric art may simply be due to the fact that the subject held no iconographic appeal for the Geometric artist. It is worth pointing out, however, that the few scenes of horse-drawn *ekphora* on vases do none the less provide 'a rare and striking case of a contradiction between Homeric practice and Geometric representation' (Snodgrass 1970, 163), in so far as in Homer the corpse is carried to the place of interment by pall-bearers. More direct evidence for the occasional use of wheeled hearses in Geometric times is provided by the discovery of iron rings from two graves in the Kerameikos which have been identified by Müller-Karpe (1962) as 'bindings for wheel-knaves'. Since at least four such objects have been found in each grave, it is clear that they belonged to a four-wheeled hearse.

To the early post-Geometric period belongs a terracotta model of a four-wheeled horse-drawn cart found at Vari in South Attika (fig.9). A driver stands at the front of the cart (missing horses) which transports a bier covered with a lavishly decorated pall. The body is hidden under a shroud, also decorated, in the form of a lid which lifts off to reveal a clay figure beneath. Four mourners stand on the cart, one at the head and at the foot and one on either side, their arms raised to their heads in attitudes of mourning. A child rolls on its back on top of the shroud in an ecstasy of grief, and a bird perches beside it. The model is dated to before the middle of the seventh century and was probably used in a ceremony performed in connection with offering trenches (see below).

The *ekphora* is also represented on two black-figure *kyathoi* (cups) found in Italy and dated to the late seventh century B.C. On one the corpse is drawn to the grave on a cart pulled by mules, and on the other by four bowed pall-bearers dressed in long *himatia*. In both cases the deceased is wrapped in an *epiblêma* with his head uncovered and resting on a pillow. The cortège accompanying the cart consists of seven figures in all: two women sit beside the bier, three others and a man walk beside it, all beating their heads; and a bearded *aulos* (flute)-player brings up the rear. On the other *kyathos* two mourning women accompany the pall-bearers, an ephebe on horseback follows behind, and the rear is brought up by an old man on foot; a woman and white-robed *aulos*-player wait at the grave. The last representation of an *ekphora* occurs on a crude terracotta plaque reportedly found in the Peiraios and perhaps of Classical date. The deceased, his head bare and wrapped in an *epiblêma*, is borne along in a cart drawn by two horses. The cortège is led by a woman carrying a vase on her head. She is perhaps an *enchytristria* (see below p. 36). Behind the bier walks a man wearing a conical helmet and breastplate but carrying no weapons who appears to be holding a

Fig. 9. Terracotta model of an *ekphora*. The tiny bird perched on top of the pall is perhaps intended to represent the 'soul' of the deceased.

conversation with the corpse, possibly, as Rayet (1884, II no. 75 p. 6) suggests, reproaching him for having abandoned his relatives. Alongside the bier walks another female mourner supporting the head of the deceased in her left hand and beating her own head with her right hand. An *aulos*-player and two more women also attend.

From representations in art, supplemented by literary and epigraphical evidence, the following can be deduced about the *ekphora*. It was customary in some communities to make a sacrifice either to the dead or to the underworld deities before the cortège set out, but probably by the Archaic period the practice had been abandoned. On Keos, however, this *prosphagion* as it seems to have been called was expressly permitted by a fifth-century law. In early times the procession to the place of interment took place in daytime, which is why Solon regulated that it must be held before sunrise. The law was evidently upheld, for on the black-figure bail-*amphora* by the Sappho Painter lamps are shown blazing away as the dead man is lowered into his coffin. If unchecked, the mourners did not proceed in silence to the cemetery, but would make frequent halts at street corners so as to attract the maximum amount of public attention. Solon prescribed that men should head the cortège and women follow behind. He also imposed the same restrictions on the

attendance of women at the *ekphora* as at the *prothesis*. He does not, however, seem to have banned flautists, although it is possible that he limited their number to ten. The corpse would be transported to the grave either in a hearse drawn by horses or mules, or, more frequently, by pall-bearers known as *klimakophoroi* (ladder-carriers), *nekrophoroi* (corpse-carriers), *nekrothaptai* (corpse-buriers) and *tapheis* (buriers or grave-diggers). Originally the pall-bearers were probably members of the deceased's family, but in later times they were hired. Sometimes *ephêboi* (youths) were specially selected for the purpose. If the dead belonged to a coterie, his colleagues might have provided the convoy: we are told that the corpse of the philosopher Demonax was borne to the grave by sophists. Hired musicians accompanied the body to the grave playing what is obscurely referred to as Carian music.

The deposition

Inhumation and cremation were practised concurrently from the eighth to the fourth century B.C., though their relative popularity varied greatly over the period. The only method used for disposing of the dead in Homer is cremation. The verb *thaptô* (bury), which implies inhumation, is in fact used exclusively of cremation, as is seen from Elpenor's plea to Odysseus, 'Don't leave me unburied (*athapton*), but burn me' (*Od.* 11.72f.). There is some evidence to suggest that embalming was not unknown to the Greeks of Homer's day. As has long been recognised, the means by which the bodies of Achilles, Sarpedon and Hektor are preserved by Thetis, Apollo and Aphrodite is in fact reminiscent of the art of the Egyptian embalmer. Both inhumation and cremation were common in Geometric Greece, but in the Archaic period adults were more frequently disposed of by cremation. Evidence from the Classical period reveals no preference either way. In tragedy, however, the usual form of burial is cremation. In the Hellenistic period inhumation seems to have predominated, just as it had in the Protogeometric period some six hundred years previously. As Kurtz and Boardman (*KB* 96) note with regard to the Classical period, 'There is no apparent difference in either the rites or offerings which have been associated with the grave, and the predominance of one method over the other varies from place to place.' Nor can economic factors be held entirely responsible for the choice either, since some of the most expensive grave-gifts dating to the Archaic period have been found in connection with inhumations.

Increasing evidence is coming to light which demonstrates that in exceptional circumstances ritual slaughter took place at the graveside from the Protogeometric through to the Classical period. Homer's description of the funeral of Patroklos as performed by Achilles refers to the slaughter of twelve Trojan youths, two dogs and four horses, sacrificed upon the dead man's pyre. Bruck (1926, 31), who believed that human sacrifice was a feature of Minoan and Mycenaean burial practices, used this passage to justify his theory. He regarded the covering of Patroklos' bier with hair-offering by the mourners as an 'ersatz human sacrifice' and the presence of mourning women at the funeral as illustrative of a diminution in the strength of the ancient ceremony which originally had required their sacrifice. Though there is little if any evidence to support Bruck's theory for the Bronze Age, recently excavation undertaken jointly by the Greek Archaeological Service and the British School of Athens at Lefkandi on Euboia has provided startling corroboration of Homer's description for Dark Age Greece in the case of the heroic dead. A shaft grave belonging to what has been identified as a heroön or 'hero shrine' dated to the tenth century B.C. comprises two compartments, one of which contains the skeletons of at least three horses, apparently thrown head first into the pit. The other compartment holds two burials: the skeleton of a woman, and an *amphora* containing the dead man's ashes alongside which were an iron sword, a spear head and a whetstone. Clearly the warrior hero whom the tomb complex celebrated had been buried accompanied by his consort and his horses. Human sacrifice was certainly exceptional but horse-burials, sometimes with traces of the hearses which the horses had drawn before being slaughtered and buried with the deceased, are also known from Salamis in Cyprus dated to the eighth and seventh centuries B.C. Instances of the same practice are also reported from the Classical and Archaic periods. Herodotus relates that Kimon Koalemos, who won an Olympics 'hat-trick' in the four-horse chariot race on three successive occasions, and who is alleged to have been assassinated by the sons of the tyrant Peisistratos in 527, was buried outside the city of Athens in the deme of Koile with his horses 'opposite him'. In addition, two horses were buried in the Kerameikos around the turn of the fourth century B.C.

Deposition is rarely represented on vases. *Lêkythoi* sometimes show the act being performed by the winged Hypnos and Thanatos. A unique non-mythological representation occurs on a black-figure *loutrophoros amphora* by the Sappho Painter which depicts a coffin being lowered into a grave by two men dressed in a *himation*. The man on the right who is holding a shroud leans forward apparently in the act of depositing it in the grave. Two others stand inside the grave extending their hands upwards in order to receive the coffin from above. Scenes of cremation on vases are even rarer.

About what happened during this final, most critical, act in the whole drama, we are very imperfectly informed. So far as we know no priest was required to be present, and it may be that his office banned him from attendance at the graveside even in a private capacity. In early times women known as *enchytristriai* probably officiated in some capacity or other, perhaps in connection with blood-sacrifices made to the dead. It is hardly conceivable that the bereaved proceeded without the benefit of any established liturgy or approved form of words, though what prayer or utterance was deemed suitable and to whom it was addressed is nowhere stated. It seems likely, whether or not the corpse was borne to the grave with the head exposed, that the coffin-lid was not actually sealed until the moment of deposition. A small libation was made to the dead at the grave: in discharging her abbreviated rites over the body of her brother Polyneikes, Antigone does not omit to pour *trispondai choai* (thrice-poured offerings) to the dead as she scatters earth upon his corpse (S. *Ant.* 431). Both in Homer and in real life wine was used to quench the remains of the funeral pyre, after which the ashes were gathered up by the nearest relative and placed in a cinerary urn. Offerings were then made to the dead. The bail-*amphora* by the Sappho Painter shows a typical selection consisting of baskets of food, a *hydria* (waterjug), an *alabastron* (ointment flask) and *lêkythoi*. Such items were deposited either in the grave itself or in a place near the grave. To the end of the eighth century B.C. date two shallow, brick-lined ditches found in the Kerameikos containing burnt deposits including sherds of late Geometric date. Such 'Opferinnen' or offering trenches, which vary in length from two to twelve metres, continued to be constructed into the Classical period and beyond, though the richest examples are Archaic. From the discovery of fragments of carbonised wood found inside post-holes it seems probable that the offerings were once set out on wooden planks. In addition to large quantities of burnt pottery, remains of small animals, birds, especially fowls, and shells have been found among the debris. Mourners probably lined up alongside the trench while this rite was performed, the climax to the whole ceremony of burial.

A progressive deterioration in the quality of goods deposited in the grave is detectable from the Classical period onwards, reaching its lowest ebb *c*. 400 B.C. in the replacement of the white-ground *lêkythos* by the fusiform *unguentarium* (vessel for holding ointments). However, this cut-back in expenditure on offerings made to the dead is no absolute measure of a popular disinterest in their welfare. In a grave on Lenormant Street in Athens dated to around the second century B.C. were discovered thirty-one *unguentaria* of careless manufacture which, in the words of the excavator, seem to indicate that 'the mourners had sought to make up by numbers for the insignificance and dullness of the vessel itself'.

The Kean lawcode states that after the conclusion of the burial service, men and women should leave the cemetery separately, although textual difficulties make it unclear who left first. *Prima facie*, however, we should expect the men to stay behind to finish the construction of the tomb, while the women returned to the house of the dead in order to supervise the preparation of the banquet (*perideipnon*) which was to be held in his honour.

4

Between Worlds

From trita to triakostia

Anthropologists have frequently observed that many peoples believe that the soul of the deceased does not reach its final destination immediately after death but remains for a time marginally between two worlds. Plath (1964, 308), for instance, relates how the spirit of the Japanese dead, even after the flesh has decomposed, 'polluted by death and potentially dangerous, may wander for many weeks. It is purified and made safe by a series of rites that ordinarily culminate on the 49th day after death. However, sometimes the living find it necessary later to perform additional rites to make certain that the soul has securely entered the ranks of the departed ...'. Likewise Hertz (1907, 34), describing the beliefs of the peoples of the Malay Archipelago with particular reference to the practice of secondary burial, reported that in the initial period after decease, the soul 'must first undergo a kind of purgation during which it stays on earth in the proximity of the body ... it is only at the end of this period ... and thanks to a special ceremony, that it will enter the land of the dead ...'. The interval between death and integration in the spirit world is widely regarded as critical for the safety of the soul, whose diminished powers of resistance leave it exposed to attack from malignant spirits. Van Gennep (1909) has suggested that it is largely to secure the welfare of the deceased in this taxing and troublesome liminal period that the ceremonies which he categorises as rites of transition are performed.

Evidence for belief in the marginal condition of the dead in Late Helladic Greece was detected by Mylonas (1948, 98), who, pointing out the disrespectful attitude of the Mycenaeans towards previous burials, and contrasting it with the meticulous care shown to the body at the time of burial, explained this difference by claiming that the spirit of the Mycenaean dead remained sentient until the body had decayed, but that after this period had elapsed it had no further contact with its corpse. This observation accords with the finding of Hertz (1907, 47), who noted that, 'in several Melanesian Islands it is believed that the soul remains weak for as long as putrefaction lasts ... Death is fully consummated only when decomposition has ended; only then does the deceased cease to belong to this world so as to enter another life.'

The period of transition for the Athenian dead may be deemed to have lasted at least until the performing of the thirtieth-day rites called *triakostia, triakas* or *triakades,* the ritual which concluded mourning held approximately one month after decease. When it began is less easy to establish, though it is possible that a dying person, or even one who was condemned to death, was considered to be no longer fully integrated in this world. An intermediary stage in the transitional period was perhaps reached with the completion of the funeral which clearly marks the passing of a critical stage in the life-cycle of the dead. Certain taboos were now lifted and the deceased for the first time passed out of the sight as well as out of the exclusive care of the living, an event alluded to in scenes on Attic white *lêkythoi* which show the brothers Thanatos (Death) and Hypnos (Sleep) raising the still-unconscious body out of the grave.

That the dead were not finally disposed of by virtue of burial is suggested by what we know of the ceremony called *perideipnon,* a banquet shared by the relatives after the funeral at which, according to Artemidoros (5.82 *T*), the dead himself was believed to be present in the capacity of host. Communal post-funerary meals are known from many cultures. They serve, in the opinion of van Gennep (1909, 164), 'to reunite all the surviving members of the group with each other, and sometimes also with the deceased, in the same way that a chain which has been broken by the disappearance of one of its links must be rejoined'. At the *perideipnon* the bereaved wore garlands and delivered eulogies on behalf of the dead. Possibly as well they sang songs. Probably the banquet took place immediately after the return of the relatives from the *ekphora*. According to Lucian (*Luct.* 24), it brought to an end a period of fasting which had lasted three days (i.e. from the time of decease).

This meal shared by the living and the dead is to be sharply distinguished from banquets prepared at the tomb, from which the living may have been debarred from partaking for the fear they might pass under the influence of the spirit world (see below p. 110ff.). The meals prepared at the tomb during this transitional period were known as *trita* and *enata* (or *ennata*), the third- and ninth-day rites. Exactly when these feasts were reckoned from we do not know, but if the living were excluded from participating, we should naturally expect the *trita* to postdate the *perideipnon*, since their exclusion would clearly indicate that they and the dead no longer shared the same family circle. We know next-to-nothing about what happened during these ceremonies, but there is no reason to suppose that they were essentially different from those performed at the graveside at other times during the year. Though the *enata* are mentioned more frequently than the *trita*, this does not provide us with grounds for assuming that the former were more important than the latter, for if the *trita* took place on the same day as the burial, perhaps soon after the *perideipnon*, reference to an *ekphora* might automatically have implied the conclusion of the day's proceedings with the holding of the *trita*. On the thirtieth day after death the rite known as *triakostia* was performed. The lawcode of Ioulis on Keos banned the keeping of thirtieth-day rites, but there is no other reference to the observance in any surviving legislation. Attic writers only infrequently allude to it. It seems to have been customary to deposit 'sweepings' (*kallysmata*) from the house on the grave when performing the rite. *Triakostia* are associated with the worship of Hekate as well as with the tendance of the dead. The word was also the name for a ritual performed regularly each month, either on the thirtieth day or on the death-day of the deceased.

It seems probable that in Athens the thirtieth-day rites marked the final stage in the obsequies. A passage in Lysias (1.14) refers to a charge being laid against a woman who applied make-up to her face 'although her brother had been dead not yet thirty days'. Elsewhere in Greece the period of mourning was of different duration. At Gambreion in Asia Minor, the law prescribed that mourning should not exceed three months for men and four for women, whereas at Sparta only eleven days were allowed. We should not necessarily expect all relatives of the deceased to observe the full statutory period, however. As van Gennep (1909, 147) points out: 'Mourning requirements are based on degrees of kinship and are systematised by each people according to their special ways of calculating kinship.'

Later writers refer to a meal called *kathedra* (sitting), which marked the conclusion of mourning and the resumption of normal life in the community. This was held in honour of the deceased by relatives who sat (rather than reclined) in accordance with the custom that prevailed in Homeric times. Three further *kathedrai* were celebrated at monthly intervals. When the practice was first established, and at which commemorative banquet the dead person's full and final transfer to the next world was celebrated, is not known, but it may be that the Greeks had no strong or settled views on the matter, since anthropologists have shown that the conclusion of mourning does not invariably correspond to the final departure of the deceased. But the lifting of mourning would have marked the end of a period of uncertainty, danger and special concern for members of the deceased's family. From then on – if the explanation proposed here is substantially correct – acceptance in Hades was a mere formality.

The corpse as a taboo object

Taboo ideas, as Nilsson (1925, 82) observes, 'accumulate more than elsewhere about the critical points of human life, about birth, death, and marriage, when man is more exposed than at other times to the attacks of "power" or "the powers" '. The polluting effect of the Greek corpse was by no means an obsession. In Homer it could even be regarded as a thing of beauty. In a passage of extraordinary boldness, Hekabe describes Hektor's corpse as 'dewy-fresh' (*herséëis*), a word used elsewhere in the poem to describe the lotus (*Il.* 24.757). What appears to be the earliest testimony for the idea of the contagiousness of physical decay occurs in Hesiod who cautions against having intercourse after returning from 'the ill-omened funeral' (*Erg.* 735). The degree of contagiousness of the Greek dead varied from polis to polis, as reference to pollution in codes of funerary practice make clear. The fifth-century legislation from Keos ordained that the polluted were the mother of the deceased, his wife, sisters, daughters, a maximum of five other women, 'children of daughters and of cousins' (text uncertain). As Moulinier (1952, 77) has observed, the Kean code seems to have regarded miasma as a right and privilege which needed to be restricted to a few, rather than as a baleful influence from which one should seek a speedy release. It is possible that the limits of pollution were also laid down in the rules drawn up *c.* 400 B.C. by the priestly phratry of the Labyadai at Delphi, which stated according to one interpretation that there was pollution up to the moment until the *thigana* (coffin lid?) was closed. Since the closing of the *thigana* took place at the *sêma* or tomb, it would appear that exposure to the noxious presence of the dead was judged to be the true source of pollution. The Labyad rules, unlike the Kean code, do not define which members of the family were the polluted, and it is possible that we have to do here with a more overtly pathogenic interpretation of miasma, in contrast to the view which saw it as an automatic condition of close kinship with the deceased.

In Athens a law attributed to Solon appears to have granted entitlement, if that is the correct word, to a wide group of persons by permitting women over the age of sixty and those within the degree of second cousin (*anepsiadai*) to enter the house of the dead and to take part in the funeral. The Athenian lawcode also required relatives, or, failing relatives, the demarch, to 'purify the deme' if the body had not immediately been taken up for burial.

Fear of the polluting effect of the dead, though widespread, was not universal throughout Greece. Plutarch (*Lyk.* 27) says that the lawgiver Lykourgos put an end to superstition (*deisidaimonia*) in Sparta by permitting people to bury their dead inside the city and to erect grave-monuments near sacred places. In this way he familiarised young people with the sight of death 'so that it did not trouble or frighten them, as if touching a corpse or walking among graves caused pollution'. It is also interesting to note that in Euripides' *Alkêstis* the fact that a death has recently occurred in his host's house in no way deters Herakles from sitting down to a hearty meal, though naturally it would be methodologically unsound to draw any general conclusions from this singular instance inasmuch as Herakles' name was a by-word for gluttony.

Hertz (1907, 76) has observed that 'the horror inspired by the corpse does not spring from the simple observation of the changes that occur in the body'. Such a rationalistic explanation of pollution, he argues, is inadequate on the grounds that 'in one and the same society the emotion caused by death varies extremely in intensity according to the social status of the deceased. There is some slight evidence to suggest that this principle holds true of ancient Greece as well and that the corruptibility of a dead body varied in proportion to the social standing of the deceased. In the case of the infant dead, it is perhaps because the risk of pollution from a child's corpse was regarded as negligible that children continued to be buried intramurally at a time when extramural burial was insisted upon for adults. Young (1951, 133) has noted that although the burial of adult dead within the city of Athens comes to an abrupt end *c.* 500 B.C., child-cremations and urn-burials continued to be made within this area right down to Hellenistic times. Though urn-burials of infants could, as Young points out, easily have been made clandestinely, cremation would obviously arouse public notice. The conclusion must therefore be that this practice was condoned by law. But while a belief in the innocuousness of the infant dead provides us with a possible explanation for the exceptional treatment of child-corpses, economic, hygienic or purely sentimental reasons may also be partly responsible for the distinction.

Equally unsatisfactory and ambivalent is the evidence relating to persons of high social status. Herodotus (6.58) tells us that after the death of a Spartan king had been announced, two freeborn persons from every household – one male and one female – had to perform the rite of purification (*katamiainesthai*). While Herodotus plainly intimates that the custom arose out of fear of pollution rather than as an outward sign of mourning, it is difficult to resist the impression that it was intended chiefly as a mark of honour to the royal dead.

Cathartic measures against the dead

Customs observed in Athens while the corpse still lay in the house during *prothesis* included placing a bowl of water (*ardanion*) brought from outside the house so that visitors could purify themselves upon entering and leaving; hanging a cypress branch, or alternatively a lock of hair, on the door (possibly merely to serve as a warning that a corpse lay within); placing *lēkythoi* around the bed of the deceased (perhaps intended as a purification of both living and dead alike); and finally, most important of all, bathing the corpse (above Chapter 3). It is interesting to note, as we have already seen, that touching and fondling the body were essential features of the ritual lament – a clear indication that the corpse was not held in complete abhorrence.

While the body remained unburied, purificatory measures could reduce, but not eliminate altogether, its polluting effect. Perhaps immediately after the funeral, it was the custom in Athens for relatives of the deceased to perform a ceremony known as *aponimma* (washing). This involved digging a trench on the west side of the grave, pouring in water, and reciting the following formula: '*Aponimma* (water) for you to clean yourself with – you for whom it is meet and right.' Afterwards myrrh was poured into the trench. From Athenaios' observation that *aponimma* was used by the Athenians to describe 'rites performed in honour of the dead' as well as for ceremonies of purification, it would appear that this ritual was intended to benefit both living and dead.

It was customary for relatives of the deceased, upon returning home after a funeral, to take a bath. What further purificatory measures were enjoined by Athenian practice is not known, but we can be certain that the deceased's house had to be cleansed in some way. According to the Kean inscription, the day after the funeral a freeman had to purify the house both with sea-water and some other substance. The ceremony terminated with offerings to Hestia, the goddess of the hearth. Possibly as well the placing of sweepings (*kallysmata*) on graves once a month was intended to remove any lingering impurities from the home, though the significance of this curious ritual remains unclear.

For doubtful cases, there existed at Athens interpreters of religious law (*exêgêtai*) whose business was to pronounce upon the correct religious procedure concerning death or purification where the circumstances of a person's demise were in some way irregular. In the speech *Against Evergos* (47.68) by Pseudo-Demosthenes the plaintiff claims that when an old nurse of his died from manslaughter at the hands of the accused, he consulted the *exêgêtai* 'in order to learn what ought to be done'. They inform him that after making all necessary arrangements both for her funeral and the prosecution of her killer he should purify himself and his house. The wording of their answer suggests that they regarded being polluted as an obligation at least as much as a physical taint or infection.

Cathartic measures against the dead had to be taken not only at the time of decease but on other commemorative occasions during the year as well. As already noted, the lexicographer Photios states that at the Choës, the Athenian festival held on the second day of the Anthesteria, the *psychai* of the dead were believed to wander abroad and that in order to counteract their noxious influence people would chew buckthorn (*rhamnos*) and smear the doors of their houses with pitch.

Gods as well as humans could become infected by the dead. Artemis abandoned her favourite Hippolytos in his dying moments because, she declared, it was not lawful (*themis*) for her to see the dead or to infect her eyes with their last gasps. Similarly her brother Apollo had to leave the house where Alkestis was dying so that the miasma in the house should not touch him. Not only the gods but also all holy places had to be kept clean of death. Numerous inscriptions from all over the Greek world ban from temple precincts those who have been in recent contact with the dead. A second-century B.C. inscription from Eresos on Lesbos decreed that those who had purified themselves after a funeral of a member of their own family must wait twenty days before entering the temenos area; non-relatives of the deceased, on the other hand, after performing the necessary ablutions, could be admitted after only three. An inscription from Attika dated to the second century A.D. which relates to the cult of Men laid down that the impurity of a corpse lasted ten days. An unknown cult at Lindos (possibly oriental) of similar date decreed that forty days had to elapse 'after the funeral of a member of one's own family' before one could return to normal life. From an inscription found near the Propylaia in Athens we learn that it was an ancestral custom (*patrios nomos*) that 'no one should either give birth or die in any temple precinct'. It is, moreover, a striking fact that at Rhamnous in northeast Attika, where a line of tombs over one and a half miles in length extends from outside the fortress wall, no tombs are actually to be found opposite the temple area itself. Finally, we may note that the reason for Sokrates' lengthy stay in prison was a law which stated that while the sacred embassy (*theôria*) to Delos was taking place, 'the city had to remain pure and no public executions were to take place'. The sacred island of Delos, the birthplace of Apollo, was first purified in 543 B.C. by the tyrant Peisistratos who dug up all the graves that were within sight of the sanctuary and had the bones conveyed to another part of the island. Possibly in order to avert a further outbreak of the plague which had ravaged Athens in 430 B.C., Nikias carried out a second purification of the island in 426, removing all the dead and ordaining that 'no one was to die or give birth on the island, but they must be conveyed to Rheneia (a small island nearby)'.

At least some priests were forbidden all contact with the dead. Those who presided at the Eleusinian Mysteries were debarred from entering a house of mourning, visiting a grave, or even attending a funeral banquet. Similar restrictions were placed on the priestess of Demeter on Kos. The cult of Zeus Polieus on the same island prescribed that if a priest attended an *ekphora*, five days had to elapse before he could resume his functions again.

Explanations of pollution belief

Having examined some of the evidence for the existence of a taboo upon the Greek dead, it remains for us to consider how such a belief first arose. We will now need to look at miasma in a wider context than that aspect of it which has merely to do with the corpse.

Nilsson's theory of pollution, which I quoted at the beginning of this chapter, was that pollution arises from exposure to attack from hostile power or powers. These powers had been defined by Rohde before him as *daimones* (spirits), namely 'uncanny forces surrounding men and stretching out after them with a thousand threatening hands into the darkness' (1897, 296). Principal among this sinister band of spirits was the goddess Hekate, whose favourite haunt was cemeteries and places of ill-omen, and who was present both at childbirth and at death, when the *psychê* either enters or leaves the body.

However, the notion that the dead are dangerous because subject to the influence of *daimones* is unsupported by any real evidence. In Homer *lymata* were conceived of as a material which could be scraped off, washed away or burned out – a substance, in fact, rather like dirt. That fear of pollution is essentially fear of dirt and catharsis a reflection of a desire for hygiene is the explanation which has been proposed by Moulinier (1952). This physiological interpretation at first sight seems to provide the most natural and satisfactory solution to the question. After all, what could be more logical than that the unpleasant changes which quickly overtake a dead body in a hot climate should give rise to the belief that the dead should be treated circumspectly? However, the theory fails to explain why the same feeling should attach to the other dramatic moments of life such as birth and marriage.

Jane Harrison (1921, 10) fittingly described the attitude of mind which a taboo object like a corpse inspires as one of 'mingled attraction and repulsion, desire and shrinking'. Pollution in effect is merely another aspect of purity – and both conditions must be treated with extreme caution. This interpretation is supported by etymology. The Greek *hagos*, the postulated root of *hagnos* (pure) and *agos*, the usual word for pollution, have been shown by Chantraine and Masson (1954) to derive from a common source, as the ancient grammarians had also postulated. As Vernant (1974, 124) puts it, 'the meanings of *hagnos* and *hagios* are not fundamentally different from that of *agos*. They refer to what is forbidden, prohibited in the sacred'.

The idea that the corpse was a sacred object, or at least that it became so through the performance of certain rites, demonstrably existed in the Classical period. Antigone's act of sprinkling dust over the corpse of Polyneikes is, for instance, judged sufficient to consecrate his body to the gods below (S. *Ant.* 247). Cremation as well as inhumation performed this function: the body of Klytaimnestra is described as having been 'rendered *hagnos* by fire' (Eur. *Or.* 40). For those returning from the dead, the process took place in reverse. Admetos is told that he is not permitted to hear Alkestis speak until the third day comes and she has been 'deconsecrated' (*aphagnistêtai*) to the underworld gods (Eur. *Alk.* 1144ff.).

The corpse is taboo because the corpse is sacred, and it is sacred because the dead person, in the initial period after his decease, lacks a proper social identity in either world. Even a moribund is not fully of this world. As Thanatos points out: 'For *hieros* (sacred) to the deities below is he from whose head this sword has consecrated (literally 'made *hagnos*') a lock' (Eur. *Alk.* 75f.).

It would, however, be unwise to insist upon too precise an explanation of pollution beliefs. The sentiments surrounding a corpse in the period between death and burial, a time when rapid changes are taking place in the body, are *ipso facto* more fluid and uncertain than those which attend the final condition of the dead when entry to the afterlife has been fully achieved. It seems inevitable that considerations of hygiene, fear of unknown powers and a sense of guilt should at least have contributed to the suggestiveness of the taboo upon the Greek corpse, which, judged overall, seems to have aroused practical, rather than pathological, concern.

5

Life in Hades

According to Christian teaching, death offers the way to salvation. 'Verily, verily, I say unto you, except a corn of wheat fall into the ground and die, it abideth alone: but if it die, it bringeth forth much fruit' (John 12:24). In certain circumstances, a Christian can, with easy conscience, actively foster his own death, as most obviously in the case of a martyr dying in defence of his faith. The prospect of what follows death may therefore stand as a consolation for the awfulness of this life. Paganism, by contrast, produced no martyrs. Though one might die defending a principle, as did the mythological Antigone and the historical Sokrates, in so doing one acted entirely on personal initiative, without the backing of either a theological framework or divine exemplar. To a practising pagan, religiosity offered a means of worldly assistance and advancement in which contemplation of the afterlife played no part. It followed that if one had acted heedlessly or disrespectfully towards the gods, one did not have to wait until the hereafter to be informed: it was here and now that the powers above would supply or withold their favours. Though belief in a system of alternative afterlifes, corresponding to Christian ideas of Heaven and Hell, did exist to a limited degree – witness Orphism and the Eleusinian Mysteries – such a belief was by no means fundamental to the spirit of paganism and represented only a relatively late stage in its development. While largely spared the horrors of a Christian Hell, the dying lacked as well the consolation of a better lot in the hereafter. It is therefore difficult to imagine that they can have contemplated their arrival in the world below with a more positive attitude of mind than that of restrained foreboding. Mythology taught that mankind had not always been dispatched to the underworld upon the completion of its earthly cycle. According to Hesiod (*Erg.* 153), the race of bronze, the originators of violence and warfare in the world, were the first to descend to 'the misty house of cold Hades'. To this limited extent, therefore, Hades, the place of darkness, was viewed by the Greeks as man's reward for Original Sin.

Topography

In Homer both the god and his kingdom are expressed by the single word *Aïdês*, to give the name its proper epic form. Excluding Earth and Olympos, whose sovereignty the gods shared, the 'murky darkness' as it is otherwise known in Homer, was one of three areas of the universe ruled by an individual deity, along with *aithêr* and the sea, ruled by Zeus and Poseidon. It was possible to approach *Aïdês* either by land or by sea, its location being variously described as 'at the bounds of Okeanos' and 'beneath the depths of the earth'. For the first *Nekyia* in the *Odyssey* Kirke gives Odysseus the following instructions: he must sail across Okeanos till he comes to the wild coast and groves of Persephone 'where the tall poplars grow and willows that quickly shed their seeds'. Then, after beaching his ship, he is to seek the rock where the rivers Pyriphlegethon (Blazing-like-fire)and Kokytos (Wailing) flow into Acheron. In the second *Nekyia*, Hermes leads the suitors slain by Odysseus by a land route which takes them 'along the dark, mouldy ways'. They arrive at the streams of Okeanos, and we learn of a white rock, the gates of Helios, and the region of dreams. The topography is sufficiently unfamiliar that we might be pardoned for suspecting that we had not arrived in Hades at all, but the conversation which follows the suitors' arrival is expressly stated to be taking place in that region. Hesiod contributes little to our understanding of the geography of Hades, except to tell us that it contains echoing halls and that it is icy. As noted, he also informs us that the men of the bronze race were the first to descend to the underworld, their predecessors, the races of gold and silver, becoming 'pure spirits living on earth' and 'blessed spirits of the underworld' respectively. It is surely significant that later Greek literature has left us with no picture of the underworld which might be considered representative of ordinary Greek belief. In fact the first extant literary description of the topography of Hades after Homer is provided by Aristophanes in the *Frogs* (117ff.). Inquiring of Herakles by what route he descended to the underworld to fetch Kerberos, Dionysos is informed that he will first come to a fathomless lake which he must cross in Charon's boat, and then to 'serpents and beasts in thousands', a 'mass of mire' and 'everlasting dung'. Proceeding further, he will hear the sound of flutes and behold the myrtle groves where those initiated into the Eleusinian Mysteries reside. On arrival at the lake, Dionysos is greeted by Charon who calls out the names of the places for which his barque is bound: the plain of Lethe, the Donkey's Shearing, Kerberia, Crowland and Tainaron.

Our other principal literary source is the myths of Plato. According to the doctrine put forward in the *Phaedo*, the majority of dead, all those, that is, who are judged to have lived a neutral life remarkable neither for its goodness or badness, are conveyed in boats to the Acherusian Lake, where they dwell, undergoing purification, until such time as they are sent back to be born again as living creatures. In the myth which the resurrected Er relates in the *Republic*, by contrast, the dead upon arrival in the underworld first come to a huge meadow, from whence, after judgment, they proceed seven days later to a 'place of choosing' where sample lives are put before them. They then journey, afflicted by a terrible heat, to the plain of Lethe, a desert waste where they spend the night, before being borne away to their new births. Though there are undoubted echoes of popular belief in Aristophanes' and Plato's description of Hades in so far as they duplicate each other in certain particulars, at the best they merely serve as eccentric variants on a popular theme.

We should also include in our discussion of the geography of Hades the so-called 'Orphic' gold leaves, which Zuntz has now demonstrated to be Pythagorean in origin. One such *lamella* found near a grove at Pharsalos which also contained a bronze vase of Attic workmanship dated *c.* 350-320 B.C. declares: 'You will find on the right in the house of Hades a spring, and standing beside it, a white cypress. Do not go near the spring. Further on, you will find cold water flowing from the lake of Memory ...'. It is at this latter spring, the text continues, that the dead are to relieve their thirst. We are to conclude, it seems, that there is a parting of the ways at the entrance to Hades – a view shared incidentally by Sokrates in the *Phaedo*, who instances the need for guides (*hêgemones*) in its favour.

Below or beyond Hades is Tartaros, the place of punishment for disobedient gods. Dark, windless and seemingly subterranean, it is the pit (*barathron*) into which Zeus cast the Titans together with his father Kronos. In the *Iliad* it is both 'as far beneath *Aidês* as heaven is above earth' and 'at the uttermost limits of earth and sea'. In the *Theogony* it is situated 'in the depths of the broad-wayed earth' and 'as far beneath earth as heaven is above earth'. Hesiod states that a bronze anvil, if dropped from heaven, would take ten days to reach earth and then a further ten to arrive at Tartaros. The darkness of this region is such that 'night is poured around it in three rows like a collar round the neck, while above it grow the roots of the earth and of the unharvested sea' (*Th.* 726ff.). Tartaros does not figure prominently in the imagination of later writers. In the pseudo-Hesiodic *Aspis* it is used merely as a synonym for Hades. The theogonist Pherekydes says that it was guarded by the Harpies and Thyella. In Aeschylus it is both a place of punishment for disobedient gods and the home of the Eumenides. In the *Oedipus at Kolonos*, Oedipus calls upon 'the dread paternal Erebos of Tartaros' to curse his son Polyneikes. Finally, in the *Phaedo*, Plato depicts Tartaros as a cavern which all subterranean rivers flow in and out of, an image which possibly reflects its etymological connections with *tarassô*, 'stir' or 'agitate'.

Sculptural and pictorial representations of Hades for the period and area under study are rare, though they do occur later, notably in the series of large Apulian *amphorai* of the latter fourth century which exhibit Pluto and Kore enthroned in a shrine surrounded by mythical personages. It is particularly instructive that no Attic white *lêkythos* portrays a scene set in the underworld. Though Hermes and Charon sometimes figure, it is as if the artist's imagination stopped at the banks of the River Acheron, as Pottier (1883, 82) has aptly remarked.

It seems clear that the Greeks were not much concerned to produce a consistent and clearly mapped-out picture of the landscape of Hades. Nor did they expend much creative imagination upon the topography. That the region was regarded as dark and windy, and that it contained a great river we need not doubt, but how much further can we safely proceed in attempting to establish an essentially popular conception of the underworld? Landmarks such as the white rock, the myrtle groves, the plain of Lethe, the white cypress and the lake of Memory may all derive from a common tradition, but since we learn of their existence from such a diversity of literary sources, and since no poet or painter has provided us with a synthesised view, it is perhaps safer to assume that the Greeks were as much in the dark about Hades as they have left us.

Ministers of Hades

Only gradually did those responsible for the smooth running of

Hades begin to acquire the stamp of a distinctive identity. Significantly, Homer, who gave the Olympian gods such vivid personalities, barely makes reference to their underworld counterparts. Hades, for instance, the 'lord of those below' and brother of Zeus and Poseidon, is barely differentiated from the realm which he governs. We are merely told that he is 'implacable' (*adamastos*) and 'relentless' (*ameilichos*), 'most hated by mortals of all the gods', 'monstrous' and 'strong'. Probably as god rather than as place he is on several occasions described as 'famous for his steeds', but why is not clear. We learn, too, that Hades was once wounded in the shoulder by an arrow from the bow of Herakles and had to ascend to high Olympos to receive the ministrations of the divine healer Paieon, but that was in the dim and distant past (Hom. *Il.* 5.395ff.).

The Homeric *Hymn to Demeter*, probably to be dated to the seventh century, provides us with a rare graphic detail when it refers to the god as being dark-haired, a characteristic which he shares with his brother Poseidon. The hymn recounts in detail the only mythological story known to be connected with Hades, namely his abduction of Persephone, the daughter of Demeter, whom he transported to the underworld to be his queen. It is here, too, for the first time that we encounter the use of euphemistic titles for Hades, such as 'all-receiving' and 'ruling over many', a clear signal that in the Archaic period it was considered unlucky to refer to the god by name. In Pindar we witness a momentary instance of bureaucratic confusion when he takes on both the role and *rhabdos* (magic staff) elsewhere assigned to Hermes *Psychopompos* (Leader of Souls), leading the bodies of the dying down 'the hollow way'.

It is a distinctive feature of Greek eschatology that Hades rarely, if at all, assumes the role of tormentor of the wicked dead. Aeschylus alone assigns him a judicial role when the Chorus in the *Eumenidês* describe him as 'a great chastiser (*euthynos*) of mortals below the earth' who 'overlooks everything with his recording mind' (273ff.). Even in Aeschylus, however, his role is ambivalent: in the *Suppliants* (157ff.) he is identified as 'the most hospitable Zeus of the dead' to whom the Danaids promise to present themselves, having duly committed suicide, if the Olympian gods do not honour their appeal for protection in the world above. Neither Sophokles nor Euripides suggest that Hades performs the function of judging the dead, though in Sophokles' *Antigonê* (451) it is stated that Dike (Justice) shares residence with the gods below. This essential neutrality of Hades is reflected in the type of epithets which are applied to the god in tragedy. He is 'common to many' and 'where all must sleep'. Once only he is described as bloody, but this is by Apollo who has a personal grudge against him.

In the Classical period 'Hades' always refers to the god, never to his realm, descent to which is described as '*es Haidou*' ('to the house of Hades'). It is also in this period that the king of the underworld acquires the alternative title of Plouton or Pluto, a word etymologically connected with *ploutos*, 'wealth' and possibly an honorific, awarded in recognition of his beneficent powers. Under this title the god is occasionally invoked for aid, either to assist in a dangerous project or to hasten the moment of one's death. In inscriptions Hades as god of the dead does not figure before the fourth century.

Representations of the god in art are rare. An early appearance is on a sixth-century black-figure lip cup by Xenokles in the company of his two brothers, Zeus and Poseidon. He is shown without any attribute but with averted head; perhaps he has just been assigned to the underworld, as Vermeule suggests, and is registering his displeasure at the apportionment. A vase from Volci in the British Museum depicts him as a benign, white-haired old man, holding a cornucopia. On the *Nekyia* vase, an Attic red-figure calyx *kratêr* dated *c.* 450 B.C., Hades appears with Persephone in the company of other famous underworld figures, including Herakles, Hermes, Perithoös, Theseus, Elpenor, Ajax and Palamedes. The abduction of Persephone is also infrequently depicted on vases. A rare sculptural representation of the god dated to the fourth century shows him reclining at table beside Persephone who is seated on his left: no longer a raffish rapist, but a quiet, family man.

It is well-known that Hades had no generally recognised cult – hence the force of Kreon's taunt in Sophokles' *Antigonê* (777) that it was he alone of the gods whom Antigone in her perversity chose to worship. There is no record of any offerings being made in his honour, and it is doubtless merely a poetical conceit on Euripides' part that in the *Phoinissai* (1574ff.) drops of split blood on the battlefield constitute a libation to the god. According to Pausanias, it was only at Elis where a cult developed, and even then the worship took on an aura of mystery: the temple was opened once a year and only the priest was allowed to enter. In addition a Ploutoneion, or shrine of Pluto, is referred to in an inscription from Corinth, though generally this word signifies an inlet to the underworld, exuding mephitic vapours. A cave, sacred to Pluto, exists most famously at Eleusis.

Likewise Hades' assistants only gradually took on shape and identity. The earliest to do so was Kerberos, whom Homer, while not mentioning him by name, describes as 'the hound of Hades whom Herakles stole from Erebos'. In the *Theogony* Kerberos is named as the offspring of Typhaios and Echidna, 'an eater of raw meat, the bronze-voiced dog of Hades, fifty-headed, relentless and strong' (311). His role as warder is vividly portrayed: he fawns 'with tail and ears' when the dead enter the underworld, but is ready to devour them if they should try to leave. Kerberos is occasionally mentioned in tragedy, sometimes with scepticism regarding his existence.

Kerberos first appears in art on a Corinthian bowl (now lost) dated *c*. 600 B.C. On Attic vases, representations of him – usually two-headed – almost all belong to the last quarter of the sixth century. His abduction by Herakles is a popular subject. The best example is a red-figure *amphora* attributed to the Andokides Painter dated *c*. 530 B.C. A crouching Herakles is in the act of tentatively putting forth his right hand to stroke the monster, while in the other he holds a chain with which to bind him. A colonnaded portico and, oddly, an olive tree, provide the setting. Sculptural representations are rare but not unknown.

Hermes *Psychopompos* is also known in Homer, but from a passage which is suspected to be a late interpolation (*Od.* 24.1ff.). He is described as carrying 'a fair gold wand (*rhabdos*)', an implement intimately associated with necromancy, with which he 'charms the eyes of those he wishes, while others who sleep he wakes'. Hermes not only conducts the dead to their new home, but also releases them again to the light of day – such at least would appear to be the meaning behind a fifth-century Attic white *lêkythos* in Jena which shows the god standing beside a giant *pithos* (storage jar) half-buried in the ground, out of which issue forth winged spirits of the dead.

In the capacity of Hades' factotum, Hermes figures both in the *Hymn to Demeter*, as his charioteer, and in the *Hymn to Hermes*, as his special messenger. In neither poem does he figure as *psychopompos*. On the other hand, he is frequently referred to in this capacity in Greek tragedy with the epithet *pompaios* (leader) or *chthonios* (of the underworld).

On Attic *lêkythoi* Hermes appears only infrequently. Sometimes he conducts the dead to Charon's waiting boat on the banks of the Styx; less commonly he comes all the way to the grave to collect his charge, looking on while Thanatos (Death) and Hypnos (Sleep) perform their duty. Especially memorable is a painting dated 440-430 B.C. which shows him seated on a rock while a woman adjusts her hair in preparation for her final journey (fig.10). As *psychopompos* Hermes rarely appears on gravestones, and I know of only one certain example: a marble Attic *lêkythos* erected to a woman called Myrrhine dated *c.* 420 B.C.

In addition to fulfilling the role of conductor of souls, Hermes in the plays of Sophokles is also invoked to assist in the passage of death. Ajax, for instance, prays to the god to enable him to die without painful convulsions; Oedipus calls upon him to lead him to the sacred tomb where he is destined to be buried; and in a somewhat different vein, Elektra enlists his services, together with those of Hades, Curse and the Erinyes (Furies), to avenge the murder of her father. A further duty performed by the god in his chthonic capacity is that of 'weigher of souls' in scenes of *psychostasia* (soul-weighing) on vases of the late Archaic and Classical period.

Representations of Hermes, often in the form of a stone pillar with carved head and male genitals known as a *herm*, were occasionally placed over graves or carved on *stêlai*, presumably as a way of committing the dead to the care and protection of Hermes *Chthonios*. Examples of sculptures of this kind have been found in Attika, the Peloponnese, Thrace, Macedonia and the islands of the Aegean. Because *herma*, a 'foundation', 'prop' or 'support', could also signify a funerary monument which in its simplest form might simply be a heaped pile of stones, Nilsson (*GGR*[3] I, p. 503) suggested that the name Hermes means in effect 'he who is in a heap of stones'.

Charon, the ferryman of the dead, makes his first appearance in Greek mythology at a much later date than either Hades, Kerberos or Hermes. According to Diodorus Siculus, he entered Greece via Egypt, but it is possible that his origins should be sought among the Greeks of Magna Graecia. One of the earliest, perhaps the first reference to him is in an inscription from Phokis dated to between the sixth and fifth centuries B.C. It reads: 'Hail, Charon, no one slanders you even when they are dead, you who release many men from toil.' The citation, though brief, strikes one as odd, since the credit for releasing mortals from toil would more naturally go to Hermes *Psychopompos*. In the *Seven Against Thebes* (856ff.), Aeschylus describes Charon's boat as 'ever plying its way across Acheron with black sails ... to the land where Apollo may not set foot, the sunless regions ...' In the epic poem *Minyas*, which is possibly of fifth-century date, Charon is referred to as 'the old ferryman' and was thus represented by Polygnotos in his paintings for the Lesche (Painted Hall) of the Knidians at Delphi. In Euripides' *Alkêstis* he is described, interestingly, as 'a *psychopompos* holding an oar' and 'an elderly *nekropompos* (leader of corpses)'. Once again there seems to be a confusion of roles among the ministry suggestive either of diffidence or – more probably – indifference regarding the actuality of the next world on the part of the Greek imagination.

On Attic *lêkythoi* Charon is the most frequently represented mythological personality. He is shown in his boat waiting patiently while the dead, sometimes accompanied by Hermes, approach. On what is perhaps the earliest *lêkythos* which figures such a scene, the ferryman's appearance has been aptly described by Fairbanks (1914, I 189f.) as 'repulsive' in contrast to the ennobled features of Hermes who escorts a woman to Charon's boat 'almost with a look of kindly pity'. Later representations show him in a more favourable light, and on some vases he has the refined features of a Quattrocento John the Baptist. In general, there are two distinct Charon 'types' on Attic *lêkythoi*, stern Charons and kindly Charons, though the latter predominate. The ferryman of the dead is a particularly common choice of subject for the Sabouroff Painter, and for artists of the Reed Workshop, which flourished in the last decade of the fifth century. On later Attic *lêkythoi* he becomes less popular.

The Charon of Greek art may instructively be contrasted with the Etruscan Charun. Whereas the Greek ferryman appears calm and pensive, his Etruscan counterpart is of frightening appearance and less subtle in approach, being armed with a heavy hammer with which to club his recalcitrant victims to death. His characterisation in Greek literature is slight and insignificant: in Euripides' *Alkêstis* he is impatient; in Aristophanes' *Frogs* he is courteous and obliging. Rare sculptural representations include a rather clumsy funerary *stêlê* in the Kerameikos in which he is shown simply as an old man.

The role and status of Thanatos, the personification of Death, are nowhere clearly defined. The famous passage in the *Iliad*, where, in the company of his brother Hypnos (Sleep), he comes to remove the body of Sarpedon from the battlefield, almost seems to suggest a kind of tenderness. In the *Theogony* we learn that he is the son of Nyx (Night), and that he numbers among his brothers not only Hypnos, but also Moros (Fate), Ker (Fate of Death) and Dreams. The name of his mother is never divulged. He is also described as 'having a heart of bronze' and being 'hateful even to the gods'.

Fig. 10. Attic *lêkythos* *c.* 440-430 B.C. showing Hermes as *Psychopompos* patiently awaiting his charge.

The most detailed literary portrait of Thanatos occurs in
Euripides' *Alkêstis*, where he is described as dark-browed, winged
and black-robed. He is armed with a sword with which he
consecrates those destined to die by symbolically cutting off a lock of
their hair. Apollo describes him as 'hateful to mankind and loathed
by the gods'. What is not understood is Thanatos' status and dignity
vis-à-vis the other underworld powers – or even, more crucially,
whether he is to be regarded as a totally independent figure distinct
from Hades. The ancient commentators on the *Alkêstis* clearly
thought that he was not, for they substituted his name for that of
Hades in their discussion of the play. The problem of his identity has
largely to do with a crucial passage in which the doomed Alkestis
imagines she sees a winged figure who has come to haul her off to
Hades. Whereas in earlier passages in the play the task of conducting
the dead to the world below is assigned to Thanatos, now in her
reverie it seems to be Hades, the underworld king, who himself
performs this menial role.

Elsewhere in the play Thanatos tells us that he possesses rights
(*timai*) to whose enjoyment he is entitled as much as others, and a
privilege (*geras*) which increases in proportion to the youthfulness of
his victim. On the other hand, he cannot act on his own initiative,
having received orders to kill 'whoever needs killing' as he
engagingly puts it. The problem of determining his exact status from
the evidence of Euripides' play is further complicated by the fact that
it would be dramatically inconsistent to represent him other than as
'an ogreish creature of popular mythology', since, as Dale (1954, 54)
points out, he has to wrestle with the glutton Herakles and be
worsted by him. To what extent this somewhat grotesque portrait of
Thanatos is derived from popular belief is, of course, impossible to
tell, since there exists no adequate comparison in the whole of Greek
literature. To be sure the contrast between the Euripidean image on
the one hand, and the impression received from Homer and Greek
vase-painting (see below) on the other, is considerable, but the
irreconcilability of the two does not entitle us to conclude that they
could not – or did not – co-exist. Indeed if Euripides' inspiration did
not ultimately derive from popular mythology, it is difficult to
imagine what other source it might have had.

References to Thanatos elsewhere in tragedy are rare. In
Sophokles' *Oedipus at Kolonos*, the Chorus refer to him as 'the saviour
who comes at last to all alike'. He is perhaps to be identified with the
son of Earth and Tartaros who is invoked by the Chorus later in the

same play, though previously, as noted above, he is called the son of Nyx. Thanatos is invoked by Ajax before he falls upon his spear; by Philoktetes in the hope that he will put an early end to his misery; and by Hippolytos who sees him as his only cure. In addition we are told that he keeps Polybos in the grave and begets the poison which kills Herakles.

In the late sixth and early fifth century Thanatos and Hypnos appear in Attic vase scenes carrying off dead mythical figures such as Sarpedon and Memnon. On Attic *lêkythoi* they carry away ordinary Greeks as well, though women do not begin to figure as their victims until the end of the fifth century. Where named, Thanatos and Hypnos are sometimes contrasted as older and younger types respectively, but the distinction is not enforced. On one occasion, on a *lêkythos* by the Reed Workshop, a bearded and menacing Thanatos is shown pursuing a woman at a tomb who recoils in horror while Hermes watches on: a rare example of a pre-emptive strike by a chthonic deity against a helpless victim. This scene may be compared with the description in the *Iliad* (18.535ff.) of the personified Ker who 'grasping one man alive, recently wounded, and another unwounded, drags a third just dead through the fray by his feet', a passage memorable in its unique depiction of the furious onset of death.

A sculptured drum from one of the columns belonging to the temple of Artemis at Ephesus shows a winged figure which might conceivably be Thanatos, but apart from this doubtful case, no known sculptured portrait of the god has survived. There is, however, in Pausanias (5.18.1) a portrayal of Thanatos in the company of Hypnos and Nyx on a carved cedar-wood chest which was deposited in the temple of Hera at Olympia by the Kypselids of Corinth, in gratitude for the saving of their founder.

Like Hades, Thanatos was not normally the recipient of a cult established in his honour. He is described as 'the god who does not receive libations (*aspondos*)', and the only one who does not like presents. Only once, at Sparta, do we hear of a temple being erected to him. But the practice was decidedly odd, and the Spartans were odd people for doing it, as Plutarch (*Kleom.* 9) intimates, for they also erected temples to Laughter and Fear.

What is perhaps most remarkable about the picture of Hades and its agents which emerges from literary and iconographical sources is its lack of distinctive colouring. The functionaries who ran it, no less than the kingdom over which they presided, if joyless, were hardly intimidating. Not that the Greek mentality wholly shyed away from the prospect of more macabre delights in the world to come than those so far discussed. The description of the repulsive Eurynomos in Pausanias' account of the *Nekyia* by Polygnotos at Delphi – 'a spirit (*daimôn*) who eats the flesh off corpses' and 'whose skin is of a colour between blue and black, like that of flies which settle in butchers' shops' – provides a rare but welcome glimpse of the Greek imagination taking a robust interest in the horrors of putrefaction and decay.

Retributive punishment

Death in Homer is the consequence of, rather than the punishment for, reckless behaviour – and any divine intervention is explicitly ruled out. Thus Odysseus' companions perish through having devoured the sacred kine of Hyperion and Aegisthos for having slain Agammemnon and wedded Klytaimnestra. *Atasthaliai* (presumptuous acts) are the only crime which brings such retribution, and it is significant that it does not elicit any moral judgment from the poet. Persons who commit it are merely described as *nêpioi*, 'children', because they should have known better. However, with death all retribution ceases. There is no hint of a reckoning on the other side of the grave. Good and evil alike lead an equally cheerless existence. Thus the activity of Minos, judge of the underworld, who is described as 'pronouncing to the dead (*themisteuonta nekussin*)', is evidently confined to settling law-suits among their number. The traditional sinners Tantalos, Tityos, and Sisyphos are punished not because they committed normal offences such as murder, theft or rape, but because they insulted the dignity of the gods. They are therefore held up both as an example and as an exception to the general rule.

   A lot differentiated from that of the rest of mankind is reserved for Menelaos alone. The sea-god Proteos prophetically informs him on the shores of Egypt: 'But in your case, Zeus-born Menelaos, it is not fated that you should die and meet your doom in horse-rearing Argos, but the immortals will convey you to the Elysian plain and to the bounds of the earth, where fair-haired Rhadamanthys dwells, and where life is easiest for men. There is no snow there, nor heavy storms, nor rain, but Okeanos always sends the breezes of soft-blowing Zephyros to refresh men' (*Od.* 4.561ff.). The reason why this dispensation is granted him, however, is not that he of all mankind is especially deserving but that he has relatives in high places.

It is interesting to compare this passage with the description of the Isles of the Blest which Hesiod provides. In the *Works and Days* he tells us that the race of heroes, the fourth generation to inherit the earth, were accorded a twofold destiny. Some were 'enfolded in the end of death', dying in battle, but to the rest 'Zeus, the father, son of Kronos, gave a livelihood and a dwelling, separate from men, and settled them at the ends of the earth; and there they lived, free from care, in the Isles of the Blest by deep-swirling Okeanos' (166ff.). Here, too, the blessed heroes (*olbioi hêrôes*) who achieved translation are awarded this destiny seemingly not in recognition of personal merit, but rather in consequence of having evaded death on the field of battle.

The earliest example in Greek literature of belief in a system of rewards and punishments in the next world is to be found in the *Hymn to Demeter*, which is probably dated to the seventh century B.C. Towards its conclusion the poet declares in what is a climax to the whole hymn, 'Prosperous (*olbios*) is he among men who live on the earth having seen these things; but he who is not initiated (*atelês*) and who has no part in the mysteries (*hiera*), never has the lot (*aisa*) of such things, once he has perished and gone beneath the murky gloom.' It has frequently been pointed out that according to the doctrine propounded here, knowledge of the holy ritual – in particular the witnessing of the mysteries (*epopteia*) – is all that is necessary to become prosperous in the life to come. Nothing is said of the merits of good conduct. Identical in tone is a fragment from a Pindaric *thrênos* in which it is stated, 'Prosperous is he who having seen these things passes beneath the earth. He knows the end of life and its god-given beginning (or 'principle', *archa*)'. Though our knowledge of the Eleusinian Mysteries is extremely incomplete, and while it is possible that the absence of reference in surviving texts to any moral requirements may be due simply to the accident of survival, this seems unlikely. Certainly Diogenes the Cynic did not believe that ethical considerations played any part in determining a person's destiny in the next life according to this system, for on hearing Sophokles' statement, 'Thrice-prosperous are those who having seen these rites pass to Hades', he sneeringly remarked, 'What! Do you mean that Pataikion the thief will have a better lot after death than Epaminondas because he has been initiated?' The only text which suggests that morality did play some part in the

mysteries comes in a passage in Aristophanes' *Frogs* (353ff.) where
the Chorus of Initiates banish from their number 'anyone whose
mind is impure ... or who takes pleasure in ribald quips which are out
of season', as well as all who are corrupt, venial and unpatriotic.
Though this may be a garbled version of the official proclamation
made at the commencement of the celebrations, there is no reason to
suppose that the classes of persons enumerated by Aristophanes'
comic Chorus were singled out for censure at the mysteries
themselves. As Adkins (1960, 145) points out, it is the business of a
comic Chorus to castigate all those guilty of corruption and venality,
and this they do whether or not they are adopting the persona of a
Chorus of Initiates. The only category of offenders who we can be
certain were not permitted to participate in the festival were
murderers and those awaiting trial for murder, and even these were
not excluded on moral grounds, but simply because the shedding of
blood made them ritually impure.

Another religious movement which believed in a dualistic afterlife
were the Orphics who traced their origin to the legendary Orpheus
and whose existence dates from around the seventh century B.C. An
allusion to an Orphic belief is made by Aristophanes in the *Frogs*
(145ff.) when he consigns to Everflowing Mud 'anyone who has ever
wronged a guest ... stolen money from a child, or thrashed his
mother, or struck his father on the jaw, or sworn a false oath'. For
those who have led a life of virtue, on the other hand, the Orphic
reward, according to Plato, is 'everlasting drunkenness' (*Rep.*
2.363c). A little later he cites others who 'produce a pile of books of
Mousaios and Orpheus ... in accordance with which they perform
rituals, persuading not only individuals but states as well that there
really is remission and purification for unjust behaviour by means of
sacrifices and sportive delights for the living, whereas for the dead
there are what they call rites, which deliver us from the evils of this
world, while terrible things await us if we have failed to sacrifice'.
Though no great weight can be attached to the distinction which
Plato seems to be making between two sectaries, the passage does at
least suggest that Orphism embraced different levels of enlightenment
– though this fact was clearly not considered important by Plato. In
conclusion, the attempt to recover an ethical basis – if such ever
existed – to Orphism is as ill-served by the prejudice of Plato, as is
that of the Eleusinian Mysteries by the burlesque of Aristophanes.

Belief in transmigration (*metempsychôsis*), that is to say, belief in the
entry of the human soul into some other corporeal substance after

death, seems to have existed in Greece only as a philosophical tenet, never enjoying any popular support. Such a doctrine naturally lends itself to a belief that the soul is rewarded or punished for its past behaviour according to the evolutionary level of its succeeding incarnation. The *Katharmoi* (Purifications) of Empedokles of Akragas (*fl.* 450 B.C. ?) set out the steps by which a fallen *daimôn* must ascend the ladder of being in order to secure restoration in the heavenly abode from which it has been cast out. The fragments of this poem, however, leave many important questions unresolved. On one occasion the poet declares: 'For already I have been a boy and a girl and a bush and a bird and a fish that jumps out of the sea'. What is not made explicit is whether Empedokles believed in a *post mortem* judgment coming at the end of each incarnation in order to determine the fallen *daimôn*'s level of existence at its next birth. Though Zuntz (1971, 264) claims that such a doctrine 'was inherently given when incarnation was conceived', the assertion made in another fragment that a *daimôn* 'has to wander far from the blessed ones for thirty thousand years, being born throughout that time in the manner of all mortal creatures' suggests that merit did not enable one entirely to short-circuit the cycle of births. Moreover, even if we accept Zuntz's attribution of an Empedoklean influence to the gold leaves found at Thourii, the reference to 'the sojourn of the pure' to which two of the souls expect to be sent is in my view far too vague a term to entitle us to claim that we here have evidence of 'an elaborate doctrine of the afterlife centring on the belief in a judgment after death and reincarnation of souls' (ib. 337). Equally unproved is Keuls' theory that the water-carriers as, for instance, represented in an underworld scene on a black-figure Attic *lêkythos* in Palermo, should perhaps be regarded in view of their 'jaunty air' not as damned sinners but as blessed initiates undergoing purification (*katharmos*) rather than punishment (1974, 38 and pl. 2).

More explicit of a belief in a judgment after death is Pindar's *Olympian* 2, written for Theron of Akragas in 476, in which the poet declares (56ff.): 'If a man having wealth knows the future, that immediately after dying on earth the lawless spirits pay the penalty, and sins committed in this kingdom of Zeus are judged by one both sternly and inexorably' – such a person, Pindar tells us after a short digression, having succeeded in keeping his *psychê* free from acts of injustice three times in both worlds, is translated to the Isles of the Blest. A further statement by Pindar on the destiny of the *psychê*, in which he alludes to Persephone's exaction of payment for an 'ancient sorrow (*palaion penthos*)' from those souls which she restores to the sunlight, prompts from Sokrates the observation that, according to this theory, one ought to live 'as holily as possible (*hosiôtata*)'.

Belief in a *post mortem* judgment is not wholly absent from Greek tragedy. In the *Suppliants* of Aeschylus, Danaos declares (230f.) that anyone who tried to force one of his daughters to marry would have to pay the penalty for his crime in the next world, where, 'it is said, another Zeus makes final judgment on wrongdoing among the dead'. In the *Eumenidês*, when the Furies threaten to carry off Orestes to Hades for the crime of matricide, they tell him (269ff.): 'There you will see all other mortals who have impiously sinned against a god or a guest or their parents, each receiving the deserts for his crime. For there is a great Hades beneath the earth who is a chastiser (*euthynos*) of mankind and who oversees everything with his recording mind'. It goes without saying, however, that such a belief is by no means integral to the theological framework of the *Oresteia*, since the dramatic form of the trilogy enabled Aeschylus to demonstrate both the deferment – yet ultimate triumph – of justice here on earth.

A further reference in tragedy to the dead having to face a reckoning in the next world is provided by the seer Theonoe in the *Helen* of Euripides, who says: 'For indeed such deeds are paid for both by the dead and by all men in the world above. For although the mind (*nous*) of the dead does not "live", it floats in the eternal ether (*aithêr*) and has an eternal reason (*gnômê*)' (1013ff.). These lines, however, lacking as they do any internal coherence, do not go so far as to support a belief in a doctrine of rewards and punishment after death, but rather seem to constitute 'a piece of high-toned but vague mysticism appropriate to Theonoe' (Dale 1967, ad loc.). Elsewhere in Euripides the belief is tentatively put forward that virtue is rewarded in this life. More categorically, death is seen as a punishment for the wicked.

There is a resemblance between the type of offenders referred to by Aeschylus in the *Eumenidês* passage cited above and those who figured in Polygnotos' *Nekyia* in the Lesche (Painted Hall) of the Knidians at Delphi. In addition to superhuman offenders and the uninitiated, Pausanias noted a man who had maltreated his own father being throttled by him in turn, and another who had committed acts of sacrilege being poisoned (10.28.5). Likewise a certain Aristogeiton is described in Pseudo-Demosthenes (25.53) as a man 'unlikely to receive mercy from the gods of Hades, but to be

Fig. 11. The 'handshake motif' on an Athenian *stêlê c.* 330 B.C. Prokles (right), dressed as a soldier, either greets or says farewell to his parents.

cast out among the impious because of the depravity of his life'. The crimes of which Aristogeiton is accused include failing to bury his father, attacking his mother, and selling his sister for export.

The most complete expression of faith in the doctrine of retributive punishment in the afterlife occurs, however, in the Vision of Judgment with which the *Gorgias* concludes. Sokrates (523c) narrates how in former times, when men were judged while still alive by living judges, false verdicts were being given since their *psychai* were veiled by physical beauty or wealth. Consequently Zeus decreed that *psychai* should be judged naked after death by Minos, Rhadamanthys and Aiakos. It is noteworthy, however, that the notion of a judgment in the world to come is evidently not regarded even by Plato as a particularly effective deterrent against criminal activity. In the *Laws*, for instance, with its discussion of the secular sanctions needed to curb misconduct and vice, there is no mention of eternal punishment meted out in the hereafter.

To conclude, though the theory of a division of the dead into two categories occupied a position of some importance in the Eleusinian Mysteries, it seems elsewhere to have played a relatively minor role in the history of Greek eschatology. Further, while belief in Hades as a place of punishment for certain crimes persisted from the time of Homer to the Classical period and beyond, criminally speaking the Greek underworld never became fully democratised: crimes of average venality excited neither dispraise nor retribution.

Nevertheless it would be rash to be dogmatic about an area of man's thinking which so lends itself to the formulation of privately held beliefs. Many Greeks would doubtless have sympathised with the cautious optimism with which Hypereides concludes the funeral speech delivered over the Athenian dead in the Lamian War in 322 B.C.: 'But if there is conscious life in the kingdom of Hades and divine care, as we suspect, then it is reasonable to hope that those who defended (i.e. unto death) the honour of the gods should meet with loving kindness at the hands of the divine power'.

The family reunion

A popular, indeed perhaps the most popular, Classical belief about what happened in Hades is the notion of the family reunion whereby the long-established dead greet new arrivals. The earliest literary reference occurs in the *Agamemnon* of Aeschylus. Having just killed her husband, Klytaimnestra declares that it will fall to Iphigeneia,

Fig. 12. A modern *dexiôsis*: grave monument of Marina and Dinos in Athens.

their dead daughter, to greet him in Hades – lines delivered, as Fraenkel (1950, ad loc.) notes, with 'horrible mockery', since it was Agamemnon who dispatched her to Hades in the first place. The prospect of meeting one's dead kin in the world below was not normally quite so unattractive, and might even be anticipated with pleasure. Antigone cherishes the hope that her arrival in Hades will be a welcome event for her parents and her brother Polyneikes, particularly since she has given the latter burial. Admetos instructs the dying Alkestis to wait for him in Hades and to prepare a house where they can live together, assuring her that when he dies he will be placed beside her in the same cedar wood coffin 'so that never, even in death, shall I desert you'. One of the reasons Oedipus gives for putting out his eyes is that he may not have to face seeing his parents in the house of the dead, an especially interesting comment since it implies that those suffering from physical handicaps continue to be so afflicted in the world below.

How one went about contacting one's dead relatives upon arrival in Hades we are not specifically told, but reunion was perhaps facilitated by the practice of joint burial. Conceivably, too, it may have been partly for this reason that in the fifth and fourth centuries those who could afford it buried their dead in family plots (see below,

p. 106). The 'reunion in Hades' motif is not common in epitaphs, though it does occasionally occur.

Reunion has also been interpreted as the meaning behind the handshake (*dexiôsis*), which is so common a feature in group compositions of Classical Attic funerary reliefs (fig.11; cf. fig.12). The earliest *stêlê* on which the motif figures comes from Aegina and is dated to the very last phase of the Archaic period. It shows a standing man wrapped in a mantle shaking hands with a seated woman who is holding a pomegranate. On this occasion, however, it seems clear that the seated woman is the dead and the standing man a living survivor, the two being 'firmly united across the boundary of the grave' (Johansen 1951, 139), since the woman is shown to be slightly larger than the man. With regard to later examples, however, interpretation can rarely be so clear cut and I would suggest that the significance of the overwhelming majority lies buried in that same confused area of man's thinking which incorporates so much that has to do with death and the dead. Only exceptionally is the scene made fully explicit, as in the case of the celebrated *stêlê* of Ampharete, an Attic work of late fifth-century date, which shows a seated woman fondling her grandchild (fig.13). Here the inscription above the relief unequivocally states that both are dead, and there can be no doubt at all that the action is conceived of as taking place in Hades. In contrast to its popularity on grave-*stêlai dexiôsis* is virtually unknown on *lêkythoi* of the painted variety. It does, however, figure on the red-figure *Nekyia kratêr* discussed earlier: on the lower register, a girl still wearing her chin-strap and clasping an *alabastron* is greeted in the underworld by a young man.

Activities of the dead

The principal activities of the Homeric dead appear to be gossip, sententious moralising and self-indulgent regret. In the second *Nekyia*, which supplies the fullest picture of life in the shade world below, Agamemnon's grieving *psychê* is instructed by Achilles on the unfortunate circumstances of its death (*Od.* 24.20ff.). What a pity, the latter comments, that your wife murdered you. If you had died fighting at Troy, things would have been very different. You would have had a mound (*tymbos*) and handed down a great name to your son. In response, Agamemnon makes rueful comparisons between his fate and that of both Achilles and Odysseus, jealous of the former for

Fig. 13. *Stêlê* of Ampharete and her grandchild *c.* 410 B.C. Ampharete's extreme youth suggests that the *stêlê* was originally intended to commemorate a mother and her daughter.

his glorous funeral, and of the latter for his faithful wife.

To judge from objects found in tombs, it seems that Hades was a place where one might pass a quiet hour playing a game of draughts (*pessoi*). Miniature gaming-boards made of terracotta have occasionally been found in Attic offering places of the seventh and sixth century. They are marked off in squares and ornamented at the corners with mourning figures, whose cheeks are streaked with red paint for blood. Sometimes, too, a die is found. Vermeule (1979, 80) believes that the custom 'suggests that for certain Greeks gaming was, as for the Egyptians, a metaphor of chance ... the ultimate game with the last opponent', but this interpretation is too tendentious and in my view it is unnecessary to interpret the boards differently from any other type of grave-gift: an essential, or at least desirable adjunct to a pleasurable existence in the next world. Playing *pessoi*, horse-riding, gymnastics and playing the lyre constitute the range of cultural activities which, according to a fragmentary Pindaric *thrênos*, await those of the dead fortunate to be admitted into paradise.

The pleasures awaiting the dead in Hades are also suggested by the series of so-called 'Totenmahl' (death-feast) reliefs which would have us believe that life below was one long drinking-party. This is in striking contrast to the Homeric picture, where nobody eats or drinks except when summoned by the living to partake of an irregular sacrifice. The principal compositional features of the series include a man reclining on a *klinê* on the right, a table beside him laden with various kinds of food, including cakes, fruit, pomegranates and eggs, and a seated woman on his left. The exact schema, as Thönges-Stringaris (1965) notes, can be traced to a frieze from the North Palace of Assurbanipal at Nineveh. The inspiration for the series seems to derive from votive reliefs carrying representations of feasting deities and heroes, like the one of Pluto and Persephone discussed earlier in the chapter. These make their first appearance in Greece towards the end of the sixth century. The earliest Totenmahl relief appears to be a *stêlê* found in the Peiraios dated *c*. 400 B.C. (fig.14). The series comes to an end *c*. 300-280 B.C. Examples have been found not only in Attika, but all over the Greek world, including Sparta, Argos, Corinth, Boeotia, Aetolia, Poteidaia, Melos, Delos, Thasos, Samos, as well as Asia Minor and Italy. They could be erected to members of both sexes, as their inscriptions prove. Other compositional features include the head of a horse in a square box in the top left-hand corner of the relief, the dead man's arms and armour suspended in the background as though hanging from a wall,

Fig. 14. A *Totenmahl* or 'Death feast' relief *c*. 400 B.C., showing the deceased as husband and wife drinking together. On the left a slave with an *amphora* attends. On the right a survivor watches on.

and a snake, either coiled under the table and perhaps raising its head in the direction of the food, or else entwined around a tree. Sometimes a wine-pourer attends.

What finally remains unclear is whether the figures represented on the reliefs are conceived of as enjoying in the afterlife the pleasures of earthly existence or whether they are frozen in life, caught at a characteristic moment, as it were, as their friends remembered them and as they themselves would wish to be remembered. Lending some support to the theory that they are in fact supposed to be dead is Sokrates' comment in the *Republic* quoted above that according to the Orphics the reward for the just in Hades is 'everlasting drunkenness' (2.363d).

Despite the emphasis on food and drink, bowels do not abound in Hades, as Vermeule (1979, 27) has sensitively observed – a point of contrast with the Egyptian notion of the afterlife, in accordance with which the dead were occasionally provided with both bathroom and lavatory so that they should feel 'perfectly at home' (Scharff 1947, 18).

If the appetite for food and drink remained unimpaired in Hades it is natural to inquire whether the dead had sexual relations with one another. 'The grave's a fine and private place, but none, I think, do there embrace.' Marvell's sentiments were certainly not shared by· the Etruscans as is demonstrated by a spectacular fourth-century sarcophagos from Volci showing husband and wife in eternal embrace. In the case of the Greeks, the lyric poet Anakreon gives utterance to a very reasonable anxiety when, adopting the persona of an old man who sees death approaching, he complains that whereas descending to Hades is an easy operation, getting up from it is not. The verb *anabainô* which he uses to convey the latter activity has sexual overtones, and it has been suggested – not wholly convincingly – that the poet intends a play on words. Approximately contemporary is a grave-relief from the island of Kos (*c.* 530 B.C.) on which the dead are shown to have surmounted this obstacle. Even if the dead are occasionally represented as having sex with one another, it seems likely that they produced no issue. Underworlds are not noted for their fecundity. Pluto and Persephone are themselves childless, and Theseus in Euripides' *Suppliants* heaps scorn on the Theban decision to deny burial to the Argive dead by interpreting it as the reflexion of a fear that corpses might produce children in the bowels of the earth (543ff.).

On the evidence of the so-called *loutrophoros*, a vase used in the ceremonial bridal-bath preceding a wedding which also stood as a stone-marker over the graves of those who died unmarried (see fig.15 and below p. 87), scholars have alleged that the Greeks believed in the possibility of finding a marriage partner down in Hades. Although the practice of denoting the graves of such persons in a special way is not in dispute, the significance of the *loutrophoros* as a grave-marker is by no means fully understood and does not necessarily point to a belief in the concept of marriage in death. Occasional allusions in the tragedians to a marriage taking place in Hades all serve, in my view, to accentuate the pathos of early death, as in the case of Antigone who is to become the bride of Acheron, Glauke who is to marry the underworld deities, and Iphigeneia whose bridegroom, we are told, is none other than Hades himself. Such a travesty of true marriage can hardly have formed a part of belief, and it is surely a sense of outrage at the unfairness of early death which prompts Megara to exclaim over the bodies of her murdered children, 'Fortune (*tychê*) has given you fates of death (*kêres*) for brides and me tears for the holy water used for the bridal

Fig. 15. Marble vase in the shape of a so-called *loutrophoros* dated *c.* 320 B.C. The handles are modern.

bath (*loutra*)' (Eur. *HF* 480ff.), rather than some half-baked theory about the way that weddings are celebrated down in Hades (see further below p. 87).

We have yet to consider whether Hades is hierarchical or exclusive. In Homer, as Vermeule (1979, 36) points out, it seems to be reserved for the Greek aristocracy, for we never hear of the unheroic or barbarian dead. Nobody seems to enjoy special privileges though Menelaos, as noted above, because of his family connections as son-in-law to Zeus, will avoid death altogether and be miraculously transported to the Elysian plain. In Greek tragedy, by contrast, it is at least intimated that the dead preserve the same status which they enjoyed on earth. The ghost of Dareios claims that it 'shares mastery' with the chthonic powers (Aes. *Pers.* 691) and alleges that it is for this reason that it has been permitted to leave Hades at the summons of his wife Atossa: one is led to the conclusion that it was precisely this privilege that was not granted to hoi polloi. Likewise Orestes in the *Choêphoroi* laments the fact that his father did not die fighting at Troy, since then he would have been 'an august ruler conspicuous beneath the earth and a minister of the greatest underworld deities who rule there' (356ff.). In contrast to Dareios' claim, this statement suggests that the status of a king was on a lesser footing than the chthonic powers themselves. Finally, in Sophokles' *Elektra*, Amphiareos, having been avenged for his death at the hands of his wife, is described as 'a great soul (*pampsychos*) ruling under earth' (841).

Death is an eternity. But is eternity timeless? Such little evidence as we possess suggests that the Greek notion of the afterlife was precisely this. In both Homeric *Nekyiai*, as Keuls (1974, 14) notes, 'the *psychê* of the dead is frozen in time at the moment of death, in appearance as well as in experience'. Eternal rancour and regret are the properties of the *psychai* of Ajax and Agamemnon respectively, and eternally blood-bespattered are the warriors who have died in battle.

Disbelief in Hades

Evidence for disbelief in Hades first occurs in the plays of Euripides. In the *Trojan Women* Andromache defines death as 'like never having been born' (636) and Hekabe dismisses expensive funeral gifts (*kterismata*) as 'an empty vanity to satisfy the living' (1248ff.). Elsewhere in Euripides' plays the dead are spoken of as 'nothing', and actions performed on their behalf as 'a worthless effort' (*Helen* 1421).

To what extent such statements shocked or offended Athenian sentiment we can only speculate. Plato in the *Phaedo* asserts (69e-70a) that most people (cf. ib. 77b) think that 'when the *psychê* is released from the body, it ceases to exist anywhere', but a philosopher is partial and the claim is moreover belied by indications that the Athenians did regularly provide their dead with the necessities of life (see Chapter 7). What is not in dispute is that the belief in the underworld did not go entirely unchallenged in the Classical period and that a new idea grew up, probably in the first half of the fifth century, of the *psychai* of the dead being transported up to heaven. The epitaph on the Athenian dead at Poteidaia in 432 B.C., for example, states that 'ether (*aithêr*) received their *psychai*, but earth their bodies'. A fourth-century inscription from the Peiraios reads: 'The moist *aithêr* holds the *psychê* and proud spirit of Eurymachos, but this grave holds his body'. It is to be emphasised, however, that in neither instance is there any suggestion that the *psychê* retains its consciousness or indeed its individuality. On the contrary, such epitaphs merely serve as an explanation for the separation of bodily constituents after death, rather than as a basis for a new doctrine of immortality. Occasionally, however, celestial translation does offer the assurance of individual immortality, as in the case of the following Athenian epigram of possibly fourth-century date which asserts: 'Earth holds the bones and flesh of this sweet boy, but his *psychê* has gone to the chamber of the pious'. Sometimes, too, the dead were transformed into stars. Kastor and Pollux were perhaps the brightest dead in this category, but on a clear night one might also pick out a minor tragic poet such as Ion of Chios, whose celestial effulgence is observed by Trygaios in Aristophanes' *Peace*. It is to be noted, however, that belief in the ascent of souls to the sky was never prominent among the Greeks, and was never a serious rival to more traditional beliefs.

Categorical denial of the existence of Hades is the subject of an oft-quoted epigram by the Hellenistic writer Kallimachos which takes the form of a dialogue between the living and the dead: ' "What's it like down below, Charidas?" "Very dark." "Is there any way up?" "A lie." "And Pluto?" "A fairy tale." ' But despite the incredulity of the refined Kallimachos it seems clear that in the Hellenistic period belief in Hades still prevailed. Regarding the Roman period, Plutarch claimed that in his day few people, except mothers and nurses, suffered from a 'childish terror' of the fangs of

Kerberos or having to carry water in leaky pots (*pithoi*), but this assertion is contradicted by Lucian, who declared that 'the general mob, whom the wise call the laiety, believe Homer and Hesiod and the other fabricators of myths ... and assume that there is a deep place under the earth called Hades, and that it is large and commodious and dark and sunless'.

Though Plutarch is likely to be a more reliable indicator of ordinary Roman belief than the satirist Lucian, fear of Hades was not finally laid to rest. An anonymous fragmentary papyrus dated to the end of the second century A.D. provides what is certainly the grisliest description of the underworld to come down to us from antiquity. It tells of the descent of a man to the world below in search of his dead wife or mistress. Proceeding along an 'oblique pathway', he comes to a place where dogs are seen devouring dead bodies. He crosses a river and arrives at the Shores of Ugliness. There he sits down on a rock and proceeds to fish, using a corpse's hair for bait. A break in the text brings him to a vast plain populated by beheaded and crucified bodies, together with other dead who have met violent deaths. Furies laugh at the spectacle and there is a terrible stench of gore. What is instructive is that the perilous descent (*katabasis*) is undertaken not with the object of restoring the woman to the light above, as in the case of the Orpheus and Eurydike myth, but so that she may be upbraided for her deceitfulness and expensive tastes. Marital grievances, like infernal mythology, die hard.

Finally, the Greeks saw nothing inconsistent in cherishing a belief in the dead living in Hades alongside the more straight-forward idea of their continued existence within or in the vicinity of the tomb. Such a belief forms the basis of the pious hope uttered by Menelaos in the *Helen* of Euripides, that 'if there are gods and they are wise, when a brave man dies at the hands of his enemies they make the dust on his tomb light, but cast out the wicked on to rocky ground' (851ff.). Not infrequently in literature there is confusion and even overlap, as when Hades and the path leading down to it are described as 'mouldy', or when the dead are referred to as 'lying in Hades'. Such inconsistency should come to us as no surprise: afterlifes, after all, are not the creatures of logical positivists.

6

The Special Dead

Up till now we have concentrated mainly on the treatment of and beliefs concerning the ordinary Greek dead. The object of this chapter is to investigate how funerary practices might be modified in the case of certain specific categories of the dead who were regarded as special because of their age, or their social position, or the peculiar circumstances of their demise.

Aôroi

An early demise is often lamented in tragedy and very commonly alluded to in epitaphs. The word used of a person who dies in his prime is *aôros* which means literally 'untimely', and the pathos of his condition is sometimes intensified by the use of the superlative *aôrôtatos*. Unlike Roman epitaphs, however, Greek epitaphs rarely record the exact age at time of death except in cases of extreme longevity.

The criterion for being judged to have died *aôros* depended, it is suspected, not only upon age but also upon the nature and appropriateness of the individual's death. Faced with a choice between dying on the battlefield and achieving deathless fame (*kleos aphthiton*), or alternatively surviving to inglorious old age, the Homeric hero was in no doubt as to which fate was preferable – and no Greek would have pitied him for having died an *aôros*. The same sentiment is reflected in a poem by Tyrtaios which states that it is bad when old men rather than young men die in battle (Fr. 10 *IEG*). At no period in Greek history are those who die defending their country counted among the *aôroi*, doubtless so as not to discourage the virtues of patriotism and self-sacrifice.

Humphreys (1983, 145) has suggested that in the Archaic period there may have been a dread of old age which was even greater than the dread of death. If so, it was not shared by everyone. According to Solon (27.17f. *IEG*), seventy was the age at which 'a man could receive the apportionment of death, not being *aôros*'. In the Classical period it was certainly considered a mark of good fortune (*eudaimonia*) to have lived to a great age. A woman called Chairestrate describes herself in an epitaph as *eudaimôn* for having lived long enough to become a grandmother, and a man called Litias, who claims to have reached a hundred, declares he has left behind a 'timely grief' (*ôraios penthos*) for his children. To fix an upper age limit for a woman after which point she could no longer be classified as *aôros* would clearly have been invidious. Alkestis still considers herself to be *aôros* even though she has reared children to an age where one of them at least is deemed to be capable of reflective thought (Eur. *Alk.* 167f.; cf. 393ff.). Especially to be pitied were those who outlived their children and had to give them rites of burial, an unavoidable hazard in the case of parents who were themselves immortal (Eur. *Rhes.* 980ff.). As in our own culture less sentiment attached to the plight of the very elderly. '*Tymbogerôn*', a pejorative compound of 'funeral mound' and 'old man', suggestively intimates that such a person had outstayed his welcome and was over-ripe for burial.

Archaeology records two distinctive practices in the case of the infant dead. In the first place, though exceptions are occasionally found (see fig. 16), in the majority of cases much less care and expense is expended on the graves of children than on those of adults. Simple pot-burials are regular from the Geometric period onwards, the principal shapes being coarse-ware *pithoi, hydriai* and *amphorai*, occasionally with incised decoration but often left plain. In the Classical period, though the practice of pot-inhumation persisted, infants are often placed in a pair of clay tubs, one being inverted over the other. The fashion of burying children cheaply persisted into Roman times. The museum at Vrana near Marathon contains a child-burial dated to around the beginning of our era which utilises a pair of bee hives placed end to end (fig. 17). In the light of this evidence, it is difficult to resist the impression that any serviceable container was acceptable for the body of a child.

The second distinctive practice pertaining to child-burial is that instances of cremation are practically unknown (but see below, p. 82 for certain exceptions). In their excavations undertaken in the Kerameikos Brückner and Pernice (1893, 188) did not record a

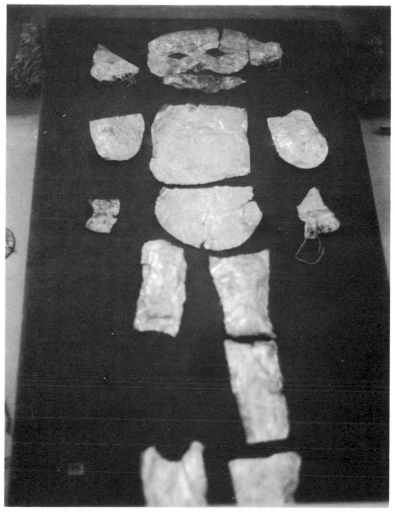

Fig. 16. Gold sheets placed over a baby found in a Mycenaean tomb.

single child-cremation, and the experiences of other archaeologists have confirmed that this was no local aberration. Though the difficulty in discovering traces of possible infant-cremation must be taken into account, the exclusive practice of inhuming the infant dead receives confirmation in later times from Pliny who states: 'It is a universal custom not to cremate a person before the teething stage' (*NH* 7.72).

That infants constitute a special category of the dead is widely recorded by anthropologists. Hertz (1907, 84), observing that only abbreviated rites are commonly performed on their behalf, accounted for this event as follows: 'The deaths of children ... provoke only a very weak social reaction which is almost instantaneously completed. ... As (the children) have not really been separated from the world of spirits, they return there directly ... without a period of painful transition appearing necessary. The death of a newborn child is at most an infra-social event; since society has not yet given anything of itself to the child, it is not affected by its disappearance and remains indifferent'. Hertz in effect proposed two distinct explanations to account for the phenomenon which he described: one rests on an assumption about the meaning of funerary ritual itself (viz. that it is primarily intended to facilitate the transfer of the dead to the next world), and the other implies that the parents of a dead child, having coolly assessed what they have so far invested, come to the rationalistic conclusion that its departure signals no great loss. This latter theory may be compared with Lawrence Stone's hypothesis that in view of the high rate of mortality among children less than one year old in England up until 1750 'to preserve their mental stability parents were obliged to limit the degree of their psychological involvement with their children' (1977, 57).

Unpleasing though it undoubtedly is to entertain the supposition that in societies which pre-date the 'demographic transition' an infant's death caused little distress even to the parents of the deceased, mere sentiment must not be allowed to obscure the existence of certain evidence in its support. The practice of exposure (*ekthesis*) is after all a familiar theme of Greek legend, the best known example being that of Oedipus whose ankles were pinned together to minimise his chances of survival. It has long been argued that an Athenian father possessed the legal right to expose his newborn children. Though Bolkestein (1922) sought to disprove the existence of this practice by invoking demographic evidence to demonstrate that there was no necessity for it ever to have been introduced, we cannot assume that an Athenian would have calculated in precisely this way. We are dealing with a question of social ethics rather than of population control. What needs therefore to be asked is the following: is there any evidence to suggest that the practice of exposing newborn infants, far from arousing condemnation or disapproval, was actually tolerated and condoned by Greek society?

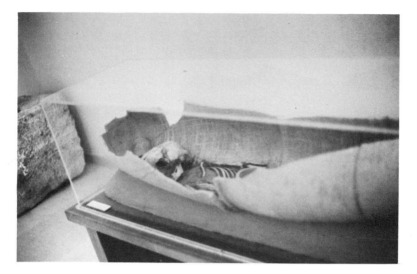

Fig. 17. Child burial in two bee-hives found near Marathon.

The literary statements in its support have been recently discussed by Rudhardt (1963, 18). Strongest in its favour is Sokrates' comparison of an argument put forward by his interlocutor to an infant which he might have brought to birth. Sokrates says, 'We must look at our offspring from every angle to make sure we are not taken in by a lifeless phantom not worth rearing. Or do you think that your child must be reared in any case and not be exposed?' (*Tht.* 160e). As Rudhardt remarks, the meaning of such a comparison would be lost if Athenian sensibilities were too delicate to tolerate contemplation of such an act. Poseidippos, writing in the third century, also provides a valuable testimony despite his comic exaggeration: 'If you have a son, you bring him up, even if you're poor, but if you have a daughter, you expose her, even if you're rich' (Fr. 11 *CAF*).

If the right of exposition did exist in Athens – and in my view the question cannot be resolved either way – it probably only covered the period in a child's life up until his *amphidromia*, the naming-ceremony for an Athenian child which was held on the fifth or tenth day after birth, especially in view of Aristotle's statement that 'the majority (i.e. of deaths in infancy) occur before the child is a week old' (*HA* 7.588 a 8). Nor can there be any serious doubt that girls would have been the victims of such a practice much more commonly than boys.

The Spartan state not only tolerated but actually demanded

exposure in the case of malformed infants. Plutarch (*Lyk.* 16.1-2) informs us that the father of every male child had to present his offspring before the council of elders (*gerousia*) for examination. If it was strong and lusty, he was required to raise it; if it was not, he had to expose it at the foot of Mount Taygetos 'in the belief that the life of that which nature had not provided with health and strength right at the beginning was of no value either to itself or to the state'.

The traces of infant-cremations found in the southwest quarter of the Athenian agora between the Areopagos and the Hill of the Nymphs dated to the fourth and third centuries B.C. (viz. to a period when no other intramural burials have been found in Athens) may perhaps be connected with the deaths of those infants who had been exposed by their parents or who simply died prematurely. If the deaths of very young Athenian children possibly produced only a very weak social reaction, it seems clear that keen sympathy was felt for those who, while perhaps surviving their *amphidromia*, none the less died before attending their first Anthesteria, the festival held in the spring on the 11th-13th of the month Anthesterion. On the second day of this festival, the day which was known as the Choës, a child, upon reaching its third year and being *choïkos* (i.e. of an age to take part in the festival), would be presented with a wreath, a wreathed *chous* (fig. 18) or juglet, and a small cart. This ceremony was a solemn occasion, having something of the quality of a religious confirmation, for the child would here experience its first taste of wine, thereby being formally admitted to the religious community. H.R.W. Smith advanced the attractive hypothesis that one who died in childhood without having undergone this important rite de passage received in compensation a miniature *chous* in his grave because, in the words of a child's epitaph, 'a *daimôn* had arrived in advance of the Choës'. Such vases are frequently illustrated with scenes in red-figure from the Choës festival. The majority of *choës* were found in Attika and date to the fifth and fourth centuries B.C., though a quantity has also been found in Eretria in what are judged to be graves of Athenian children. In addition, there are a number of Italiote *choës* manufactured in South Italy, which show similar scenes to those found on Attic vases of the same shape. A particularly popular theme is that of a child's cart. Other children or animals, principally goats or rams, sometimes pull a child along inside it. Games, such as ball-throwing, also figure prominently. Other *choës* are decorated with scenes that are overtly sepulchral. On one a mourning woman seated on the steps of a tomb is being consoled by

Fig. 18. An Athenian *chous* illustrated with a scene of children at play.

a young man dressed in a short cloak (*chlamys*) and a broad-brimmed hat (*petasos*): the schema is identical to that found on white-ground *lêkythoi*. On another two children are shown drunkenly revelling in front of a *stêlê* standing in the background. Hardly could the pathos of early death be more keenly expressed. In addition to the *chous* juglet, another offering commonly placed in the graves of children during the Classical period is the so-called 'feeder', a small black-spouted pot, which touchingly often shows signs of use. It is perhaps to be compared with the gift of a scraper (*strigil*) in the tomb of a young man, an item perhaps so personal that it was judged to be inseparable from the dead.

Further on the subject of special gifts placed in children's graves mention should be made of the burial of a child beneath the floor of a Geometric house in the agora at Athens – if the interpretation is correct. With the child were found the bones of what may have been his pet piglet. I would also draw attention to a fifteenth-century Mycenaean pit grave of a girl aged one and a half who had been showered with gifts by her parents. In addition to a large quantity of pottery was found a necklace with a gold pendant exhibiting a formalised lily motif.

A lament for a dead child is preserved in Euripides' *Trojan Women*, where Hekabe grieves for the infant prince Astyanax, who was perhaps himself *choïkos* at his death. What distresses her particularly is that he had not known 'youth or marriage or godlike sovereignty' and had scarcely been introduced to his *psychê* (1171f.).

There are several *stêlai* of Classical date erected to commemorate the deaths of small children, but I know of none that was erected in the Archaic period. Especially noteworthy is an Athenian *stêlê* containing a representation of a naked boy aged eight to ten years in the company of his dog. Though the carving itself is unexceptional, the epigram upon the architrave strikes a highly personal note. It informs us that the deceased, who bore the same name as his grandfather Philostratos, was a consolation (*paramythion*) to his parents who nicknamed him Little Chatterbox or Neollarion, 'but a *daimôn* snatched you away to be missed by all'. Occasionally a small child forms an element in a funerary composition, as in the case of the sumptuous *stêlê* found at Vari erected in memory of Mnesagora and her little brother Nikochares (fig. 19). Nikochares himself, aged about four or five years old, stretches his hand out in the direction of a small bird which his sister is holding. The *stêlê*, which may have served as a cenotaph, perhaps commemorates a joint death either as a result of some accident or illness obliquely referred to in the epitaph as the fate (*aisa*) brought on by a *daimôn* which snatched them away.

Commemoration of a dead baby is demonstrated by the famous *stêlê c.* 410 found in the Kerameikos showing Ampharete holding her dead grandchild (fig. 13). It is worth pointing out that the fourth

Fig. 19. *Stêlê* of Mnesagora and her brother Nikochares *c.* 430 B.C.

century B.C. witnessed an increased artistic interest in children and a corresponding improvement in their visual portrayal, both in painting and in sculpture. It is from this period that a *stêlê* survives commemorating Xenokleia who died from grief brought on by the death of her eight-year old son.

Representations of dead children are certainly rare on white-ground *lêkythoi*, but those that exist are none the less poignant and affecting: a well-known example by the Painter of Munich 2335 shows a child standing on a small hill and waving to his mother as Charon's boat draws up alongside to take him away (*AWL* pl. 42.1). As Kurtz comments, 'even Charon himself seems to be touched by the pathos of the child's untimely death' (ib. 218). In conclusion, all the evidence suggests that the death of a Greek child was a painful and disturbing event.

Whether any particular fear was felt towards the infant dead as constituting a category of vagrant spirits is difficult to establish. *Aôroi* are expressly invoked in *katadesmoi* (curse-tablets), but, as argued above (p. 6), those whose services were enlisted in this way did not themselves possess awful powers, but were seen as suitable couriers to those who did. The only explicit testimony about the fate of the infant dead in the hereafter dating to the Classical period is provided by the myth of Er, in which Sokrates refers to 'things not worthy of record' which are said about children who perish in earliest infancy (Pl. *Rep.* 10.615bc). A similar vision is reported in Plutarch by Timarchos, who, on descending into the oracle of Trophonios' cave, experiences an oracular dream in which he hears 'the wailing of innumerable infants' (*Mor.* 590f). In his *Consolation to his Wife* on the death of their daughter Timoxena who died at the age of two, Plutarch compares the soul to a captured bird which over the years becomes tamed to this life (ib. 611e). No *choai* are brought to children who die in infancy nor are *ta nomizomena* performed for them precisely because their souls do not remain beside their bodies but depart instantly to their proper habitation: in sum, they have no portion of the earth or of earthly things. It will be observed that the explanation for the omission of funerary rites in the case of young children here advanced bears a striking resemblance to Hertz's own suggestion discussed above (p. 80), though it is to be emphasised that Plutarch's theory was not necessarily widely accepted in the late first or early second century A.D.

Young adults, as Humphreys (1980, 104) notes, constitute the largest group of persons for whom Archaic funerary monuments were set up in Attika: of twenty inscriptions which record the relationship between the commemorator and the deceased, thirteen indicate dedications by parents to their children. It is also interesting that there are few Archaic sculptural representations of men and women in middle life (see Jeffery 1962), though we cannot rule out the possibility that this is a reflection of artistic convention. In the Classical period persons of all ages are commemorated, frequently in family groups comprising occasionally as many as five members. Oddly, no *stêlai* set up to a husband and wife jointly survive from the Archaic period. Throughout the whole series of Athenian funerary monuments, men are far more commonly honoured than women (by a ratio of over 2:1 in the fourth century).

Historians have eloquently extolled the special sympathy felt by the Greeks towards the unmarried dead. Gardner (1896, 115), for instance, wrote: 'No sentiment is more often expressed in epitaphs, none more strongly affected the Greek heart, than the sadness of the fate of these young men and women to whom death came in the place of that marriage which was regarded as the consummation of earthly happiness. When the marriage vase was used for funeral libations, then indeed the bitterness of fate was felt by every bystander.' The marriage vase to which Gardner refers, now known as a *loutrophoros*, has been identified with the type of tall, wide-brimmed, narrow-necked vase with thin, curving handles ending in volutes. As a funerary monument it is carved both in relief and in-the-round. So commonly is it found in cemeteries, however, that it has been suggested that the vase normally thought of as a *lebês gamikos* (bowl for mixing wine specially used at weddings) should properly be regarded as a *loutrophoros*. Equally plausibly '*loutrophoros*' may have been a general word for any vase used for *loutra* (sacred water for washing-ceremonies), as has been proposed (*KB* 152).

There is another more serious problem which has to do with the identification of a special marker placed over the grave of the unmarried dead. In Demosthenes (44.18 and 30) the speaker offers as proof that a man died unmarried the fact that a *loutrophoros* stood upon his grave. The only other Classical reference to *loutrophoros* is in Menander (*Sam.* 730f.), where it occurs in a passage in which women and a flute girl are also mentioned. It seems natural to assume that the word here signifies 'a bearer of *loutra*' on the analogy of *hydriaphoros* (water-carrier) and *kanêphoros* (basket-carrier) (*KB* 152). If this is also the meaning of the passage in Demosthenes, the inference must be that a carved figure was set up over the grave.

Later writers, such as Pollux (8.66) and Harpokration (s.v.) imply just this, though no such sculptures, to my knowledge, have been found.

Heroes

Only brief mention can be made here of heroes and the war dead, two highly significant categories of the dead both deserving of individual treatment. The Greek hero is defined by Farnell (1921, 343) as 'a person whose virtue, influence or personality was so powerful in his lifetime or through the peculiar circumstances of his death that his spirit after death is regarded as a supernormal power, claiming to be reverenced and propitiated'. The origin of the worship of heroes in Greece is not known, though it has long been emphasised that the conception of a transfigured soul endowed with prevision and the power to dispense or withold blessings has no place in the Homeric poems.

Hêrôa, shrines erected for the worship of heroes beside earlier graves and sometimes containing votive material, date from the Geometric period onwards. It is a characteristic of heroes' graves (and, hence, of *hêrôa*) that they are frequently incorporated within the city, sometimes in the agora or town hall (*prytaneion*), or even built into the wall beside the city-gate; alternatively, a hero might be buried within a sanctuary, as in the case of Pelops whose grave is situated in the Altis at Olympia near the great altar of Zeus.

Hero-worship came to prominence in Athenian state religion under the tyrant Peisistratos in the second half of the sixth century B.C. The belief was vigorously adhered to at the time of the Persian Wars when the practical participation of heroes like Theseus and Ajax at Marathon and Salamis was counted as having played a major part in securing the Greek victory.

Sophokles' description of the death of Oedipus provides the fullest account of the beliefs surrounding the last moments of a hero's life that has come down to us. Having been informed by Ismene that the gods intend to raise him to heroic status, he is able henceforth to foretell the future. Oedipus is summoned to death by virtue of a sign which he has long ago been instructed to expect. He knows the exact spot where he is to die and can himself reach it unaided. Only the preparatory funerary offices are carried out, namely ritual washing and clothing of his body. None of his kin is permitted to be present at his death and he receives no burial gift. The location of his tomb –

Fig. 20. Fragment of a war memorial erected in honour of Athenian soldiers who died near Corinth and at Koroneia in 394/393 B.C. The memorial was found beside the *Dêmosion Sêma*.

judged to be sacred (*hieros*) like those of the *dioblêtoi* (struck by lightning – see below) – is to be kept a closely-guarded secret by Theseus and his descendants. It is to be avoided at all times and his spirit, unlike that of the ordinary dead, is not to be invoked.

The war dead

Among the specially commemorated war heroes were those who fell at Marathon for whom a cult was established under the polemarch. In addition, a procession was held annually in honour of the dead at Plataia, maintained even in Plutarch's day (Plu. *Arist.* 21). Those who died in both these battles were buried on the spot, an exceptional honour in the eyes of the Athenians. Ordinarily the Athenian war dead were given a state-burial in Athens itself. Such a ceremony permitted both an extension and elaboration of normal funerary routine in several important respects, as we see from Thukydides' account (2.34) of the funeral held on behalf of those who died in the first year of the Peloponnesian War: first, the *prothesis* lasted three days instead of the customary one; secondly, waggons instead of pall-bearers were employed to transport the dead to the place of interment; and thirdly, any female relative of the deceased was permitted to attend the funeral (cf. p. 42 above). Most important, the funeral was organised along tribal and civic lines – the state in effect claiming what was properly the right of the family.

At what period this ceremony, described by Thukydides as an ancestral custom (*patrios nomos*), was first established has been much debated. Jacoby (1944b, 52) argued that it was first introduced by a new law after the Athenian disaster at Drabeskos in 465 B.C., whereas Gomme (1956, II 98) thought it was 'a good deal older than the Persian Wars'. Jacoby's second point, that public burials took place on the 5th Boedromion (i.e. September) as part of the festival of the Genesia, is also refuted by Gomme (ib. 100). Nor indeed do we know when the practice of delivering a funeral speech (*epitaphios logos*) over the war dead by a man chosen by the Boule began at Athens. The earliest known example was delivered by Perikles on behalf of those who died fighting against the Samians in 439. Late sources, without good grounds, inform us that the custom began shortly after the Persian Wars, or even, according to the rhetor Anaximenes, in the time of Solon. In addition, funeral games (*agôn epitaphios*) were celebrated annually in Athens on behalf of those who died in war under the supervision of the polemarchos or war-lord (Arist. *AP* 58.1).

With the exception of those who died at Marathon and Plataia, the Athenians according to Thukydides (2.34.5) buried their war dead 'in the loveliest suburb of Athens' on both sides of the road leading from the Dipylon to the Academy. Before the middle of the fourth century this so-called *Dêmosion Sêma* (People's Grave) was rebuilt in the form of a ceremonial way 39 metres in width aligned with both *polyandreia* (communal graves) and tombs of distinguished individuals.

Perhaps also to be regarded as part of the *patrios nomos*, though not mentioned by Thukydides, was the practice of inscribing the names of the war dead of the whole year on ten individual *stêlai*, one for each tribe, standing side by side on a common base. The earliest such 'casualty list' is dated to 465/4 B.C. and records the names of the Athenians and their allies who died at Drabeskos, Thasos and in the Chersonese, though the practice probably began earlier. A minimum of thirty such lists have been identified, all with one exception fragmentary, and few that can be dated with positive certainty. It is possible that the war dead of each year were also honoured by a carved monument (fig. 20). Though none has

Fig. 21. *Stêlê* marking the cenotaph of Dexileos who died in a cavalry action near Corinth in 394/393 B.C. (see also fig. 22).

conclusively been identified as such, Clairmont (1970, 43f.) has suggested that the relief in the Villa Albani in Rome, the famous Dexileos relief (figs. 21 and 22), and another in Berlin, owe their inspiration to a monumental prototype erected by the state. Mention should also be made of Boardman's thesis that the Parthenon frieze is a monument to the dead at Marathon. From an inevitably selective count of the participants in the cavalcade which yields him a total of 192 figures – the exact number of Athenians killed at that battle – he argues that the frieze 'shows the fighters of Marathon celebrating the prime festival of their goddess on the temple dedicated to her as a thanksgiving for her aid at Marathon and afterwards, and in a manner which indicates the heroic status of those who fell there' (1977, 44). Athens was by no means the only Greek state to award special honours to the war dead, who were sometimes accorded the title *agathoi andres* (good men) or simply *agathoi* (the good).

If a military engagement took place within or not far from the borders of one's land, the bodies of the fallen were probably transported home in carts, there to be prepared for burial by the relatives of the deceased. In the fifth century, however, when Athens built up her maritime empire, there were numerous occasions when the only course available was to cremate the dead on the field of battle and then ship the ashes back home. The famous passage in Aeschylus' *Agamemnon* (437ff.) in which the war god Ares is given the title 'gold broker of corpses (*chrysamoibos*)' paints a pitiful picture of the arrival back home of 'cinerary urns (*lebêtês*) containing ashes that are easily stored in place of men' – a situation doubtless all too familiar to members of the poet's audience. It is interesting to note further that the war dead were not cremated communally but separately, for Aeschylus makes it clear that their ashes were stored in individual urns which could easily be identified by their labels.

Such practices were not universal throughout Greek history. The Homeric poems preserve the memory of a time when it was acceptable to bury the cremated dead on foreign soil. This was true of heroes no less than of ordinary soldiers. Hence, the tombs of Achilles, Ajax, Antilochos and Patroklos were intended to become, and indeed did become, well-known landmarks in the Troad. Ordinary soldiers, on the other hand, were cremated communally. In a passage which may have been inserted into the *Iliad* at a late date, the Greeks and the Trojans make a truce and search the battlefield for their respective dead. Two pyres are built facing one

Fig. 22. The Kerameikos looking west. On the far right is the *Tritopatreion* (see fig. 1) and to the left the cenotaph of Dexileos (see fig. 21).

another and the dead are cremated. On the recommendation of Nestor, the Greek army erect a *tymbos* around their pyre. The fact that the Achaean dead could be disposed of on foreign soil had much to do with the fact that Homeric society did not practice a cult of the dead. Athenian society of the fifth century, by contrast, most emphatically did, and it is for this reason that the return of their dead was of such vital importance to the living.

The murdered dead and their killers

In the case of the murdered dead, it was the duty in Athens of the nearest relative of the deceased to carry a spear at the *ekphora*, to make a proclamation at the tomb indicating an intention to prosecute those responsible for the murder, and then to guard the tomb for three days. Attention was also drawn to the fact of a person's murder on his funerary monument. A pair of open hands carved on a *stêlê* inscribed with an imprecation was clearly intended as 'a gesture of prayer invoking divine vengeance upon those responsible for the murder' (Couilloud 1974, 277 and no. 485). It was an offence against the gods to let a murderer go scot-free.

Victims of murder constituted a category of the unquiet dead, their salient characteristic being anger. This they directed both against their murderers and against those who do not avenge their killing. According to the orator Antiphon (*Tetr.* 1.3.10; 3.4.10) both the murdered victim himself and the person (or god) to whom he turned as suppliant for a vengeance-killing were thus known as *prostropaioi* (turning themselves aside). Ensuring that the murderer be brought to justice was a solemn undertaking. Plato in the *Laws* (9.866b) recommended that if the next-of-kin failed in performing this duty, he should be banished for five years 'inasmuch as the dead man demands atonement for his death'.

Unfortunately the majority of our evidence regarding the condition of the murdered dead derives from poetic sources and is to be regarded with considerable suspicion. From tragedy and epic poetry we learn that a murderer was well-advised to take precautions against the vengeful spirit of his victim by performing a savage rite known as *maschalismos*. This involved cutting off the extremities (termed *maschalismata* or *exargmata*) and stringing them around either his own or the murdered man's neck. So Jason, when he slays Absyrtos, cuts off the murdered man's *exargmata*, licks up his blood and then spits it out three times 'as it is right to do to propitiate for the outrageous crime of murder' (A.R. 4.470ff.). Whether such practices were actually current in the Classical or Hellenistic period archaeology does not reveal. Evidence from tragedy suggests that the status of the murdered dead was radically affected by the fact of their killing. Unavenged a murdered king was deprived of all his majesty; avenged, he ruled 'as a mighty soul (*pampsychos*)'.

The celebrated invocation of the Erinyes or Furies by the murdered Klytaimnestra in the *Eumenidês* (115ff.) of Aeschylus has suggested to some scholars that these sinister chthonic deities performed the singular function of avenging premeditated consanguineal homicide. There exists little evidence to support such a hypothesis. Despite Rohde's claim (1897, 179) that the Furies were 'auxiliaries attached to the souls of murdered men', the more cautious view of Farnell (1907, V p. 438) that their close association with the murdered dead derives solely from the fact that they were the physical embodiment of Curses is more consistent with the evidence outside the play (e.g. Hom. *Il.* 19.259; Hes. *Erg.* 803f.).

Murderers, as well as their victims, were among the unquiet dead. Klytaimnestra's ghost complains that it is condemned to shameful wandering because 'the fact that I am a murderess is a disgrace, among the dead' (Aes. *Eum.* 96ff.). Yet this is not so much a disgrace, as the ghost later goes on to say, as the fact that her death remains unavenged by the Furies. Of Orestes it is alleged that as a mother-slayer he will have to pay for his crime in Hades, but there is no evidence that ordinary murderers were so treated.

We do not know what burial procedure was adopted in respect of murderers. Plato in the *Laws* recommended that they should be executed and their corpses cast out of the victim's country unburied (9.874b). More stringent regulations were to be applied to anyone found guilty of patricide, matricide, fratricide or infanticide, who should be 'put to death and his body dumped naked outside the city at an appointed place where three roads meet. There all the magistrates in the name of the state should cast a stone on the head of the corpse in expiation of the crime. The corpse shall then be carried to the border and be thrown out by legal sentence without burial' (ib. 873b). Xenophon (*Hell.* 1.7.22) tells us that the Athenians denied burial to traitors and tomb-robbers, whose bodies were deposited in what was officially known as the *barathron* (pit). Situated in or near the deme of Melite, the *barathron* is perhaps to be identified with a long depression beside the Northern Long Wall near the so-called Hill of the Nymphs. In Sparta the place for the bodies of condemned criminals was called the Kaiades, which was probably near Mistra. What happened to such corpses subsequently is not recorded. Rohde (1897, ch. 5 n. 32) thought that 'it is incredible that they could have wished to leave (them) to putrify in the open air', though there is no evidence that they did not actually do just this.

Suicides

Lasch (1900) distinguished four categories of belief in respect of suicides: (1) suicide is judged to be a normal act and the fate in the next world of the person who has committed it is no different from that of the ordinary dead; (2) it is rewarded as an act of valour (cf. Jainism); (3) the suicide has to wander between the world of the living and that of the dead, being denied entry to the kingdom of the dead; (4) he is punished in the next world. Belief in the miserable fate of suicides in the next world is widely reported among many peoples. A suicide often places his community in grave peril from which it can only be released by ritual cleaning. There is a fear that the evil may be contagious. For this reason the tree on which a suicide hangs himself may have to be uprooted and burnt.

Fear of and hostility towards the suicide are by no means confined to so-called primitive societies. Christian condemnation of the act dates from the fifth century A.D. Augustine (*Civ. Dei* 1.17) declared it to be a crime except in the case of victims of rape, and at the Council of Arles in 452 A.D. it was branded as the work of the Devil. A century later at the Council of Braga in 563 the church ordained that suicides were to be refused Christian burial and that no mass was to be said for the repose of their souls. In England the practice of driving a stake through the body of a suicide and then burying it at the crossroads was finally abandoned in 1823. But it was not until 1961 that the Suicide Act abrogated a law that had been in force since 1554 which declared suicide to be a criminal act. It is self-evident that the moral and intellectual evaluation of suicide has changed very slowly, the fears which it has inspired in Christian society being apparently similar to those which exist in Africa and elsewhere.

It is difficult to assess to what extent the Greeks regarded suicides (*autocheires* or *biaiothanatoi*) with either fear or loathing. In Homer suicide receives only slight reference and never with any blame attached. Epikaste, the wife of Oedipus, the first literary suicide, is presented as merely reacting to an intolerable situation (*Od.* 11.271ff.). Despite Rohde's claim (1897, 3) that 'to turn aside from life altogether never enters the head of anyone in Homer', Odysseus' despair, Helen's shame and Achilles' grief are sufficient to give rise to suicidal thoughts – or at least to fears among their friends for their safety. The tragedians suggest that in certain circumstances suicide is an appropriate and indeed desirable response. Hekabe, for instance, blames Helen for not putting an end to her miserable existence (Eur. *Tro.* 1012ff.); and it is noteworthy that the Chorus, though seemingly apprised of Phaidra's intention to take her own life, take no steps to prevent her from doing so (Eur. *Hipp.* 782ff.). Of other characters in Greek tragedy, Ajax, Jokaste and Leda all kill themselves out of shame and fear of evil repute. Eurydike dies upon learning of the death of her son who has himself committed suicide out of violent remorse. Alkestis and Makaria offer their lives in self-sacrifice. Menelaos and Helen form a suicide pact to perish together if their escape plan fails. Suicide wishes are uttered with monotonous regularity, and the threat of suicide may sometimes be used as a form of blackmail.

It is the *Ajax* of Sophokles that provides the most detailed discussion of the ethics of self-destruction. The hero's wife, whom we would expect to produce the most passionate and persuasive arguments against suicide, urges her husband to reflect upon the kind of life to which she will be confined in the eventuality of his death; begs him to think of his other family ties; emphasises her dependence as a captive upon his protection; and concludes with a reminder of the debt of kindness which is owing to her in return for the happy life they have shared together. But that is all. There is no criticism of suicide as such, merely an appeal for the avoidance of an action bound to react harmfully upon family and friends. In the final address to Ajax before he delivers his speech on Time, the Chorus, observing the gloomy despair which has now replaced his former frenzy, comments that a man in his condition would really be better dead, thus in effect almost sanctioning the act which is to follow. The reaction of Ajax's friends and associates to the fact of his suicide can be briefly summarised as follows: in the case of the Chorus, a feeling of guilt at having failed to recognise his intention earlier; in the case of Tekmessa, an acceptance of the fact that this is what heaven willed and what he himself sought; and in the case of Teukros, some degree of guilt, but mainly an indulgent self-pity at the prospect of the unpleasant task of having to break the sad news to his parents. It is instructive to note that in the lengthy debate which occupies the whole last third of the play and which centres around the hero's entitlement to his funeral dues, the fact that he is a suicide is never referred to at all.

The Christian objection to suicide rests largely on the concept that God has given man an allotted span of life to fulfil. Popular Greek religion shows little trace of such a belief. In Homer, as Athene herself admits, the gods are unable to protect their friends when the fate (*moira*) of death comes upon them (*Od.* 3.236ff.), and Zeus' scales in which he places the fates of death (*kêrê*), one for the Greeks and one for the Trojans (*Il.* 8.68ff.), are clearly to be understood as something distinct from the god and over which he has no control. An exception should perhaps be made in the case of heroes whose deaths the gods do seem to overseer: Hyllos, though willing, is unable to shorten his father Herakles' life because it is ordained by Zeus (S. *Trach.* 1022). Orphism, Pythagoreanism and Platonism, however, did condemn suicide on the grounds that it was interfering with divine dispensation. On being asked to explain the paradox why death is counted a blessing but suicide is judged to be wicked, Sokrates (Pl. *Phd.* 62b) declares that he can only repeat the doctrine that is told *en aporrhêtois* (in secret): namely that the gods who are our guardians have put us in a kind of prison (or garrison) which we must not try to escape from (or desert). The comment is probably a reference to the Orphic doctrine that the body is a tomb in which the soul is incarcerated, but there is no reason to suspect that it does not reflect Sokrates' own views on the subject, despite the ironical deference which introduces it. In addition the Pythagorean Euxitheos is said to have taught that the souls of all creatures were imprisoned in the body as a punishment and that 'the gods had ordained that if they refuse to remain in the body until he releases them, they will be plunged into further and more terrible torments' (Ath. 4.157c).

'Legal theory', notes Devereux (1961, 293), 'views the suicide as an anti-social being (*felo de se*), whose act deprives society of the services of one of its members'. The custom in Athens, as Aischines (3.244) informs us, was to cut off the right hand of the suicide – a measure presumably adopted to render the spirit of the deceased harmless. Possibly other distinctions in the form of burial accorded to a suicide were also observed in the Classical period. Plato in the *Laws* (9.873d) discriminates between those on the one hand who commit suicide because they are compelled to do so by a state injunction, or because they have suffered an intolerable misfortune or disgrace, and those on the other hand who do so out of indolence (*argia*) or unmanly cowardice. In the latter case he recommends that their next-of-kin should consult the *exêgêtai* to determine 'what further rites must be adopted in the matter of purifications and burials'. He also prescribes that suicides should not be buried in cemeteries but 'in the nameless regions ... without a gravestone or an inscription to mark the tomb', and that they should have no companions in the grave. Plato, as a moralist, has a vested interest in outlawing the suicide. According to Aristotle (*EN* 5.1138a) Athenian law did not explicitly condemn suicide, though *de facto* it treated it as illegal. He draws this conclusion from the fact that legal penalties were imposed in the case of those who made unsuccessful attempts at suicide, involving a fine as well as loss of civil rights. In his attempt to explain the rationale behind the legal practice, Aristotle comes to the conclusion that suicide was regarded as an act of social irresponsibility.

In the Athens of Plutarch's day the bodies of persons who had hanged themselves, along with their clothing and the noose itself, were thrown into the *barathron*, together with the bodies of common murderers (Plu. *Them.* 22.2). Elsewhere a more liberal attitude prevailed. Livy (37.54.21) reports that in Massalia, a Phocaean colony which had preserved its Greek traditions 'as though its inhabitants lived in the very navel of Greece', anyone wanting to commit suicide merely sought permission to do so from the senate, and if his reasons were judged adequate, he was provided with hemlock free of charge. According to Strabo (10.5.6) a Kean law decreed that anyone over the age of sixty was compelled to drink hemlock so that there should be enough food to go around for all. Suicide in the Roman period could be a very public affair. Valerius Maximus, who knew of a Kean suicide law resembling that which operated in Massalia, tells of a woman from the town of Ioulis on that island 'of the greatest dignity but already very old' (viz. over 90), who, having explained to the citizen body her reasons for committing suicide, issued an invitation to Sextus Pompeius to attend her self-poisoning in the belief that his presence would render her death 'more distinguished' (2.6.8).

Dioblêtoi

Any object struck by lightning was treated with reverence in the Greek world, and it is thus not surprising that distinctive burial procedure was adopted in the case of persons who met their death in this way. They were known as *dioblêtoi*, 'those smitten by Zeus', it being the belief that Zeus, the wielder of the thunderbolt, had deliberately marked them apart in this way. In mythology these include Herakles, Kapaneos and Semele. Of Kapaneos it is said that both his corpse and his *tymbos* were *hieros*. *Hieros*, as Rohde notes (1897, 580f.), never has the meaning of 'accursed', like the Latin word '*sacer*'. It is possible that *dioblêtoi* were thought to dispense blessings on the community in which their bodies resided: it was presumably for this reason that the body of Kapaneos was buried in front of the palace – a distinction, as noted above, normally reserved for heroes. Certainly in later times such a person, according to Artemidoros (*Oneirokr.* 2.9 *T*), was 'honoured like god'. Plutarch tells us (*Mor.* 665c) that the bodies of *dioblêtoi*, being believed to be incorruptible, were not necessarily accorded cremation or burial but were sometimes left where they were struck by lightning, within an enclosure; even dogs and birds, he reports, would not touch them.

It has been suggested that the three gold leaves found in the tumulus known as the Timpone Piccolo (height 5m; circumference 52m) in Thourii were buried with persons who had been struck by lightning. They are inscribed with minute lettering in the Greek language containing many errors. The gold leaf classified by Zuntz as A1 which preserves the most careful text of the three contains the statement: 'Fate (and the other immortal gods) and the star-flinger subdued me with a thunderbolt' (*DK* no. 18a; Kern 1922, no. 32c). Zuntz, who takes this literally, is of the opinion that the tumulus was first erected over the grave of a single person killed by lightning 'and that two others who later found their deaths in the same way were buried in this most appropriate place' (1971, 136).

Unfortunately the tumulus was poorly excavated in the last century and only summarily reported, and consequently its stratigraphy is only imperfectly understood. None the less certain facts about the burials which it contained are plainly established: first, the dead were all inhumed, not cremated; secondly, the tombs were low and plain, being constructed of tufa and then painted white; thirdly, they contained no grave-gifts other than a single gold leaf apiece; and fourthly, traces of ashes found outside the tombs provide evidence of commemorative sacrifices performed at the funeral or subsequently. In view of the distinctive funerary procedure conducted on behalf of Kapaneos as commented on above, which is supported as well by the testimony of Pliny (*NH* 2.145), the information that the bodies of the dead were all inhumed lends considerable support to their identification as *dioblêtoi*. On the evidence of letter-forms, and because on A1 the ending *-ou* is expressed by the single letter *-o*, Zuntz suggests a date for this plaque, which he believes to have accompanied the earliest burial in the tumulus, of 'not later than the middle of the fourth century' (1971, 295f.).

Deuteropotmoi

Sokrates in the *Republic* (10.614b) tells a story about a Pamphylian soldier called Er, apparently killed in a battle, who revived on the twelfth day after his supposed death while awaiting immolation on his funeral pyre. Thereupon he related what he had seen in the world beyond. *Deuteropotmoi* (or *hysteropotmoi*), 'second-fated ones' (or 'persons with two fates'), as such people were called in later times, were 'those for whom an *ekphora* had been held and a tomb constructed on the assumption that they were dead' (Plu. *Mor.* 264f). Also included in this category were those reported to have died abroad but who subsequently returned home. Being considered impure, Plutarch explains, they were forbidden to mix with other people or to enter any sanctuary (or merely the sanctuary of the Semnai (Holy ones) according to Hesychios). In order to secure release from the ban, as the Delphic oracle informed a *deuteropotmos* called Aristinos, it was necessary to undergo 'all that a woman in childbirth does when she produces', that is to say, being washed, wrapped in swaddling clothes, and breast-fed, before making a sacrifice to the 'blessed gods' (Plu., loc. cit.): in other words, to repeat the life-cycle all over again from the start. As Jane Harrison (1908, 245) pointed out, the reasoning behind the ritual is that something is seriously wrong with the *deuteropotmos*: 'he is rejected by the powers below and unfit to mingle with his fellows in the world above; he is highly taboo ... the only chance is for him to be born again.' Likewise Alkestis, not rejected by but already consecrated to the powers below, might be described as a born-again *deuteropotmos* at the end of Euripides' play (above p. 47).

Ataphoi

In Euripides we may detect traces of the belief that the unburied dead (*ataphoi*) could not enter Hades but were condemned to haunt this earth to which they remained indissolubly bound. In later times the souls of the unburied dead could be invoked in the service of magic, their wanderings only coming to an end when the rite of burial had been duly performed.

The importance, or rather necessity, of conducting burial rites on behalf of the Greek dead, and the corresponding insult to human dignity if they be omitted, is so frequently alluded to both in the tragedians and the historians that it scarcely needs any illustration. Recognition of the due of burial, described by Theseus in Euripides' *Suppliants* as being 'a Panhellenic law' (526), extended to the almost invariably upheld custom of returning the bodies of one's fallen enemies on the battlefield. Only in exceptional cases do we learn that the right was denied, as after the battle of Delion in 424 when the Boeotians initially refused to return the Athenian dead on the grounds that they had occupied a sanctuary in the course of the campaign. It is conceivable that the Athenians denied burial to the Persians after the battle of Marathon, for although they claimed to have honoured their enemy dead, Pausanias was unable to find the grave. But the possibility that the Athenians simply chose not to mark the spot cannot be ruled out.

In Athens, according to a law ascribed to Solon, if a boy were hired out as a prostitute by his father, he was released from the obligation of having to provide his father with sustenance and a home in his old age; but he was still required to give him burial and to carry out *ta nomizomena* (Aischin. 1.13). If a formal interment was found to be impractical, at least a light covering of earth had to be sprinkled over the corpse – the rite performed by Antigone on behalf of her brother. Aelian (*VH* 5.14) states that this duty was even required of a stranger. In times of crisis there were, naturally, specia˙ pressures.

Thukydides (2.52) tells us that when the plague broke out in Athens in 430 B.C., many people neglected to hold proper funerals. Some threw their dead on to a pyre that belonged to someone else and then set light to it; others threw their corpse on to one that was already burning, and then ran off. The importance of according the dead proper burial receives further confirmation from the fact that if the body for some reason could not be recovered, a fictitious burial took place and a cenotaph (*kenotaphion*, or *kenon mnêma*) was erected over an empty grave. Cenotaphs were among the graves which lined the *Dêmosion Sêma* which led to the Academy. They received offerings like other graves, a stone in some cases serving as a substitute for the body of the deceased.

It remains to consider why the performing of the due of the dead (*geras thanontôn*) was so important, and why omission was so shocking to Greek sentiment. Or more accurately, since almost all societies stress the need for respectful treatment of the corpse, we need to try to determine what feelings and beliefs underlay its significance in Greek eyes.

As we might expect where matters of religion are concerned, no single belief prevails to the exclusion of all others. This can easily be exemplified by reference to the lengthy debate in the *Ajax* of Sophokles as to whether the hero, by willing the deaths of his military commanders, has forfeited his right to burial. The debate turns upon many issues. Upholding Ajax's claim, the Chorus accuses Menelaos of being a violator by proposing to override it. Teukros says vaguely that Ajax's burial is justified, but Menelaos, who classes him among the enemy, complains that if Ajax is interred a murderer will prosper. Menelaos is cautioned not to insult the gods and warned darkly that if he mistreats the dead, he will be punished. What is interesting about the debate is not only the points it raises, but also those it omits. It is striking that no eschatological argument is advanced on Ajax's behalf. Nowhere either in this play or, for that matter, in the *Antigonê*, which poses an identical problem, does Sophokles argue that the soul of the unburied dead could find no peace in Hades – a point of contrast with the *Iliad* in which Patroklos appears to Achilles demanding burial so that he can gain admission to Hades (*Il.* 23.71ff.). Instead Sophokles directs all our thoughts to the sheer horror of treating a human being like a carcase. Equally illuminating is the omission of any reference either to the malignant influence of the unburied dead or to the necessity for burial on utilitarian, hygienic grounds. It is as an offence against humanity and against the gods that claims for burial, according to Sophokles, chiefly rest. In conclusion, it hardly seems necessary to point out that the degree of enlightenment ascribed here to Sophokles may not have been shared by the poet's contemporaries.

Finally, in addition to the *ataphoi* there were also the *apotaphoi*. The exact significance of the title is not fully understood, but it is likely that those designated in this way were buried separately, whether as a mark of distinction or, alternatively, as one of disfavour.

7

Visiting the Tomb

The regular visiting of the tombs of one's dead relatives was for an Athenian of the Classical period an act of almost comparable importance to that of interment itself. Its omission by a son, or adopted son, and heir was a matter of such gravity that this circumstance might be adduced as evidence in a case of disputed inheritance to prove that the claimant had no genuine kinship with the deceased. Conversely it was of vital concern to an Athenian that he should leave behind him who would not only attend to his burial but also perform the customary rites at his grave. The anxiety with which he contemplated the omission of these rites could be so acute that it might induce a childless man to adopt an heir with the express object of ensuring that his mortal remains did not want attention from the living. The importance which Athenian society as a whole placed upon the proper observance of tomb-cult is indicated by the fact that before a citizen could pass the examination (*dokimasia*) which he had to undergo before appointment to public office, he had to prove to the satisfaction of his assessors that he had regularly discharged this obligation. As in the case of interment, those most responsible were the immediate family of the deceased. On vases, those who visit the cemetery are predominantly female.

There does not appear to have been any expression in Greek reserved exclusively for acts of devotion performed at the tomb. *Ta nomizomena*, which is used generally to mean customary practices performed on behalf of the dead, are defined by their context, and sometimes refer to the laying-out of the body and the funeral, and at other times to the cult of the tomb. Other expressions used include *ta nomima* and *ta hiera patrôa* (ancestral rights).

In addition to rites conducted at the graveside on the third, ninth and thirtieth days after death, commemorative visits were paid both monthly and annually. In the case of annual rites (*eniausia*), we do

Fig. 23. *Peribolos* or family plot of two brothers called Agathon and Sosikrates in the Kerameikos. The front wall was originally covered with stucco painted white. The high central *stêlê* records the names of the dead buried within the plot.

not know in the majority of instances whether they were performed on the anniversary of the deceased's death, on the anniversary of his funeral, or on his birthday. We know also of an annual event called the Genesia, which is described by Hesychios (s.v.) as 'an Athenian festival of mourning' and said by Herodotus (4.26) to be 'known to all the Greeks'. Jacoby (1944a, 67) has convincingly argued that the Genesia was originally a private festival celebrated annually and privately on the deceased's day of death. Solon, however, anxious to cut down the display of private grief in the capital, in his re-arranging of the Athenian religious calendar, appointed that the Genesia should become a national festival held every year on the 5th Boedromion, thereby preventing celebrants from carrying out rites in more than one cemetery. In addition to the Genesia, lexicographers also refer to a festival called the Nemeseia, described by Photios (s.v.) as 'a night-long festival (*panêgyris*) held in honour of the dead' which could involve the kin in lavish financial outlay (see below).

Greek tragedy makes it clear, however, that irregular as well as regular visits were paid to the dead throughout the year. Elektra, for instance, promises to bring drink-offerings to her father's tomb on

the occasion of her wedding, whenever that should be (A. *Ch.* 486ff.).
It is clear, too, that advice and even assistance were sometimes
sought from the dead at the place of interment. Though the offerings
brought to the cemetery on these occasions could have been quite
cheaply procured and doubtless were in the majority of cases, we
gain some insight into the expense that might be lavished upon the
dead even in the fourth century from the fact that the defendant in
Demosthenes' speech *Against Spoudias* claims that his wife paid out a
mna of silver on her father's behalf at a certain Nemeseia (41.11).

Self-evidently, visiting the graves of one's deceased relatives is
facilitated by the practice of burying them in the same plot of ground.
Tomb grouping can be traced in mainland Greece as far back as the
late Middle Helladic period. Grave Circle B at Mycenae, one of the
earliest known examples, consists of a parapet wall built of large
limestone orthostats enclosing an area with an estimated diameter of
28 metres. Within the enclosure were twenty-four graves thought to
belong to members of the ruling class. The grave circle is dated
between the end of the seventeenth and first half of the sixteenth
century B.C. Evidence exists for a resumption of the practice in both
the Geometric and Archaic periods, in the shape of both round and
rectangular mounds, but it is in the last decades of the fifth century
that among the well-to-do in Athens there arises what might
justifiably be termed a craze for family enclosures. The majority of
such *periboloi* date to the fourth century B.C. and the finest examples
are to be found in the Kerameikos (fig. 23). Of these the most
prestigious aligned the so-called Street of Tombs, which constituted
a section of one of the busiest thoroughfares in ancient Greece
carrying traffic to and from the busy port of Peiraios. Along here as
well passed the Dionysiac and Eleusinian processions, and there can
be no doubt that all this greatly enhanced the prestige of those
families which could afford to bury their dead in this area. In recent
years, another important series has come to light in connection with
the ancient deme of Rhamnous to the north-east of Athens. Here,
periboloi extend for a distance of over one and a half miles, aligning
both sides of an ancient road which led to the deme of Marathon in
the southwest. The number of persons buried within a plot rarely
exceeded six, though many *periboloi* enclosed only two or three.
Likewise overwhelmingly the majority of funerary inscriptions
commemorate a maximum of four persons. Rarely is there evidence
for tomb-groupings extending over more than three generations,
which suggests the average dead Athenian could realistically expect

Fig. 24. The faithful protector of the dead: a stone watchdog on perpetual guard at one of the corners of the family plot of Lysimachides of the deme Acharnai in the Kerameikos.

to receive *ta nomizomena* from his children, rarely from his grandchildren, and only exceptionally from his great-grandchildren. If this estimate is correct, the situation in Classical Athens was not substantially different from that which currently prevails, one suspects, in modern Britain.

Though piety towards the dead doubtless contributed in prompting an Athenian family to erect a costly funerary monument, there can be no doubt at all that earthly considerations were also to the fore. The siting of *periboloi* along major thoroughfares, the fact that they were often fronted by a wall several metres in height, and the use of intimidating symbols of strength and power to define their boundaries, together with the fact that when Demetrios of Phaleron banned all but the simplest form of grave-marker in 317 B.C., his motive was to curb unnecessary expenditure, all seem to indicate that a *peribolos*, whatever else it might have been, constituted a status-symbol, both intended and adapted to display wealth to maximum effect (figs. 23-5).

Our principal source of information for the Athenian cult of the tomb is provided by the series of white-ground *lêkythoi* with funerary iconography, supplemented by the frequent descriptions of tomb-visits in plays which focus on the story of Elektra. In the initial period of their manufacture *lêkythoi* were simply regarded as household items, the scenes which decorated them being either mythological or domestic. From the 460s to 410s, however, they became the most popular offering to the dead and developed an iconography which was predominantly funerary (fig. 26). Largely this was due to the influence of the Achilles Painter, whose long career lasted from *c.* 460 to the 430s, and who seems to have done more than any other artist to make the *lêkythos* the Athenian grave-gift par excellence in the latter half of the fifth century. As Kurtz (*AWL* 51) has suggested, it may be that its spectacular rise in popularity at this time was due to restrictions on more expensive forms of funerary art.

Representations of tomb-visits on *lêkythoi* display a marked uniformity. In the centre is a *stêlê* decorated with ribbons. From either side, two, or rarely three, persons approach, the vast majority of them women. They bring offerings, display themselves in various attitudes of grief, extend their arms in greeting, and perform other pious acts of devotion. The gifts are transported in a wide, shallow basket of circular appearance with sloping, slightly concave sides, made out of reed or cane known variously as *kaneon* or *kaniskion*. Invariably the basket-carrier (*kanêphoros*) is a woman. Sometimes, it is suspected, the dead is represented at the tomb as well. Tomb-visits also appear occasionally on black-figure *lêkythoi* and on vases of other shapes. In the latter case the persons participating are mainly heroic.

Although the *lêkythos* ceased to be a popular grave-gift *c.* 410 B.C., there is no reason to suppose that visits to the grave were any less popular in the fourth century than in the fifth. Indeed the evidence from the orators testifies to their continuing importance throughout the Classical period. Similarly, no eschatological explanation need be sought for the disappearance of the *lêkythos*, which, in Kurtz's words (*AWL* 74), 'marks a change in fashion, not a change in mortuary practice'.

From the late fourth century onwards in Asia Minor and in the islands of the Aegean, however, commemoration of the dead took on a new aspect. It became the practice to bequeath a sum of money for the establishment of a foundation whose aim was to guarantee periodic rites held in honour of the deceased in perpetuity. The philosopher Epikouros, for instance, who died in 270 B.C., set aside a yearly income (*prosodoi*) from the capital bequeathed to his heirs for an offering (*enagismata*) to be made to his brothers, his parents and himself (D.L.10.16ff.). An inscription known as the Will of Epiktete

Fig. 25. Funerary monuments were designed to impress the passer-by: hence, their backs were left uncarved.

of Thera dated *c.* 200 B.C., records the foundation of a three-day feast to be held annually in honour of the Muses and the heroes, the latter group comprising Epiktete herself, her husband and their two sons. Some twenty-five initial members of the foundation, both male and female, are mentioned in the will. Bequests of this kind were especially common among those who wished to be remembered as benefactors of their polis. But it would be wrong to view commemorative foundations purely as exercises in public relations. The Will of Epiktete lays down precise instructions as to the nature of the offerings to be made to the heroes, which include an animal sacrifice (*hiereion*), a special type of sacrificial cake known as *ellutai*, and a *statêr* of cheese, all of which had to be burned. It is thus reasonable to assume that the idea of contributing to the welfare of the deceased and securing their continuation by means of periodic offerings of food and drink persisted into the Hellenistic period.

Feeding the dead

There can be little doubt that although the wreathing, be-ribboning and anointing of the *stêlê* formed a major part in the rites, the tomb feast was the principal manner of honouring the dead and delighting his ghost, in view of the fact that sensual pleasure, of which a banquet was the chief element, was commonly regarded in antiquity as the supreme reward for a virtuous life. Whether the dead was cremated or inhumed, male or female, remains of burnt deposits in and around graves illustrate that a meal was equally acceptable to all. Artemidoros (*Oneirokr.* 1.4*T*) tells us that the only category of the dead not invited to attend such feasts were suicides. The meal as a whole seems simply to have been known as *daïs* or *deipnon*, and those who partook of it as *eudeipnoi*. More technical expressions in use include *enagismata enagizein* and *choas cheisthai*. Sometimes the two phrases are coupled together, in which case *enagismata* clearly refers to the food offering and *choai* to the drink. Lexicographers, however, regularly define *enagismata* so as to include *choai* as well, and when the word stands alone it should probably be taken in this comprehensive sense. As Farnell (1921, 354) has suggested, it may be that its etymology indicates that food reserved for the dead was put under a taboo which barred its use from the living, the natural explanation of *enagizein* being 'to put an *agos* (pollution) into the food' or alternatively 'to put things that are under an *agos* into the grave'. Herodotus (2.44.5), who is our earliest authority for the use of the

Fig. 26. Attic white-ground *lêkythos* depicting women setting out for a cemetery with baskets laden with gifts for the grave.

word, opposes *enagizein*, which is something you do on behalf of a hero, to *thuein* (sacrifice), which is something you do on behalf of a god.

There is, however, no clear evidence to indicate whether or not the living also partook of the meals which they served to the dead. Farnell (1921, 354), who believed that table-fellowship with the dead was considered unlucky and likely to bring one under the influence of the spirit-world, adduced in support of his view the fact that at

Sikyon the sacrifice made to Herakles as a god was shared among his worshippers, whereas that which was consecrated to him as a dead hero was tabooed for use by the living (Paus. 2.10.1). What prevailed in the case of heroes, however, may not have prevailed in the case of the ordinary dead. The *perideipnon*, or feast held in the dead man's house immediately after the *ekphora*, does not clarify the issue either, since the dead at this point were judged to be marginal. It is true that the Will of Epiktete permitted the relatives who gathered in the shrine (*herôon*) to share in the sacrificial feast of the dead, but it is noteworthy that separate portions were assigned to each group.

The end panel of the Late Middle Helladic Ayia Triada sarcophagus in Herakleion Museum provides what is perhaps the earliest representation in Greek art of a sacrifice performed on behalf of the dead. A procession of five figures moves towards a shrine before which a slaughtered bull lies trussed on a table. The earliest literary description of a sacrifice to the dead occurs in the *Odyssey* (10.526ff.) where Odysseus is recommended by Kirke to make an offering of a ram and a black ewe to 'the glorious tribes of the dead'. Although the sacrifice is atypical in that its intention is not to administer to the needs of the deceased but to restore them to consciousness, and in particular to revive prophetic utterance in the seer Teiresias, there is no reason to doubt that what Homer has in fact provided us with is a description of a regular sacrifice to the dead.

Blood sacrifices were known as *haimakouriai*, although the expression *sphagia entemnein* (cut up the victims) was also used. Even in Homer's day, however, the flesh of animals was not the only kind of food offered to the dead. Literary evidence suggests that the most common victim was a sheep or an ox, but judging from the bones found in graves, it is clear that cows, pigs, goats and hares were also offered to the dead, at least in the Geometric period. Only female or castrated animals were considered appropriate offerings, and the preferred colour of the victim was black. The animal was slaughtered over a trench with its head looking downwards so that the blood trickled directly into the earth. It was then skinned and its carcase burned. Sacrifices to the dead were generally made at sunset or at least before nightfall, although exceptions are known.

Solon's ban on the sacrifice of an ox at the *ekphora* leads one *a fortiori* to suspect, however, that this kind of offering was forbidden in Athenian tomb-cult from the early sixth century onwards (Plu. *Solon* 21) – if indeed commemorative visits were paid to Athenian graves in the Archaic period. The complete absence of any reference to animal sacrifice on Attic *lêkythoi* provides grounds for infering that in the fifth century the practice as conducted on behalf of the ordinary dead was at least very rare. The large quantity of animal bones which have been found in the deposits of offering places in the Kerameikos from the end of the sixth century to the beginning of the third do not indicate that Solon's ban was widely disregarded, since the identified remains have been attributed to domestic animals, especially birds, which may have been intended to provide the dead with companionship in the next world, rather than to stave off his hunger.

In general we know very little about what food was served to the Classical dead and about how it was prepared. Lysistrate (Ar. *Lys.* 601) speaks of a honey-cake called *melitoutta*, which the scholiast fancifully explains was given to the dead in order to ward off Kerberos. These cakes are possibly represented on *lêkythoi* as small round objects projecting from the baskets which celebrants carried to the tomb. As we have seen (note to p. 70) pomegranates had a special significance for the dead. On *lêkythoi* occasionally an egg is shown being presented at a tomb. Sometimes a favourite meal was prepared for the dead: Klearchos (Ath. 8.344c) tells us that a certain flautist, remembering a fellow musician's fondness for fish, was in the habit of depositing a plate of fry on his grave. Since *enagismata* are defined by Hesychios (s.v.) as 'whole burnt offerings' (*holokautômata*), it may be that the burning of food-offerings to the dead facilitated their despatch to the next world.

While it is likely that private sacrifices were not made to the dead in Attika during the Classical period, publicly the fashion still continued. The war dead and the heroes were naturally put on a special diet. Thukydides (3.58.4) records that the Plataians who died at Marathon annually received the first-fruits (*aparchai*) of the Athenian harvest. Plutarch (*Arist.* 21.3) records that a black bull was sacrificed every year to those who died fighting the Persians at Plataia. Unfortunately no description is preserved of the *enagismata* which the *polemarchos* or war-lord offered annually to the tyrannicides, Harmodios and Aristogeiton (Arist. *AP* 58.1).

Drink offerings

Like the performing of sacrifices to the dead, the pouring out of drink offerings or *choai* in their honour can be traced back to Minoan times. A scene of drink offering is portrayed on the front panel of the Ayia Triada sarcophagus, and a libation ceremony seems to have formed a part of the funeral service performed in connection with the tholos tombs in the Mesara in southern Crete. It is likely, too, that a final toast or possibly a libation was made in Mycenaean tombs at the conclusion of the burial service, after which the *kylikes* were smashed and the passage (*dromos*) blocked up.

In the Classical period it seems to have been the *choai* which both constituted the principal offertory to the dead and provided the most effective means of summoning up the ghost. Eustathios states that 'a *choê* is offered to the dead, but a *spondê* is not'. What distinction he may have had in mind is not known, but it may have had something to do with quantity. The Kean lawcode indulgently permitted 'not more than three *choes* of wine and one of olive-oil to be carried to the grave' (*LSG* 97A.8f.). A *spondê*, on the other hand, as Lucas (1969, 62f.) pointed out, would appear to have been no more than a few drops. The passage of liquid refreshment to the dead in his grave was facilitated in some cases by the insertion of feeding-tubes made of clay-piping into the ground, a practice recorded both in the case of inhumation and cremation burials. Such devices are, however, comparatively rare in Athenian graves of the Classical period.

When a blood sacrifice was being performed, the *choai* were poured out before the victim's throat was cut. This is the order of ceremonies both when Odysseus summons the host of the dead from Hades (*Od.* 10.516ff.) and when Polyxene is offered in human sacrifice to Achilles (Eur. *Hek.* 527ff.). We learn most about drink-offerings from Aeschylus' *Choêphoroi*, although it must be emphasised that the rite is being performed on behalf of a victim of murder. So Elektra naturally judges the normal form of words which are uttered on such occasions (94ff.) – 'Grant prosperity in return to those who send these adornments, a gift to match the good they have given' – to be singularly inappropriate in view of the fact that she has been sent to offer *choai* at the grave of the murdered dead at the bidding of her mother who perpetrated the deed. She is advised by the Chorus to utter 'holy words' (*semna*) on behalf of those of goodwill and to make a plea for vengeance against her father's murderers. The ceremony thus begins with a prayer to Hermes for assistance in summoning Gaia and the underworld deities who look after her father's house. As Elektra pours the *choai* to the dead, she invokes her father to take pity on both herself and Orestes, ensure that his murderers are repaid in kind, and be a transmitter of 'good things' (*esthla*) to those on earth. So that the *choai* may 'come to flower' (*epanthizein*), the ceremony concludes with a paean to the dead.

From accounts of drink-offerings in tragedy, coupled with evidence from vases, the following re-construction can be proposed. *Choai* were usually poured at the grave, either on to the steps supporting the *stêlê* or possibly over the shaft. The liquid could be in either mixed or unmixed form, but whichever the case the ingredients were always the same: honey, milk, water, wine and oil. A wide variety of vases which might have served as containers for *choai* figure on *lêkythoi*, including *hydriai, oinochoai, phialai* and *lêkythoi* themselves, as well as drinking-vessels of various shapes. Of particular interest is an unusual-shaped vase with a high foot and swelling body, possibly to be identified as the *plêmochoê*, described by Athenaios (11.496b) as 'shaped like a top standing solidly on its base, which was used at Eleusis on the last day of the Mysteries'.

Before pouring out the *choai*, the celebrant commended both himself and his gift to the dead, thereby issuing the latter with an invitation to attend the rite being enacted in his honour. Assistance was sought in contacting the ghost of the deceased through the mediation of Hermes, Gaia and other gods and *daimones*. There followed a prayer to the dead which took the form of a general request that they be kindly disposed (*preumeneis*) towards their family and dispatch bounty (*esthla* or *agatha*) to the world above in requital for the offering being made. Doubtless it was common practice at this point to insert an appeal for a more specific boon. A prayer for evil to befall one's enemies was perhaps only made in exceptional circumstances. Other members of the party provided an accompaniment to the ritual by singing a dirge in honour of the dead. Following its conclusion, the vessels which had served as containers for the *choai* were perhaps smashed in the vicinity of the tomb.

Decorating the stêlê

Celebrants of the cult of the dead brought to the tomb not only food and drink, but also gifts and items of ritual significance with which to deck the *stêlê*. The exact purpose of the gifts is not always clear. A discus and lyre, for instance, which hang suspended in mid-air to right and left of a tomb on a vase in Boston, are perhaps intended to evoke the memory of the deceased's athletic prowess and musical accomplishment. On the other hand, the representation of a sword attached by its belt to the *stêlê* on a *lêkythos* in Athens may have been put there to indicate that the deceased died in battle. Once again we must be wary of insisting upon too precise an interpretation of the iconography.

The commonest way of decorating the tomb was by winding a broad, flat sash or ribbon around the shaft of the *stêlê* and then tying it into a knot or bow with the loose ends hanging down. Such ribbons (called *taeniai*) were provided with terminal strings which also hang loose. Few *stêlai* as represented on vases are depicted with no *taeniai* at all, and some have as many as five or six. The ribbons are painted in bright monochrome, the colours being blue, green, vermilion, black, purple and brown. Sometimes they are shown in the hands of the celebrants, held out towards the tomb in what is perhaps a formal gesture of presentation. They also figure frequently among the objects brought to the tomb in offering-baskets. In addition to the flat ribbon, a round tubular fillet appears regularly on *lêkythoi*, particularly in the work of the Achilles Painter. It has a patterned texture, made up of a series of dots interrupted by a patch of dark paint, this pattern being repeated several times. *Taeniai* of this latter type are depicted either laid at the foot of the *stêlê* or else wound into a wreath and placed upright against its base. Ribbons were not only used for honouring the dead, but occur in other religious contexts as well. Various explanations have been proposed to explain their meaning – that they possessed the power to ward off evil, elevated the object they adorned to a higher plane, or were a mark of homage – and it is probable that their durability and popularity owed something to each.

The custom of bringing floral tributes to the grave can be attested from both vases and tragedy, the earliest literary reference being found in Aeschylus' *Persai* (618). Though the practice is in general less frequently alluded to in Greek than in Latin epigrams, tombs are commonly depicted on vases either decked in myrtle branches or with a wreath or coronet placed upright against the steps. Celery (*selinon*) was an especially popular offering to the dead, perhaps even being exclusively reserved for their use. Whether any religious significance attached to the rite remains unclear, though it is possible, as Lattimore suggests, that it contains an allusion to the belief that the buried dead help fertilise the earth and in this way are repaid for their favours.

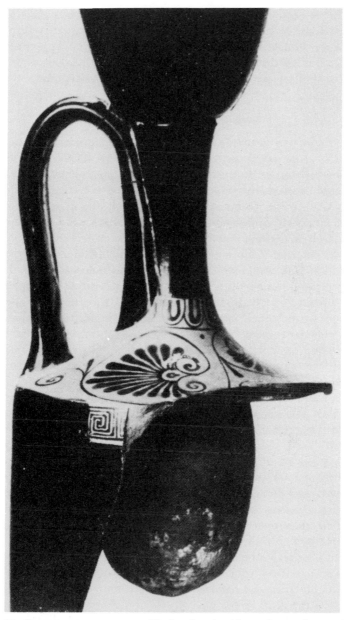

Fig. 27. Economy measures: a *lêkythos* fitted with an internal container intended to save the bereaved the expense of having to fill the whole flask with oil.

A more personal offering to the dead was the gift of a shorn lock of hair, which Orestes deposits on his father's tomb upon first returning to Argos. Iphigeneia in Tauris regrets she cannot make this offering to her brother on learning of his supposed death, whereas the vain Helen, similarly bereaved, cuts off only the tips of her hair.

The eschatology of the cemetery visit

The attempt to construct a hard and fast eschatological framework around the practices we have been considering is bound to founder for several reasons. In the first place such explanations as have come down to us from antiquity are often nothing more than aetiological inferences; in the second place, things were doubtless done at the tomb for which no explanation was ever popularly available. None the less it is reasonable to assume that at some level there must exist a mutual interdependence between ritual and eschatology, and in the belief that this is so I offer the following general observations.

In order to understand the significance of visiting a cemetery for an Athenian, it is important to do away with any preconceived notions we may have that are the result of its superficial resemblance to the modern cemetery visit. While it is tempting to view the ritual of tending the dead at the place of burial as a characteristic of all settled communities with close-knit family structures, and thereby to trace the modern visit by direct descent to its Classical predecessor, Ariès (1974, 68ff.) has conclusively demonstrated that our own cult of tombs, far from developing out of any earlier tradition, arose as a protest reaction to a very specific situation, namely the Church's casual modes of disposing of the bodies entrusted to its care in the second half of the eighteenth century. Before that date, such visits were completely unknown. It is also instructive to note that the modern cult of tombs did not grow up in the wake of any burgeoning religiosity among the population as a whole. Rather it was a lay cult, kindled and supported largely by atheists, which the clergy did little if anything to encourage.

The Classical Athenian cult of the tomb, on the other hand, would appear to proceed from the assumption that the attention paid to the *stêlê* by the living did materially and substantially affect the state of being of the dead in the next world. Iphigeneia, as she calls upon Orestes believed to be dead, describes the drink-offering as 'something soothing for the dead (*nekrois thelktêria*)' (Eur. *IT* 166), and similar phrases are used elsewhere. The care lavished on the tomb had to be a gift of love in order to be received by the dead in proper spirit. Hence, Klytaimnestra's guilty offering could only anger the dead still further (S. *El.* 442ff.). Doubtless a merely token observance was regarded as less efficacious than one which was heartfelt. For maximum effect, it should be performed by the nearest relative. The elaborate preparations for the visit, the complexity of the actual practices, and the fear of the childless man at having no one to tend his remains – all the evidence points to the conclusion that here was no token pilgrimage and that it mattered in a very real sense if the cult were neglected. Obviously we cannot exclude the possibility that sentimental motives played some part in promoting the popularity of the practice as well. Affection for the memory of the deceased is an evocative stimulant, whether or not it be reinforced by a belief in the afterlife. But the more complicated the ritual the less satisfactorily it can be explained in non-religious terms.

A further point to be noted is that although belief in the existence of Hades was certainly widespread among the Athenians of the period, it did not exclude the alternative belief in the dead having access to the tomb. The simultaneous existence of these divergent sets of ideas is of course by no means an abnormal phenomenon and certainly need not be taken as a symptom or indication of cultural hybridisation; that is to say, as providing evidence of a religious cleavage based on an original ethnic divide. Binford (1972, 237) has demonstrated that as societies develop, they inevitably foster new sets of beliefs and practices, which multiply in direct proportion to the complexity of the social system. In regard to Greek beliefs in the afterlife, it is generally accepted that an existence confined to the grave represents the earliest stage of eschatological speculation, and that Hades and other ideas were a later conception, which, although they overtook the former belief, never supplanted it entirely.

In the eyes of an Athenian, a *stêlê* was much more than a monument erected to preserve the memory of the dead. Oiled, perfumed, decorated, crowned and fed, it was a focus of devotion and an object of adoration. Whether it was conceived of as the actual embodiment of the dead or merely as a symbol of his physical presence is perhaps a question we should not seek to answer. That it was a place to which the dead would come not only for material but also for intellectual nourishment is indicated by representations of lyres on *lêkythoi,* sometimes placed at the grave and sometimes actually in use in its vicinity. The sensitivity of the Greek dead, commonly envisaged as retaining their faculties at least in the vicinity of the grave, is a characteristic feature of Greek eschatology.

The dead are reachable by the living and their destinies affected by the quality of tendance received at the hands of close relatives. This seems to be the basis of the Classical tomb-cult. Yet the '*do ut des*' basis of Greek religion ensured that it was a reciprocal arrangement. Expectation of good accruing to the living who discharged it punctiliously combined with fear of reprisals at the hands of the dead who were neglected made the cult an act of self-interest as well as piety. By uniting these two strands, by giving the living power over the condition of the dead and the dead a measure of control over the destinies of the living, Athenian eschatology re-inforced a view of the essential and enduring nature of family ties, of the reciprocity of obligation, and of our inalienable connections with those on the other side.

Conclusions

The elaborate and lengthy process by which the Greek dead loosened their connections with their kin and became integrated in the society of their own kind is perhaps an analogue for an innate Greek insistence on the preservation of a system of categorisation which, in this instance, was designed to keep the world of the living rigidly apart from that of the dead. Despite the duration and complexity of the rituals involved in disposing of the dead, at no point in the proceedings were the services of any professionals required – with the possible exception of *thrênôn sophistai* (dirge experts) and *nekrotaphoi* (undertakers) – nor were the offices of the priesthood thought to be efficacious. On the contrary, the whole business was organised and conducted on a strictly domestic and amateur basis. Prohibitions in the lawcodes on wailing, lacerating the flesh, and tearing the hair, all indicate that, if unchecked, the Greeks tended to express their grief both noisily and demonstrably. Though by the fifth century many, if not all, Greek cities had regulations covering the full range of funerary procedure from *prothesis* to post-burial commemorative rites, throughout the period under study death-rituals retained a prominent and indeed leading role in the social life of the community. In Athens, where we can evaluate its role best, the public nature of death found expression through tragedy, through public funerals of the war dead, through the siting of graves alongside the major thoroughfares outside the city, and through the celebration of communal festivals of the dead, such as the Choës festival and the Genesia.

Commemorative practices conducted on behalf of the Greek dead were not always wholly inspired by genuine *eusebeia*. Hence the need for extensive regulations to limit their conspicuousness, magnitude and duration, which, it might with justification be feared, were motivated partly at least with an eye to local or kin-solidarity at the expense of a broader-based attachment to the entire polis community. In 479, following the defeat of the Persian invasion of

Greece, Themistokles persuaded the state to erect a defensive wall around the city. The re-use of Archaic grave monuments for this project, as I suggested earler (p.4), would seem to indicate that such objects were not regarded as sacred. I would further suggest that their destruction may not have been innocent of political implications. By the 470s Athens was firmly set upon the road to full democracy. The decision in 484 to devote some of the wealth accruing to the state from the silver mines at Laurion in southeast Attika to building a fleet – a decision also taken at the instigation of Themistokles – had already brought to political prominence the lowest economic status group, the *thêtes*, since it was they who constituted the rowers. It is not improbable, therefore, that the destruction of such provocative and expressive symbols of aristocratic privilege and grandeur was a politically charged act of official vandalism.

The corpse itself inspired little horror. There are few references in Greek literature to the maggots and worms with which certain Christian theologians are so engrossed. The strictly biological aspect of death seems in fact to occupy a very minor role in the culture's consciousness. No Greek artist to my knowledge ever tried to depict a skeleton, far less a ghoulish cadaver. Further on the subject of artistic representation, it is unclear why the underworld was such an unpopular theme in the case of vases specifically destined for the grave. Perhaps religious scruples or artistic preferences militated against it. But the possibility cannot be ruled out that the layout of the infernal regions held little interest for the Greek imagination. Literary references to Hades show little regard for consistency, as is demonstrated by the fact that the discrepancies between the two Homeric *Nekyiai*, whatever their individual dates of composition, could be tolerated in the same poem.

There is no evidence that the prospect of dying filled the Greeks with much apprehension, though it may be that the rise of the mystery religions marked an increasing preoccupation with the kind of existence they hoped or feared to find on the other side of the grave. If Hades' very dreariness was the reverse image of a Greek joie de vivre, there was some compensation to be derived from the fact that the place was largely devoid of terrors.

Though in the Classical period there seems to have existed a particularly close intimacy between the living and the dead, whose comfort and well-being it was the duty of every decent and respectable Athenian citizen to look after, it is difficult to escape from the impression that the ordinary Greek dead were more to be pitied than to be feared. Sterile, deadlocked in time, conscious of loss, out of touch with the world above, lacking the sinews and strength of the living, yet preserving everlastingly their wounds, their rancour, their hatred – these are the 'ghosts of worn out mortals' (*brotôn eidôla kamontôn*) as Homer represents them. To what extent succeeding centuries modified this picture can only be guessed at, though Homer's authority was such that it is unlikely to have been completely supplanted. There is, moreover, something rather touching, even pathetic, in the bid made by the Greek dead from their graves to attract the attention of passers-by. Certainly the relationship between the various outlets available to the Greeks for the expression of grief – namely the funeral, the gifts placed in the grave, the grave-monuments and the services performed at the tomb – radically altered over the centuries: what we are not permitted to infer is that there was an overall increase in scepticism concerning the existence of the dead in the afterlife.

Infinitely was life preferred over death. Yet not life at any price. There was a right time and a right place to die: in the Homeric epic and in the Archaic period death on the battlefield was more honourable than inglorious old age. Rarely, too, might the claims of the ideal override those of life, as they do in the case of Ajax, Antigone and Sokrates. Other circumstances might also make death preferable. Foreshadowing the modern debate on the use of the respirator, Euripides wrote (*Supp.* 1109ff.):

> I can't stand people who drag out their life
> with food and drink and magic spells,
> trying to keep death out of the way.
> Since they're no use to the world, they should clear off
> and leave it to the young.

There could be no more modern utterance.

A Chronology of Greek Burial

A list of the principal innovations and developments in Greek burial practice from 2000 B.C. to 400 A.D. together with major examples of funerary art.

c. 2000 B.C.	Earliest burial in the Athenian agora.
c. 1650	Grave Circle B at Mycenae erected.
c. 1600	Grave Circle A at Mycenae erected.
c. 1520-1300	Period of the Tholos tombs.
c. 1400-1340	Chamber tomb burials replaced by cist burials in the Athenian agora.
c. 1350-1200	Inhumation remains standard but cremation becomes increasingly popular throughout Greece.
c. 1330	'Treasury of Atreus' erected.
c. 1200-1150	Cremation (mainly secondary) becomes the exclusive method of disposing of adult bodies.
c. 1100	Earliest burials made on the banks of the Eridanos Brook on the west side of Athens.
c. 900	Cremation ceases to be preferred in Attika and is replaced by simple pit inhumation.
c. 775-725	Period of the so-called Dipylon *amphorai*.
c. 725	Geometric burial enclosure erected in the Athenian agora (Young 1951).
c. 700	Primary cremation begins to predominate in Attika.
	Black-figure funerary plaque series begins (Boardman 1955).
c. 700-650	Conical or rectangular mounds of earth, gradually increasing in size, surmounted by vases, become commonest form of grave-markers.
c. 660-640	Earth brought in from outside the Kerameikos to make mounds larger.
c. 640	Overcrowding in the Kerameikos leads to reduction in the size of earth mounds.

c. 610-600	'Built tombs' of mudbrick decorated with plaque series begin to replace earth mounds.
c. 600	Decline in sumptuousness of grave-gifts begins. *Stêlai* begin to replace ceramic grave-markers. First appearance of the *lêkythos* as a grave gift.
594	Solon's funerary legislation introduced.
c. 580	New series of mounds begins in the Kerameikos.
c. 570	Series of Attic funerary *stêlai* bearing a representation of the dead person in relief begins.
c. 560	First shaft-grave dug in the Kerameikos.
c. 550	Mound G (tomb of Solon?) erected in the Kerameikos (Kübler, *KER* VII.I).
c. 540	Sudhügel (tomb of Alkmaionidai?) erected in the Kerameikos (Knigge, *KER* IX).
c. 530	Single black-figure funerary plaques replace plaque series (Boardman 1955). Sphinx finial replaced by palmette finial.
c. 510	Series of Archaic Attic *stêlai* declines. *Stêlê* of Aristion by Aristokles.
c. 510-480	'*Post aliquanto*' legislation alluded to by Cicero passed in Athens.
c. 500-430	Only isolated, mainly publicly erected *stêlai* survive in Attika from this period. The *stêlê* of the ambassador (*proxenos*) Pythagoras of Selymbria (dated just before mid-fifth cent.) is almost the only surviving monument in the Kerameikos.
c. 500	Latest burials in the Athenian agora. Probable date of ban on intramural burial at Athens (Young 1951). Cremation now becomes less frequent.
c. 480	Earliest example of *dexiôsis* motif on funerary *stêlê* (Johansen 1951, 139f. and fig. 70).
480/79	Themistoklean Wall incorporates many Archaic grave-*stêlai* from the Kerameikos.
c. 470	Earliest *lêkythos* with funerary iconography.
c. 470-410	*Lêkythos* becomes the favourite Athenian offering to the dead.
465/4	Earliest surviving 'Casualty List' records the names of the Athenians and their allies who died at Drabeskos, Thasos and the Chersonese (*IG* I² 928;

	Bradeen 1967).
465	Annual ceremony for the war dead first instituted at Athens according to Jacoby (1944b).
c. 460-430	Career of the Achilles Painter.
458	Earliest reference to a belief in a family reunion beyond the grave (Aes. *Ag.* 1555).
c. 450	So-called *Nekyia* vase painted.
c. 450-400	Kean funerary legislation introduced.
439	First known funeral speech (*epitaphios logos*) delivered at Athens by Perikles on behalf of those who died fighting the Samians (Plu. *Per.* 28.4).
c. 430-317	Classical series of Attic *stêlai*.
431	Perikles' funeral speech delivered on behalf of the Athenian dead in the first year of the Peloponnesian War (Thuk. 2.34ff.).
403	Tomb of the Spartans erected on the *Dêmosion Sêma*.
c. 400	Labyad phratry funerary legislation passed at Delphi.
	Nereid monument erected at Xanthos in Lykia.
	Earliest example of Totenmahl (death-feast) relief (Thönges-Stringaris 1965, no. 65).
	Polygnotos painted his *Nekyia* in the *Leschê* (Painted Hall) of the Knidians at Delphi.
	Rosette *stêlai* introduced.
394/3	Family plot of Dexileos erected in the Kerameikos.
	Over the next seventy-five years, large sections of the Kerameikos were divided up into family plots.
c. 350	Mausoleum of Mausolos, satrap of Karia, erected at Halikarnassos.
338	Re-use of grave-*stêlai* for walls after the Battle of Chaironeia.
c. 317-315	Funerary legislation of Demetrios of Phaleron introduced at Athens.
c. 317	System of dividing up the Kerameikos into family plots (*periboloi*) abandoned.
c. 300-280	End of series of Totenmahl reliefs.
200	Destruction of grave-*stêlai* in the Kerameikos during the invasion of Philip V of Macedon.
86	Further destruction during the invasion of Sulla.
45	Cicero reported that the ancient religious ban

(*religio*) against intramural burial still operated at Athens.

c. 400 A.D.   With the abolition of pagan rites, the Kerameikos ceased to be used as a cemetery.

Glossary

BELIEFS REGARDING THE DEAD

aithêr the upper region of air, the habitation of the gods, and, from the
fifth century onwards, of certain dead

daimôn any supernatural being; occasionally, a guardian spirit who
guides the deceased to the next world

dexiôsis a modern description of the handshake motif in Greek art
possibly intended to symbolise the theme of reunion in Hades

eidôlon an image of the dead person appearing either on earth, in
dreams or in Hades

ekei the world of the dead (literally 'there')

enthade the world of the living (literally 'here')

geras thanontôn the prerogative or due of the dead

katabasis the descent to the underworld by a living or divine being; a
description of such a descent

kêr the fate of death; one's personal doom

Nekyia the rite by which ghosts are summoned to appear; any
pictorial or literary description of the underworld

psychê the 'soul' of the dead as existing in Hades, lacking any
apparent function in a living organism

psychopompos a title applied to Hermes as conductor of *psychai*

psychorrhagêma the struggle of the *psychê* to free itself from the body

psychostasia the weighing of souls in a pair of scales

skia an image of the dead person (literally 'a shadow')

CATEGORIES OF THE DEAD

ataphos one who is left unburied

aôros one who dies young

autocheir a suicide

biaiothanatos a suicide or murderer (literally 'one who causes death
violently')

Dêmêtrioi a word used originally of the general dead, it perhaps came to be reserved exclusively for those who had been initiated into the mysteries of Demeter at Eleusis

deuteropotmos (also *hysteropotmos*) one who revived after being declared dead (literally 'a person with two fates' or 'second-fated')

dioblêtos one who was struck by lightning and whose corpse was believed to be sacred (literally 'smitten by Zeus')

makarios (also *makaritês*) a word used of the dead with particular reference to the heroized or recent dead (literally 'blessed')

Tritopatores spirits of the long departed (literally 'fathers to the third degree')

THE CULT OF THE TOMB

choai drink offerings to the dead

enagismata food offerings to the dead, or more generally all nourishment provided for the dead

haimakouriai blood-sacrifices performed for the dead

holokautômata whole burnt offerings

kallysmata sweepings from the deceased's house which were placed on the grave

kaneon (also *kanoun, kaniskion*) a round wicker basket used for transporting gifts for the dead

melikraton a mixed drink presented to the dead whose essential ingredient was honey

melitoutta a honey cake specially made for the dead

taenia a ribbon used to decorate the shaft of a *stêlê*

FESTIVALS AND RITES ON BEHALF OF THE DEAD

Anthesteria an annual festival held in the month of Anthesterion (February to March). On the third day, called *Chytroi* (Pots), the dead were thought to leave the cemetery and visit their old homes. Pots containing cooked fruit were placed on their graves

aponimma a ceremony involving water which was performed by digging a trench at the grave probably after the funeral

enata (also *ennata*) rites performed on the ninth day after either death or burial

eniausia rites performed annually

Genesia an annual festival in honour of the dead. Its etymology and significance are disputed

kathedra a banquet marking the conclusion of mourning at which relatives sat rather than reclined (literally 'a seating')

Nemeseia a festival in honour of the dead. Its connection with Nemesis (Vengeance) is unclear

nomizomena (also *nomina* and *hiera patrôa*) a general word for customary rites performed on behalf of the dead

perideipnon a banquet held in honour of the deceased after the funeral at which the deceased was believed to be present in the capacity of host

triakostia (also *triakas* and *triakades*) rites performed on the thirtieth day after either death or burial; rites performed monthly

trita rites performed on the third day after either death or burial

FUNERAL RITES

ardanion a bowl of water placed outside the house of the deceased

chous a small jug placed in the grave of a very young infant

danakê (also *naulon*) the boat-fare for Charon as ferryman of the dead

ekphora the transport of the body to the cemetery for burial

enchytristria a word of uncertain meaning describing a woman who officiated in some capacity using a pot or *chytra* at the funeral

endyma a shroud

epiblêma a loose covering placed over the shroud

epikêdeion a dirge or lament

epitaphios logos a speech delivered in honour of the war dead

exêgêtai interpreters or expounders of sacred law who gave advice regarding the pollution caused by the dead in cases of difficulty such as manslaughter or suicide

goös an improvised lament sung by relatives of the deceased

ialemos a dirge or lament

katadesmos a lead curse-tablet placed in the grave in order to bind the living by a spell (literally 'that which binds down')

kêdeia the funeral

klimakophoros, nekrophoros, nekrothaptês, tapheus corpse-bearer

klinê generally any couch but used particularly of the couch on which the corpse was laid out during the *prothesis*

kommos a formal lament in tragedy

kosmos generally any attire or specifically the attire in which the corpse was laid out during the *prothesis*

kterismata funeral gifts

loutra sacred water used for religious rituals, including the ceremonial bathing of a bride before a wedding and the washing of the corpse before the *prothesis*

loutrophoros a very tall vase with thin body, elongated neck and wide rim, used for carrying the *loutra*; a stone grave-marker in the shape of such a vase placed over the graves of the unmarried dead

maschalismos the mutilation of the corpse of a murdered victim by the murderer in order to render the spirit of the deceased harmless

othônê a chin-strap to prevent the jaws of the dead from sagging open

prosphagion (also *prosphagma*) possibly the name of the sacrifice performed on behalf of the dead before the *ekphora* set out, but also used of sacrifices at the grave

prothesis the ceremonial laying out of the body on a *klinê* in funeral attire

strôma a covering laid over the *klinê*

thrênôn exarchoi professional mourners (literally 'leaders of the dirge')

thrênos a formal lament usually sung by professional mourners

TOMBS AND CEMETERIES

barathron the pit in Athens into which the bodies of condemned criminals were cast

Dêmosion Sêma 'People's Grave', a ceremonial highway leading from the Dipylon Gate on the west side of Athens in the direction of the Academy beside which the Athenian war dead and other important individuals were buried

êrion a funeral mound or barrow; a family plot

hêrôon a shrine erected over the presumed burial-spot of a hero

kenotaphion (or *kenon mnêma*) a cenotaph

Kerameikos 'The Potters' Quarter', a district on the west side of Athens outside the city wall which constituted the city's chief cemetery

mnêma a general word for a grave (literally 'memorial')

peribolos a family plot

polyandreion a communal grave

sêma a general word for a grave (literally 'sign', hence the sign by which a grave is identified)

stêlê a rectangular wooden or stone grave-marker

tymbos a funeral mound or barrow

VASES USED IN THE CULT OF THE TOMB

alabastron a globular vase without handles used for perfume and often made of alabaster

amphora a two-handled vessel for transporting and storing liquids, especially wine or oil

aryballos a small globular vessel with one handle used for oil, scent, etc.

hydria a three-handled vessel with oval body and flat shoulder used for carrying water

kratêr a large two-handled bowl used for mixing wine and water

kylix a shallow two-handled cup used for drinking wine

lêkythos a small vase or flask with narrow neck containing oil. When presented as a gift to the dead, it was often provided with a false bottom so as to enable it to be filled with a minimal quantity of oil

oinochoê a jug used for pouring wine into wine-cups

phialê a shallow bowl without a foot or handles used for wine mainly in religious ceremonies

plêmochoê possibly the name given to a vase with high foot and swelling body known to have been used at the Eleusinian Mysteries

sakkos a sieve or strainer for wine

Notes

1. THE POWER AND STATUS OF THE DEAD

1 **Character of the Homeric dead.** Lack of *menos: Od.* 10.521 and 536; 11.29, 49 and 393. Cf. 11.207 and 19.562. Impotence of their rage: *Il.* 16.491 (Sarpedon); *Od.* 11.553ff. (Ajax); *Od.* 10.552ff. and 11.72ff. (Elpenor). Lack of *phrenes: Il.* 23.104; cf. *Od.* 10.493 (Teiresias). 'Heedless': *Od.* 11.476. Failure to recognise relatives: *Od.* 11.36ff., 141ff. and 390ff. I would not, however, go so far as to say with Jaeger (1936, 74): 'The shades of the dead which have entered Hades enjoy no conscious existence there'. They may be unaware of what is happening up on earth, but they are fully capable of conversing intelligibly among themselves. See below.

2 **Necromancy.** *Eidôlon* of Dareios: Aes. *Pers.* 744ff., 779ff., 826, 832ff. and 840ff. Aristophanic parody: Peisander was instrumental in the overthrow of the democracy and the establishment of the Four Hundred (Thuk. 8.53). His name seems to have been proverbial for cowardice (Xen. *Symp.* 2.14). It is presumably in order to recover his 'spirit', therefore, which has forsaken him, that he comes to Sokrates. Chairephon, banished by the Thirty Tyrants in 404, was noted for his pale countenance (Ar. *Wasps* 1413; cf. Pl. *Apol.* 21). Oracle of the dead in Thesprotia: for the locality see Thuk. 1.46.3-4 and Paus. 1.17.5. For the excavation see Dakaris 1973, 139ff. See also the invocation of the dead Melissa by her husband Periander as told in Hdt. 5.92 (referred to below p. 150). Necromancy is satirised in Luc. *Men.* The dead register their displeasure: Aes. *Ch.* 32ff.; Eur. *Hek.* 36ff. Message conveyed to the dead: Eur. *Hek.* 422; *IG* II² 12067 = Clairmont 1970, no. 39. Powerlessness of the dead: Eur. *Helen* 963ff.; *Supp.* 543ff.; Fr. 450 *TGF*.

4 **Tritopatores (or Tritopatres).** See Phanod. Fr. 4 *FHG* I, p. 367; Kleitodem. Fr. 19 *FHG* I, p. 363; Demon. Fr. 2 *FHG* I, p. 378; Kern 1922, Fr. 318; Phot. and Sud. s.v. The trapezoidal temenos of the *Tritopatores* or *Tritopatreion* stands in the angle formed by the junction of the Sacred Way and the so-called Street of Tombs in the

Kerameikos Cemetery, directly opposite the *peribolos* of Dexileos and the tombs of the *proxenoi*. On the evidence of letter-forms on the three *horos* markers found *in situ* (*IG* I² 870), the structure is dated to the second half of the fifth century B.C. There are no traces of an altar and only the western half of the sanctuary is preserved. See Travlos 1971, figs. 391 and 394-5. *Tritopatores* as fertility spirits: Hippok. *Insomn.* 92.

Sensitivity of the dead in the vicinity of the grave. Tomb affording protection: Eur. *Helen* 315, 324, 528, etc.; Aes. *Ch.* 540. The dead capable of detecting a hostile presence: S. *Ajax* 1393ff.; Eur. *Herakl.* 1040. Necessary to pass their graves in silence: Rohde 1897, ch. 5 n. 110; *Epigr. gr.* 119; Sch. on Ar. *Birds* 1490; Hsch. and Phot. s.v. *hêrôs*. '*Sigêlos*': Str. 9.2.10; cf. S. *OC* 130ff.; Farnell 1921, 352. For re-use of gravestones in times of national emergency, see Lykourg. *Against Leokrates* 44; Aischin. *Against Ktesiphon* 236; Garland 1982b, 127.

6   **'Nerterois meiligmata.'** See Aes. *Ch.* 15; cf. Eur. *Hek.* 535. For *choai*, see below ch. 7.

    Anthesteria. See below p. 44.

    Katadesmoi. See *Tab. Defix. passim* for *katadesmoi* from all over the Greek world. Bound lead figures inside lead coffins: *KB* pl. 45.

7   **Legal protection of the dead.** See Is. 2.47; cf. 9.37; Ps.-Dem. 43.81. Offence to speak ill of the dead: Plu. *Solon* 21. Offence to tell lies about the dead: Is. 9.6, 23 and 26; cf. Thphr. 28. Prosecution on behalf of the dead: Rohde 1897, ch. 5 n. 115; Meier and Schömann 1887, 630. Denial of right of burial regarded as an act of *hybris*: Eur. *Ph.* 1663 and S. *Ajax* 1385; cf. Eur. *HF* 708. *Kakôsis goneôn*: Dem. 24.107; cf. Xen. *Mem.* 2.2.13. Legal vengeance for the dead: Lys. 12.100 and 13.91-97.

8   **The dead must be honoured.** See Eur. *Alk.* 1060; S. *Ant.* 511 and 745. Cf. also S. *El.* 968; Eur. *Helen* 1277. Protected by the gods: S. *Ajax* 1129, 1154 and 1343f.; cf. S. *Ant.* 1070; Eur. *Hek.* 136ff. The imprecations directed against tomb-violators found especially in Phrygia, Lykia and Caria, frequently invoke the power of such deities as Zeus, Persephone, etc., in their defence (see *TGLE* 109).

    The dead as makarioi. See Ar. Fr. 488.10f. *CAF;* Hes. *Erg.* 141; Aes. *Pers.* 633; Eur. *Alk.* 1003 (with *daimôn*); Pl. *Laws* 947e and *Phd.* 115d; Xen. *Ages.* 11.8. For discussion, see Rohde 1897, ch. 7 n. 10 and Vermeule 1979, 73. Vermeule thinks that *makar* and *makarios* may be borrowed from the Egyptian *ma'khrow* or 'justified', a title applied to the Egyptian dead whose confession of innocence had been accepted by the gods of the underworld and who were therefore permitted to enter the *Sekhet Aaru* or 'Field of Reeds'. As Vermeule herself points out, however, there are etymological difficulties. Thukydides (2.51.6) uses *makarizô*, 'to pronounce blessed', of Athenians who recovered from the plague, perhaps, as Vermeule suggests, because they were deemed to have risen from the dead and considered 'practically immortal'. '*Makaria*', 'blessedness', is used ironically as an equivalent to *es korakas* ('go to the devil'), e.g. Ar. *Knights* 1151; Pl.*Hp. Ma.* 293a. In modern Greek the funeral feast served after the burial service at the house of the deceased consisting of boiled wheat, a glass of wine and a slice of bread is known as *makario* (that which is blessed), and *makaritis* (he who is blessed) is commonly used as a euphemism for the dead (Danforth 1982, 43f., 47 and 106).

10 **The dead as chrêstoi.** On Attic grave-reliefs: Clairmont 1970, nos. 25, 44 and 49; cf. Arist. Fr. 592*T*. The expression *chrêste chaire*, sometimes coupled with the title *hêrôs*, is found from the fourth century onwards especially on epitaphs from Boeotia, Thessaly, Asia Minor and Cyprus, later spreading to all areas of the Greek world (Rohde 1897, ch. 14.2 n. 30). In Athens, as in Rhodes, it is only very rarely used of citizens (see Fraser 1977, 71).

The dead as heroes. See Fr. 75 *CAF*. For discussion, see Lattimore (*TGLE* 97ff.). Lattimore notes that of the instances found in Athens of *hêrôs* being used of the dead, only one, it seems, describes an Athenian citizen (IG II² 6797).

Representations of the dead on grave reliefs. See especially Johansen 1951, figs. 35-8 and 70. *Lêkythos* of Myrrhine: Johansen, pl. 82 (Nat. Mus. cat. no. 4485). The conventions of Greek art make the identification of so-called 'worshippers' problematical. The Attic *stêlê* of Xanthippos dated *c.* 430 shows a bearded figure seated on a *klismos* holding a model of a foot. On a much-reduced scale two small figures stand beside him (*BM* cat. no. 628; Cook 1976, pl. 84). Cook is probably correct in interpreting these latter as children 'represented as miniature adults rather than with correct childish proportions' (107).

12 **Saluting the dead.** For discussion, see Pottier 1883, 58, and Johansen 1951, 161f. For refs. and illustrations, see Aes. *Ch.* 9; Eur. *Alk.* 768 and *Supp.* 772; Arias et al., 1962, pl. 126 (*loutrophoros*); *AWL* pls. 19.2, 29.3 and 34.3 (*lêkythoi*). For possible *proskynêsis*, see *AWL* 210 and pl. 31.1.

The winged dead on Attic lêkythoi. See Vermeule 1979, ch. 1 figs. 4, 5, 19 and 23. For a scene of *psychostasia* (soul-weighing) involving diminutive winged dead, see ib. ch. 5 fig. 14. Winged dead also appear on vases of other shapes but with far less frequency.

2. DYING

17 **Death certificates from Roman Egypt.** Cf. *P. Oxy.* 475, 1030, 1198, etc.

18 **Biological theories of death.** The heroes whose deaths are described by the departure of the *psychê* are Hyperenor (14.518f.), Sarpedon (16.505), Patroklos (16. 856) and Hektor (22.362). For the Homeric terminology for death, see Garland 1981, 43ff. According to Sokrates, death is separation (*apallagê*) of the *psychê* from the body (Pl. *Phd.* 64c). For Aristotle's theory of death, see Lanza 1980, 164ff., with *Resp.* 478b.

19 **Onset of death.** Death with heavy hands: Hom. *Il.* 21.548. *Thymos*-shattering death poured around a man: *Il.* 13.544, 16.414 and 580. For other metaphors for death in the *Iliad*, see Garland 1981, 46 with Tables 4 and 5. See also Vermeule 1979, 39. For Apollo's gentle arrows, see *Il.* 24.758f. For Thanatos (Death) as a personalised being, see below p. 56ff.

Psychorrhagêma. Cf. Eur. *Alk.* 20 and 143; Pl. *Phd.* 118a and Olympiod. ad loc., p. 142. For a tracing of the development of this theme from paganism to Christianity, see Alexiou 1974, 25.

Man's inability to foresee his own death. Cf. Aes. *PV* 248ff.; Pl. *Gorg.* 523d. See also Adkins 1960, 119.

References to the doom of death in epigrams. Cf. Peek 1960, nos. 37 (Eretria, 6th cent.); 44 (Thasos, 500 B.C.); 55 (Pontos, fifth cent.); 83.3 (Kerameikos, *c.* 350), etc.

20 **Prophetic power of the dying.** Cf. Hom. *Il.* 16.851ff. (Patroklos); 22.358ff. (Hektor). Sokrates prophesies to his jury after he has been condemned to death, declaring that he is 'now at the time when men most prophesy, when they are about to die' (Pl. *Apol.* 39c).

Last words of the dying. For sentimental Hellenistic epigrams (as noted by Macleod 1982), see *AP* 7.513 and 646-8. See also Eur. *Alk.* 299-325. That the words of the dying are memorable was also the belief of the Romans, cf. Tac. *Agr.* 45.5. The last words of Sokrates are perhaps intended to signify the philosopher's belief that death was a cure for life, since Asklepios was the god of healing (Pl. *Phd.* 118a).

3. THE FUNERAL

21 **Terminology for funeral.** For *kêdeia* as 'funeral', see Ap. Rh. 2.836 and Dion. H. 3.21.8. Cf. also Hom. *Il.* 23.160. The word can also mean 'mourning', 'alliance' or 'connection by marriage' (*LSJ⁹*). Its root *kêdos*, 'concern', gives also *kêdeuô*, which can be used either generally to mean 'to take charge of', 'tend', 'attend to', or in the specialist sense to mean (1) 'to attend to a corpse' (e.g. S. *El.* 1141; Eur. *Rh.* 983; *Epigr. gr.* 604), or (2) 'to ally oneself in marriage' (e.g. Aes. *PV* 890; S. *Trach.* 1227). *Kêdemôn* in Homer means 'one who has charge of the dead and his rites' (*LSJ⁹*), but later writers use it in the wider sense of 'one who cares for others' (cf. Thgn. 645 and X. *Mem.* 2.7.12). Closely linked is *kêdestês*, which Hsch. (s.v.) explains as 'a relative by marriage'. Willetts (1967, 19) interestingly notes that the first reference in Greek literature to *kêdestês* is of a bridegroom's father who has to light the funeral pyre of a dead bride (*AP* 7.712, Erinna). For further connections between burial and marriage-ties, see below p. 72ff. The association between marriage-relationship and singing the dirge is especially interesting, as Alexiou (1974, 10f.) notes, and persists (or has been revived) in modern Greece. Danforth (1982, 74) states that songs sung at weddings (*niphika tragoudia*) and funeral laments are so close in regard to 'their musical form, their narrative structure, and their iconography' that 'many songs can be sung at both death rites and weddings'.

Homeric funerals. See *Il.* 23.108ff. (Patroklos), 24.719ff. (Hektor) and *Od.* 24.43ff. (Achilles). For the details of the Homeric funeral, see Garland 1982a.

Funerary legislation. Athens: Ps.-Dem. 43.62 and Plu. *Solon* 21 (Solon); Cic. *Laws* 2.64 ('some time after Solon'); ibid. 2.66 (Demetrios of Phaleron); Ps.-Dem. 43.57-8; Pl. *Laws* 12.958d-960c. Labyad phratry at Delphi (*c.* 400 B.C.): *LSG* 77; Hainsworth 1972, no. 3; Buck 1955, no. 52; *DHR* II 28; *SIG³* 1220; Homolle 1895. Gambreion in Mysia (third cent.): *LSA* 16; *DHR* I 3; *SIG³* 1219. Gortyn (600-525 B.C.): *Inscr. Cr.* 4.22; Jeffery 1961, 315 no. 2. Ioulis on Keos (second half of fifth cent.): *LSG* 97; *LGS* II 93; *SIG³* 1218. Katana (sixth cent.): Stob. *Florileg.* 44.40. Mytilene: Cic. *Laws* 2.66 (Pittakos). Sparta: Hdt. 6.58.1; Xen. *Lak.* 15.9; Plu. *Lyk.* 27 and *Mor.* 238d (Lykourgos). Syracuse: D.S. 11.38. I am indebted to Oswyn Murray for the observation on phratries.

22   **Funerary expenses.** Lys. 31.21 mentions the sum of 3 *minai* 'for
the burial' and Dem. 40.52 the sum of 10. Cf. also the Kean code's
generous allowance of 300 dr. on funeral expenses (*LSG* 97A.5) with
the Labyad phratry's paltry 35 dr. (*LSG* 77C.3).

23   **Closing the eyes and mouth.** Cf. Hom. *Il.* 11.452f., *Od.* 11.425f.
and 24.296; Eur. *Hek.* 430 and *Ph.* 1451. Inscription at Smyrna:
Epigr. gr. 314.24. It was believed that the *psychê* could take one of
three exit routes from the body, viz. mouth, nostrils or eyes. See
Pease's (1935) extensive note on Virg. *Aen.* 4.684 ('*Extremus si quis
super halitus errat/ ore legam*') supplemented by Headlam and Knox
(1922) and Cunningham (1971) on Herod. 3.4. Cf. also Cicero's
pathetic description in *Verr.* 5.118: '*matresque miserae pernoctabant ad
ostium carceris ... quae nihil aliud orabant nisi ut filiorum suorum postremum
spiritum ore excipere liceret*'. The custom was dismissed by Servius (on
Aen. 4.684) as '*muliebriter*', but has none the less given birth to a long
and distinguished literary progeny, cf. Pope, *Eloisa to Abelard* 324:
'Suck my breath and catch my dying soul.'

       Charon's fee. See Hsch. s.v. *Naulon* and *danakê*, and *KB* 166 and
211. For bracteates, see Boulter 1963, 126 with refs. to parallel
examples. For abbreviated coin-types, see *KB* pl. 40 and Boulter
1963, pl. 45 (mid-second cent. B.C.).

       Lip-bands and chin-straps. See the interesting photograph in von
Salis (1957, Abb. 1) of an indentation made on the crown of the skull
of a woman aged between 35 and 40 apparently by a chin-strap. For
Geometric chin-straps, see Andronikos (1968, 41f., and Abb. 1).
Black-figure funerary plaque by the Sappho Painter: Boardman
(1955, no. 28) and *KB* (pl. 33). *Nekyia* vase: Vermeule (1974, ch. 1
fig. 8b). There is an extensive bibliography on chin-straps and
mouth-pieces in *KB* (p. 364).

24   **Washing the body.** Cf. S. *Ajax* 1404; Eur. *Ph.* 1667; Pl. *Phd.* 115a.
Persons about to die wash themselves: Pl. *Phd.* 116a; S. *OC* 1598ff.;
Eur. *Alk.* 158ff. Bridal-bath: S. *Ant.* 1201. Sea-water preferred: Eur.
Hek. 610 and 780; cf. *IT* 1193. Wounds of the dead washed: Eur. *El.*
1227f.; *Ph.* 1669; *Tro.* 1152.

       Feet facing the door. Cf. Hom. *Il.* 19.212 and Boardman (1955,
55f.). Van Gennep (1909, 151) records that in the case of the funeral
ceremonies of the Kol of India, 'the corpse is placed on a scaffold with
the feet facing forward so that the soul should not find the way back
to the hut, and for the same reason the procession travels by detours'.
See also Rohde (1897, ch. 1 n. 26). The custom is alluded to in the
English expression 'to carry X out feet first'. For general discussion

of the significance and usefulness of orientation as a criterion for determining a people's beliefs about the journey of the spirit to the land of the dead, see Ucko (1969, 272) who comments: 'There is no doubt that there are many examples ... where this is the aim of orientation, but this is by no means invariably true.'

Bier, bier-cloth, pillows, etc. Bier: Ahlberg 1971, 47, figs. 24, 25, 29, etc.; Fairbanks 1914, II 224; Boardman 1955, pls. 4 and 8; Zschietzschmann 1928, Beil. 13, 15, 17 and 18. Pillows: Ahlberg 1971, 48f., figs. 25f. and 27a; Boardman 1955, pls. 4 and 8; Zschietzschmann 1928, Beil. 17; *LSG* 77C 12f. Bier-cloth: Ahlberg 1971, figs. 2, 3, 4, 7, 8, etc.; *LSG* 77C 11; Zschietzschmann 1928, Beil. 18. Ribbons: *AWL* pl. 29.1; Boardman 1955, pl. 4.

Funeral garments. Cf. Ahlberg 1971, 40ff., figs. 31a, 36, 37, etc.; *LSG* 97A 3f. *Peristellô* in tragedy: Eur. *Tro.* 390 and 1143; *IT* 627; *Or.* 1066; S. *Ajax* 1170; *Ant.* 902. Cf. Hom. *Od.* 24.293. *Kosmos*: Eur. *HF* 548; *Helen* 1279; *Hek.* 578 and 615; *IT* 632; *Tro.* 1208; *Alk.* 613 and 618. *Peplos* as garment of the dead: Eur. *Hek.* 578 and 735; *HF* 329 and 702; *El.* 1227f.; *Tro.* 1143f. Colour of garments: *LSG* 97A 2; Artem. *Oneirokr.* 2.3; *LSG* 77C 6; Fairbanks 1914, II 164 (bis).

25 **Unmarried or recently married dead.** Cf. Eur. *Tro.* 1219ff.; Peek 1955, no. 1238.3. See Alexiou 1974, 5. Danforth (1982, 13) reports that in modern rural Greece it is customary to bury an unmarried girl 'wearing in death the white bridal dress and wedding crown she had been unable to wear in life'.

Burial in armour Bronze armour found in a grave at Argos dated *c.* 725: Snodgrass 1967, 41 and pl. 17 and *BCH* 1957, 340ff. Later examples: Snodgrass 1967, 48, 73 and 114.

Burial in jewellery. *KB* 61f., 101 and 207; Fairbanks 1914, II 165.

Legislation restricting clothing of the deceased. *LSG* 97A 5f.; 77C 11f.

26 **Placing a crown on the dead.** Cf. Eur. *Tro.* 1223 and 1247; Ar. *Lys.* 602; *Ekk.* 538; Plu. *Tim.* 26; Artem. *Oneirokr.* 1.77; Bion 1.75ff.; Zschietzschmann 1928, Beil. 17. Celery: Plu. *Tim.* 26. Gold crowns: *KB* pl. 39; Boulter 1963, 126.

Branches. Ahlberg (1971, 302) suggests that the origin of the action of holding branches over the corpse was possibly in order to keep insects away, but that in later times it became 'purely ritual'. This seems to me to be dubious. The action is also recorded on a *cippus* found at Chiusi (Paribeni 1938, no. 86, pl. 24.1: see below). Vine branches were placed under the corpse in some Athenian graves of eighth-century date (see Brückner and Pernice 1893, 165 and 184). Cf. also S. *Ant.* 1201ff. and Eur. *Hek.* 573ff. for refs. to burial in branches.

Birds. Pottier (1883, 22) suggests that under the *klinê* of a dead ephebe a *lêkythos* painter sometimes added the deceased's pet bird which would be carried as an offering to the tomb. Ahlberg (1971, 140) thinks that Geometric artists depict birds with inverted heads to show that they are lifeless, and therefore by implication connected with some funerary rite (see ibid., figs. 22 and 27). Cf. also the inverted bird suspended between two women on a *lêkythos* (*AWL* pl. 25.1) and the duck held by women seated at a tomb (Fairbanks 1914, II pl. 29.1). For columns of M's, see Ahlberg (1971, 146ff.). Small birds under the bier: ibid. figs. 22 and 27; *AWL* pl. 51.4.

Lêkythos in prothesis-chamber. Cf. Ar. *Ekk.* 538 and 996; *AWL* pl. 54.2.

Walls hung with sashes. Cf. Boardman 1955, pls. 4 and 5; *AWL* pl. 51.4.

Duration of prothesis. Ps.-Dem. 43.62. See also Rohde 1897, ch. 5 n. 50.

Gortyn law on prothesis. *Inscr. Cr.* 4.22. Cf. Is. 6.41.

27   **Location of prothesis.** Ps.-Dem. 43.62. Cf. Boardman 1955, nos. 4, 5, 12, 15 and 28, which show columns, a tree and birds flying overhead. Boardman also thinks that the fillets or wreaths hanging from the upper boarders of nos. 14, 17, 19, 23 and 25 'may be thought of as attached to lintels or eaves' (p. 56), but they could also be taken as decorations adorning the *prothesis*-chamber (see above). Ancient testimonies do not clarify the picture. They include Schol. on Ar. *Lys.* 611; Phot. s.v. *prothesis* and Hsch. s.v. *di'ek thyrôn*. Regarding the setting on Geometric vases, Ahlberg (1971, 299) writes: 'The *prothesis* with few exceptions took place inside the house or at a locality near the house, a court.'

28   **Scenes of prothesis on vases, etc.** Geometric: Ahlberg 1971, figs. 2, 3, 4, 7, 8 and 13, etc.; Andronikos 1968, pls. 1, 2 and 9; Zschietzschmann 1928, pl. 8. Black-figure funerary plaques and plaque series (total of 39 examples known, dated *c.* 600-480): Boardman 1955, pls. 1-8. Black-figure *loutrophoroi*: Zschietzschmann 1928, nos. 44-83, pls. 12-14. Red-figure *loutrophoroi*: ibid. nos. 95-117, pls. 16-18. *Lêkythoi*: Zschietzschmann lists 21 examples (nos. 118-137). For representations, see *AWL* pls. 29.1, 29.2, 51.4 and 54.2. A *lêkythos* depicting a shrouded figure within a 'mound-frame' by the Tymbos Painter (*ARV* p. 756 no. 66; *AWL* pl. 23.1) should also

perhaps be included in the list. *Cippi*: Paribeni (1938) lists 203 examples. Some features, as Boardman (loc. cit.) notes, such as the flautist and the action of embracing the dead (see below), may reflect purely local customs. The date of the disappearance of Attic scenes of *prothesis* corresponds approximately to the disappearance of *lêkythoi* from graves. Zschietzschmann (1928, 35) thinks that after this date it was no longer thought necessary to supply the dead with a representation of the rite being performed 'like a kind of perpetual lament', but we cannot know for certain that it does not simply reflect a change in taste.

Disputes regarding the right to hold the prothesis. Cf. Is. 6.40; 8.21f. and 38f.; Ps.-Dem. 44.32. See also Humphreys 1980, 98ff.

Actions in connection with the corpse. Feeding: Ahlberg 1971, 135 with fig. 22 (New York *kratêr* 14.130.15); *CVA* GB 14 *Ox.* 3 pl. 26 (*loutrophoros amphora*). Embracing: Boardman 1955, 56f., nos. 19 and 24. Standing on a foot-stool: Ahlberg (1971, 102f.) lists five examples on Geometric vases where 'a structure or stool is rendered to the right of the bier near the bier legs'. Boardman (1955, 57) notes that a woman identified as the grandmother of the deceased stands on a footstool behind the head of the corpse on plaque no. 28. For Homeric instances of embracing the corpse, see *Il.* 23.136, 24.712, and 724, with Macleod (1982) on l. 712.

29   **Sex of mourners.** The difficulty of establishing the sex of mourners on Geometric vases is discussed by Ahlberg (1971, 72ff.). Anatomical details are rarely included, and the presence of hair is no sure guide. The only criteria which Ahlberg recognises are: (1) the use of the two-handed mourning gesture (reserved for women); and (2) the carrying of weapons (reserved for men).

Children and slaves at prothesis. Children: examples include Ahlberg (1971, fig. 25) which shows a child standing on the bier at the foot end. Small figures also appear regularly on funerary plaques, cf. Boardman 1955, pls. 3, 4, 5, 7 and 8. See also *CVA* GB 14 Oxf. 3 pl. 26.4 (*loutrophoros amphora*) and pl. 7 (*loutrophoros* fragment). Slaves: Karouzou identifies an aged woman on a *loutrophoros* supporting the head of a dead girl in her hands as 'the Thracian nurse of the deceased' from the tattooing around her chin and her blond hair (*CVA* Gr. 2 Ath. 2 III Id pl. 22.3).

Grief displayed. Violent displays of grief on *lêkythoi* are not wholly absent, cf. *AWL* pl. 29.1 which shows a young girl tearing her hair. Tragedy also contains frequent references to beating the head, tearing the hair, and cutting the cheeks with the nails (e.g. Aes. *Ch.*

23ff.; Eur. *Helen* 374 and 1089; *Supp.* 51; *Tro.* 279f. and 1235).

30   **Solon's restrictions on the prothesis.** See Ps.-Dem. 43.62 and Plu. *Solon* 21.

Dirges. References to *goöi* in *Homer* include *Il.* 6.499f.; 18.51 and 316f.; 22.430 and 476; 23.10; 24.665, 747 and 761. For the distinction between *goös* and *thrênos*, see also Reiner (1938, 8f.) and Alexiou (1974, 12f.). For the influence of Homeric dirges on later literature, see Mawet (1975). References to *goöi* and *thrênoi* in tragedy include Eur. *Supp.* 82ff.; *Helen* 166ff.; *HF* 1025ff.

Hired mourners. See Hom. *Il.* 24.720f. Representations on Geometric vases: Ahlberg 1971, 131f. (23 exx. listed). Ref. in Aes.: *Ch.* 733. I know of no positive evidence later than Homer for the presence of professional dirge-singers at the *prothesis* apart from possibly Luc. *Luct.* 20, though their participation at the *ekphora* is well-attested (see below).

Musical instruments. For discussion see Reiner (1938, 67ff.). Although it is abundantly clear that *aulos*-playing accompanied the funerary procession to the grave (see below), it is less certain that it was used for *prothesis*. A lyre is represented on two vase-scenes depicting mythological *prothesis* but in neither case is it actually in use (Reiner 1938, 68 with n. 4). Homer mentions no musical accompaniment to either the *goös* or *thrênos*, and it may well be, as Reiner suggests, that music 'had only an accessory meaning in comparison with the spoken and sung ritual lament'. Cf. the ref. to *elegos alyros* (elegy which is not sung to the lyre) in Eur. *Helen* 185. It is possible that the figures seated around a box-like structure on certain Geometric vases holding a pair of objects are intended to be 'noise-making' (*KB* 61 with fig. 7), but the interpretation of such scenes remains problematic.

Movement around the bier. *Circumambulatio* or the rite of circling around the corpse is performed by the Myrmidons on behalf of the dead Patroklos (Hom. *Il.* 23.13f.). Cf. Andronikos 1968, 14f. As Ahlberg (1971, 300) suggests, it may be that the ritual had some kind of 'magical' significance. The Myrmidons circle the corpse three times. For the sacredness of the number three to the dead, see Harrison 1900, 114; Diels 1890, 40.

Importance of the ritual lament. For the combination of refs. to lament with burial, cf. Hom. *Od.* 11.72f.; Aes. *Ag.* 1541 and especially *Ch.* 429, where it is stated that Klytaimnestra dared to bury her husband without lamenting. See also Alexiou 1974, *passim*.

Anger expressed by survivors. Cf. S. *Ajax* 900ff., 1005ff., etc.;

Lucr. 3.898ff.

31   **Scenes of ekphora on Geometric vases.** See Ahlberg 1971, 300, figs. 53-5. All three exx. belong to *LG* I. Other instances listed by Zschietzschmann (1928, 38f.) do not contain evidence of funerary chariots.

32   **Ekphora in Homer.** Cf. *Il.* 23.131ff. See also Andronikos 1968, 18.

Archaeological evidence for the existence of Geometric hearses. Bindings for wheel-knaves: Müller-Karpe 1962, 66, Abb. 20.4-5 and 21.9-10. Vari cart: Hampe 1960, Abb. 46; Andronikos 1968, pl. 4a; *KB* pl. 16; Vermeule 1979, ch. 1 fig. 12.

Scenes of ekphora on black-figure vases, etc. *Kyathoi*: Zschietzschmann 1928, nos. 91 and 92, pl. 15. There is also a representation on a funerary plaque by Exekias of the harnessing of a mule before its departure for the cemetery (Boardman 1955, 64f.). The cart, in which a woman sits, is stationed in a courtyard beside a tree.

Ekphora on a terracotta plaque. See Rayet 1884, II 75.

33   **Prosphagion.** Permitted by Kean law: *LSG* 97A 12f. In addition to *prosphagion*, we also meet *prosphagma*, which is used both of a sacrifice made at a new grave (Eur. *Alk.* 845), at an established grave (Eur. *Hek.* 41 and 265), and to a god (Eur. *IT* 243). In Eur. *Helen* 1255, *prosphattô* describes a sacrifice made in connection with a burial (here at sea).

Regulations regarding the ekphora. To be held before sunrise: Ps.-Dem. 43.62; *KB* pl. 37. Halting at street corners forbidden: *LSG* 77C 15ff. Restrictions on attendance of women: Ps.-Dem. 43.62. Flautists limited to ten (?): Cic. *Laws* 2.59, cf. Zschietzschmann 1928, no. 92 (pl. 15).

34   **Pall-bearers.** See Hsch. s.v. *klimakophoros* and Poll. 7.195. Cf. also Cato's famous remark made at the debate on the exiles from Achaia instigated by Polybios: 'We sit here all day as if we had nothing to do but discuss whether some Greek geriatrics should be buried by us or by the Achaean *nekrophoroi*' (Plu. *Cat. Maj.* 9; Polyb. 35.6). We hear, too, of a certain Konopion who, 'accustomed to undertake such tasks for a fee', carried Phokion's body beyond Eleusis into Megara (Plu. *Phok.* 37). Ephebes specially selected: Pl. *Laws* 12.947c; Plu. *Tim.* 39 and *Phil.* 21.

Hired musicians at the ekphora. See Pl. *Laws* 7.800e. Somewhat at variance with Plato's statement is Hsch. s.v. Karinai. Poll. 4.75 intimates that they were flute-players.

Knowledge of embalming in Homer. See Garland 1982a, 73 and n. 35.

Cremation in tragedy. *Cf.* Aes. *Ch.* 682ff.; S. *El.* 54, 1113ff., etc.; *Trach.* 1195ff.; Eur. *Hek.* 896; *Or.* 40, 404; *Supp.* 936, 949. Ajax is a notable exception (S. *Ajax* 1165). Forms of burial and types of grave-offerings are discussed in detail by *KB* (*passim*) and are mentioned only summarily here.

35   **Ritual slaughter at the graveside.** Funeral of Patroklos: Hom. *Il.* 23.171ff.; Garland 1982a, 72. Hero-burial at Lefkandi: Popham, Touloupa and Sackett 1982. Salamis horse-burials: Karageorghis 1967, 117f., and Rivza 1979, 294ff. Burial of Kimon Koalemos: Hdt. 6.103 and Plu. *Kimon* 4; Humphreys 1982, 101f., and Garland 1982b, 158 with n. 73.

Deposition scene on loutrophoros amphora. *KB* pl. 36; *CVA* Athens I, III Hg, pl. 8.

36   **Cremation scene on vase.** A red-figure vase dated *c.* 500 shows Kroisos of Lydia enthroned on top of a funeral pyre making a libation while an attendant busies himself with lighting the logs (Smith 1898, 268, fig. 1; *ARV* 238 no. 1).

Enchytristriai. The function of *enchytristriai* has been vigorously contested. On the strength of the scholiasts on Ar. *Wasps* 289 and *Thesm.* 505, and the lexicographers s.v. *enchytrizein*, it was suggested by Glotz (s.v. *Expositio* in *DS*) that they constituted a professional body whose function was to expose unwanted children in pots or *chytrai*. Other suggestions include 'women who carried a vase at the *ekphora*' (Rayet 1884, II 75; Brückner and Pernice 1893, 148); 'women who caught the blood of sacrifice animals in bowls and purified the polluted' (Rohde 1897, ch. 5 n. 77); 'women who collect the bones of the deceased after cremation and place them in a pot' (Boeckh 1806, 57); 'women who interred children in pots' (Orsi 1906, 242; see also Bolkestein 1922, 229); and 'women who perform a sacrifice for the dead in a pit' (Bolkestein 1922), deriving *enchytrizein* from *chytros*, 'a hole in the ground'. The best ancient testimony for their function derives, as Bolkestein points out, from Pseudo-Plato's *Minos* (315c), where it is clearly intimated that their services were made use of at regular funerals and that they played no part in the exposure of children.

Coffin-lid unsealed until deposition. See the description of the Vari cart above (p. 32 with fig. 9). The funeral ordinance of the Labyad phratry at Delphi (*LSG* 77) contains an obscure provision which according to one interpretation refers to the sealing of the coffin-lid (rendered '*thigana*' and so translated by *LSJ*⁹) at the grave.

Wine used to quench remains of the funeral pyre. Cf. Hom. *Il.* 23.237 and 24.791. For a Geometric parallel from Ischia, see Coldstream 1977, 226. Cf. also the ban by the Ioulis code on more than three *choës* of wine being carried to the *sêma* (*LSG* 97A 8f.).

Ashes gathered up in cinerary urn. Cf. Hom. *Il.* 23.249ff.; S. *El.* 1138ff.; Eur. *Or.* 404; *Supp.* 1115ff. For archaeological evidence, see Coldstream 1977, 196 (Euboia, 715-690 B.C.) and 226 (Ischia). In Homer the calcified remains of Hektor are folded in 'soft purple *peploi*' before being placed in a golden urn (*Il.* 24.792ff.). The care with which the ashes were gathered up can be demonstrated from the cinerary urn described in Garland 1982b, no. A19.

Scenes of preparation for the tomb-visit. Bail-*amphora*: *KB* pl. 38. The subject features commonly on Attic white *lêkythoi* and is discussed in detail in ch. 7.

Offering trenches and offering places. Offering trenches: *KER* VI.I 29ff.; *KB* 65; *BCH* (81) 1957, 518 (Draphi). A cheaper version of the offering trench was the offering place, an irregularly-shaped, shallow-dug hole, which became common in the late sixth century. For a continuous series of offering places found in the Kerameikos in the region south of the Sacred Way dated from the late sixth to the end of the fourth century, see Schlörb-Vierneisel (1966) nos. 37, 40, 66, 89, 91, 92, 94, 105, 108, 109, 114-6, 136, 138, 160, 167 and 188. An especially rich pottery collection came from no.138 (pls. 48-50: dated *c.* 370-60 B.C.). Occasionally both offering ditch and offering place are found together (*KB* 75; *KER* VI.I 87f.). For wooden planks, see *KB* fig. 9.

Animal and bird remains found in offering trenches, etc. See *KER* VI.I 87 (late eighth to early sixth cents.) and Schlörb-Vierneisel 1966, nos. 40, 66, 105, 160, etc. (fifth to fourth cents. B.C.).

37   **Unguentaria.** Boulter 1963, pp. 115, 125f. and pl. 46: Grave K.

Men and women leave the cemetary separately. See *LSG* 97A 18ff.; Roux 1967, 172 n. 26; Humphreys 1980, 99 n. 3.

4. BETWEEN WORLDS

39   **Thanatos and Hypnos on lêkythoi.** See *ARV* p. 851 no. 272; *AWL* pls. 32.4 and 50.2 (Thanatos without Hypnos). For discussion of the subject on *lêkythoi*, see Fairbanks (1914, II p. 226). In the *Iliad* (16.671) they are sent to remove the body of Sarpedon from the battlefield.

Perideipnon. See Cic. *Laws* 2.63; Zen. 5.28; Hegesippos, *CAF* Fr. 1.10ff. In a talk entitled 'Poem and fee in Greek Archaic poetry, both choral and monodic' delivered to the Hellenic Society on Nov. 15th 1979, Prof. L.R. Rossi suggested that the following fragments should perhaps be identified as extracts from *perideipnon* songs: *PMG* nos. 419, 485(?), 894, 896, 907, 911; Pi. *I.* 2 (?); Anaxandrides, *CAF* Fr. 1. In Homer there is flexibility in the timing of the funeral feast (rendered *taphon dainunai*): that in honour of Patroklos is held before his body is cremated (*Il.* 23.29ff.); that of Hektor takes place after (*Il.* 24.802). Other refs. to the *perideipnon* include Men. *Aspis* 232f.; Artem. *Oneirokr.* 4.81; Aen. Tact. 10.5.

40   **Trita and enata.** For the *trita* cf. Is. 2.37 and Ar. *Lys.* 611ff. For the *enata* cf. Is. 2.36f.; 8.39; Aischin. 3.225. Earlier scholars, such as Pottier (1883, 81) and Rohde (1897, ch. 5 n. 83), calculated from the day of burial. Rohde drew support for his theory from the fact that according to Porphyrion on Hor. *Ep.* 17.48 (*nona die quam sepultus est*), the Roman *novemdiale*, 'clearly modelled on Greek custom', was held on the ninth day after burial. But a connection between the two ceremonies is by no means proved. More recent discussions, such as those of Freistedt (1928, 90ff.) and Alexiou (1974, ch. 1 n. 38), have attempted to demonstrate that these ceremonies should be calculated instead from the day of death. If this latter reckoning is correct, the *trita* would either have taken place on the day of burial after interment, or alternatively have formed a separate ceremony marked by a second visit to the grave later the same day.

Triakostia. See Poll. 1.66 and comment on *Lys.* 1.14 below. Rohde (1897, ch. 5 n. 87) comments: 'It is evident that the *triakades* were not so firmly established in Athens (at least in the fourth century) as the *trita* and *enata*: e.g. Isaios generally only refers to these last as the indispensable *nomizomena*'. But, as we have seen, there are few refs. to any of these rites in surviving literature, and certainly not enough to compare their relative importance or popularity. The banning of thirtieth-day rites by the Kean code, believed to have corresponded closely to fifth-century Athenian legislation, is here significant, being indicative of their general popularity. See Humphreys (1980, 100 n. 9).

Kallysmata. Alexiou (1974, 16) suggests that the function of the rite after a funeral was 'apparently to purge the pollution in the household of the deceased'. Hsch. renders *kallysmata* as '*sarmata*', i.e. refuse, sweepings. *Kallysmata* is possibly the reading in Thphr. *Char.* 10.6. Meuli (1946, 205 n. 1) thinks that the word has the same meaning as *loutra, choai* and *loibai*. It is perhaps merely a synonym for *katharmata* or *apolymata*, which Harp. (s.v. *oxythymia*) says were carried to crossroads 'whenever people purify their houses'. See also Schol. on Ar. *Pl.* 594, where it is interpreted as a sacrifice to Hekate.

Triakostia associated with the worship of Hekate. Rohde (1897, ch. 5 n. 88) noted that the last three days of the month at Athens were sacred to the denizens of the lower world, and hence *apophrades*. See Lys. Fr. 53 (Scheibe); *Et.Mag.* 131.13f.; *E. Gud.* 70.3ff. On these days banquets were left for Hekate at the crossroads. Cf. Ath. 7. 325a; Plu. *Mor.* 709a; *SIG³* 286.13 (Miletos, fourth cent. B.C.).

Duration of mourning period. Gambreion: *LSA* 16.11ff. See also *KB* 201 and Alexiou (1974, ch. 1 n. 54). Sparta: Hdt. 6.58; Plu. *Lyk.* 27.

Kathedra. See Lex. Rh. 268.19ff. and Phot. s.v. Rohde (1897, ch. 5 n. 86) suggests that *kathedra* may have been a synonym for *triakades*. See also Wyse 1904, 243. It must be emphasised that all the evidence for *kathedra* is late.

41   **Legislation regarding the contagiousness of the dead.** Keos: *LSG* 97.25ff.; Labyadai at Delphi: *LSG* 77C.20f.; Athens: Ps.-Dem. 43.58 and 62. The pronouncement of the Kean code upon the subject is unclear. Homolle (1895, ad loc.) reads: '*tênei d'enagos estô* which he rendered 'and let pollution remain up to this point'. This was emended by Bousquet (1966, 87) to *enatos* with the comment that the word was 'inexplicable'. Finally , West (1968, 176) took *denatos* to be an error for *de anatos* with subject *ho ototuzôn* understood: i.e. 'Let the wailer be immune from punishment'. The second part of the provision ('*ente ka a thigana posthethêi*') is also problematical. *DHR* (II no. 28) explain *thigana* as 'mound', on the strength of Hesychios' gloss s.v. *thisana* (sic). *LSJ⁹*, however, render 'cover, lid'.

43   **Purificatory measures adopted during prothesis.** *Ardanion*: Eur. *Alk.* 100ff.; Ar. *Ekk.* 1033; Poll. 8.65; Hsch. and Sud. s.v. Cypress branch or lock of hair: Eur. Alk. 1032; Serv. on *Aen.* 3.680; *KB* 146. *Lêkythoi*: Ar. *Ekk.* 1030; Moulinier 1952, 76.

Aponimma. See Kleitodemos apud Ath. 9.410a and *FGrH* 323 F14. Jacoby comments: 'the rite here described is meant for a sacrifice at an established grave, not as part of the funeral'; but he does not state how he reaches this conclusion. Besides, if we are to think of a new trench being dug each time the ceremony was performed, we should expect archaeologists to report their discovery.

44   **Bathing after the funeral.** See Schol. on Ar. *Clouds* 838. It is evidently for this reason that Teukros orders a cauldron of lustral water (*hosia loutra*) to be prepared for use after Ajax's burial (S. *Ajax* 1405). Orestes' madness is such that he omits to wash after the cremation of his mother (Eur. *Or.* 42). Bathing after a funeral was enjoined by the Kean code (*LSG* 97A 30).

Purification of the deceased's house. See Dem. 47.70, Eur. *Helen* 1430f.and *LSG* 97A 15.

Exêgêtai. The *exêgêtai*, or expounders of the law, who are sometimes mentioned in the context of correct burial procedure, seem to have existed merely as an advisory body largely with the object of clarifying responsibilities, but without, it seems, any power of enforcement. In addition to Ps.-Dem., there are four other fourth cent. refs. to *exêgêtai*, viz. Pl. *Euthyphr.* 4c and *Laws* 12.958d; Is. 8.39; Thphr. *Char.* 16.6. The earliest is Pl. *Euthyphr.*, dated *c.* 399. Of the institution in general, MacDowell (1978, 193) rightly remarks: 'On the basis of this evidence we cannot say when *exêgêtai* were first appointed, nor how many there were, nor how much of the sacred law they expounded in the fourth century.' See also *Et. Mag.* and Harp. s.v. For discussion see Rohde (1897, ch. 5 n. 139); Wyse (1904, 619); Oliver (1950, 28ff.); Clinton (1974, 89ff.).

Prophylactics against the dead during the Anthesteria. See Phot. s.vv. *miara hêmera* and *rhamnos*.; Hsch. s.v. *miarai hêmerai*. For the protective power of buckthorn, see Rohde (1897, ch. 5 n. 95). Pitch is not elsewhere referred to as a prophylactic.

Gods forbidden contact with the dead. Eur. *Hipp.* 1437f.; *Alk.* 22. For discussion see Barrett 1964, on 1437-9.

Temple precincts to be kept pure from the defilement of death. See *LSG* 124.1ff. (Eresos); 55.6 (Cult of Men, Attika); 139.13 (Lindos); *LSA* 12.6ff. (Athene Nikephoros, Pergamum, post 133 B.C.); 18.6 (Maeonia, 147-6 B.C.); 51.5ff. (Artemis, Miletos, end of first cent. B.C.); 84.6ff. (Dionysos Bromios, Smyrna, second cent. A.D.); *LSS* 91.13ff. (Lindos, third cent. A.D.); 106.3ff. (Camiros, very defaced); 115A.21-5 (Cyrene, end of fourth cent. B.C.). All these may be contrasted with *LSS* 54 (Syrian deity, Delos, end of 2nd cent. B.C.) where there is no mention of the pollution of death, doubtless, as Sokolowski suggests, 'because of the peculiar situation on Delos where burial was forbidden'. It should be noted that cathartic prescriptions regularly distinguish between those persons involved in a *kêdos oikeion* (funeral of one's own relative) and a *kêdos allotrion* (funeral of a non-relative), and that the regulations pertaining to the two groups vary accordingly. Inscription found near the Propylaia: *IG* II² 1035.10f. For location of tombs at Rhamnous, see Garland 1982b, 160ff. Delos: Pl. *Phd.* 58b; Thuk. 3.104.2.

45 **Priests forbidden contact with the dead.** See Nilsson 1925, 84. Priestess of Demeter on Kos: Herzog 1928, 8A IIa, 22-3; IIb, 37f.; IIIb, 17-22. Priest of Zeus Polieus on Kos: *LSG* 156A.10ff.

46 **Pollution in Homer.** There are only two refs. to pollution in Homer. At the beginning of the *Iliad*, when Agamemnon orders his army to purify itself because of the plague sent by Apollo, they do so by merely throwing the 'off-scourings' (*lymata*, 1.314) into the sea. After slaying the suitors, Odysseus orders his servants to clean the palace, which they do by sponging down the tables and chairs with water, scraping the top layer off the floor with a hoe, and then simply throwing the scourings out of doors (22.437ff.). After further killings, Odysseus and his men wash their hands and feet (*aponipsamenoi*, 478), and fumigate the palace with sulphur. From the very few refs., Dodds (1951, 36) argues that in the Geometric period pollution caused little anxiety, being relatively uncontagious and easily dispelled, whereas the 'elaborate and messy rituals' of professional archaic *kathartoi* betoken an age when pollution had become both infectious and hereditary. There is not in my view sufficient evidence to substantiate the theory that fear of pollution among the Greeks grew rather than diminished as time passed. Homer is an especially unreliable witness for this kind of hypothesis, since, as has been frequently pointed out (e.g. Vernant 1974, 118), it is suspected that the poet elects to suppress certain aspects of religious thought which in his day might have enjoyed some prominence.

5. LIFE IN HADES

49 **Etymology of Hades.** Farnell (1907, III p. 282) thinks that '*Aidês*' means 'the Unseen One', and that it is for this reason that his realm is thought to be gloomy. The etymology is much disputed. For discussion, see Solmsen (1909, 74ff.); Schwyzer (1939-50, I p. 266); Wackernagel (1953, I pp. 765ff.); Frisk (1960, s.v.); and Chantraine (1968, s.v.).

Descriptions of Hades in Homer. Referred to as 'murky darkness': *Il.* 21.56; *Od.* 11.57 and 155; 20.356. For *êeróenta*, 'murky', see West (1966, on 653) and Richardson (1974, on 337). The force of the epithet in combination with *zophos*, 'darkness', seems to be 'dark darkness'. Location given: *Od.* 10.504ff.; 11.13ff.; 24.11ff. and 204;

Il. 22.482. Paus. (1.17.5) believed that Homer's description of Hades was inspired by a visit to Thesprotia in western Epirus (the site of the later oracle of the dead, above p. 3), since Thesprotia had two rivers called Acheron and Kokythos, the latter of which he described as 'most unpleasant.' Since Pyrithlegethon and Kokytos are not mentioned again until the Classical period, Vermeule (1979, ch. 1 n. 6) has plausibly suggested that the ref. in *Od.* 10 was inserted in the late sixth or early fifth cent. The two *Nekyiai* are in fact among the most suspect episodes in the entire Homeric corpus. For discussion of the problems and inconsistencies, see Petzl (1969).

References to Hades in Hesiod. West (1966, on 767) notes that the formulaic epithet *êchêentes*, 'echoing', is appropriate to 'large and well-thronged houses', but hardly to Hades where the dead merely gibber (*Od.* 24.7; *Il.* 23.101). But in addition to making strange noises, like bats at feeding time, the dead do manage to converse intelligibly (see below). For the descent of the men of the bronze race to the underworld, see *Erg.* 152ff. The iciness of Hades is the point of an entertaining story about Periander of Corinth related by Herodotus (5.92). When the tyrant evoked the spirit of his dead wife to seek her advice, rather than comply with his request she complained that she was naked as a result of her clothes having been buried with her instead of burnt. To remedy the situation, the tyrant summoned all the women of Corinth to the temple of Hera, ordered them to strip, and made a bonfire of their clothes, thereafter acquiring a most co-operative shade.

The 'katabasis' theme in Greek literature. Aristophanes had already made use of the theme of a descent to Hades in a lost play called the *Gerytades*, produced three years before the *Frogs* in 408 B.C. For discussion of the plot, see Norwood (1931, 290ff.). For a detailed discussion of the *katabasis* motif in Greek mythology, see Ganschinietz, s.v. in *RE*, supplemented by Vermeule (1979, ch. 1 n. 1). Those who undertake the descent include Dionysos, Herakles, Odysseus, Orpheus, Psyche and Theseus. The theme of descent to the underworld can be traced to the Sumerian myth of Inanna's descent. As queen of heaven and goddess of love and war, Inanna apparently undertakes the journey to oust her sister Ereshkigal from the throne, and perhaps in addition to raise the dead (Kramer 1963, 491; *ANET* 52ff.).

50 **Mire and dung.** The mire and dung (*borboros* and *pêlos*) of Hades are a common topos in Greek literature. In Plato's *Rep.* (2.363d-e), Sokrates reproves the Orphics for the mundanity of the concept of

'burial in some kind of mud' as a form of punishment for the unholy and unjust. See also Plu. *De anima* Fr. 178 (Sandbach); Olympiodoros, *In Platonis Phaedonem* 69c (p. 121 Norvin).
Natural beauties of the underworld. The first reference to the beauty of Hades, or at least to a special part of it, occurs in Pi. Fr. 114 *OCT*, where we learn of 'a meadow of red roses' and 'a space before the city shaded by the incense tree and full of golden fruits'. A fragrance lies over the land 'whereas on the other side, sluggish streams of dark night belch forth measureless gloom'. Here Hades, if this is the region being described, seems to incorporate both heaven and hell. For a similar description of the scenic wonders of specific localities in Hades, cf. Virg. *Aen.* 6.637ff. and 703ff. The Isles of the Blest, by contrast, which are situated along 'the highway of Zeus' (Pi. *Ol.* 2.70ff.), would appear to be geographically quite distinct.

Lethe. For Lethe as a tract of land, see also Pl. *Rep.* 10.621a; D.H. 8.52.4. For Lethe as water, see Virg. *Aen.* 6.705; Luc. *D. Mort.* 13.6; Paus. 9.39.8; Aesop. 168.

Donkey's shearing, etc. For discussion of the meaning behind these terms, see Stanford (1958, on 185-7).

Tainaron. Tainaron (or Tainaros), the central peninsula of the southern Peloponnese, contained a cave believed to be an *Aida stoma* or 'mouth of Hades' (Pi. *P.* 4.44). The name of a 'genuine' entrance to Hades coming at the end of a list of nonsense places seems to be an example of *para prosdokian.*

Descriptions of Hades in Plato. See *Phd.* 113d; *Rep.* 10.614c-627d.

Gold leaves. For the text of the *lamella* found at Pharsalos, see Zuntz (1971, 360f.). It is to be compared especially with the *lamella* from Petelia, which is probably slightly older, though interestingly the latter puts the spring to be avoided on the left. For discussion of this puzzling variant, see Zuntz (367ff.), whom I do not find convincing on this point. The significance of a white cypress tree beside the bad spring is not understood.

Tartaros. See Hom. *Il.* 8.13ff. and 481; Hes. *Th.* 119 and 720ff.; *Aspis* 254f.; Pherekydes *DK* B5.25; Aes. *PV* 154, 221 and 1051; *Eum.* 72; S. *OC* 1389; Pl. *Phd.* 111e-114b. For etymology, see West 1966 on 1109. Mention should also be made of Erebos, believed by *LSJ⁹*, on the strength of Hom. *Il.* 8.368, to be 'a place of passage to and from Hades'. As Richardson (1974, on 335) notes, however, there is no justification for making such an assumption. Hesiod (*Th.* 123) personifies Erebos as the son of Chaos and brother of Nyx (Night).

Cf. also *h. Dem.* 335, 349 and 409. The region is rarely referred to in tragedy.

51 **Representations of Hades.** For the underworld on Apulian vases, see the bibliography provided by Keuls (1974, ch. 5 n. 3). I have not included in this discussion vases purporting to represent scenes in Hades which contribute nothing to our understanding of the geography of the region. These include the *Nekyia* vase dated *c.* 450 B.C. (Richter and Hall 1936, II pl. 135); vases which depict Herakles come to fetch Kerberos from the underworld; an Attic black-figure *amphora* in Munich (cat. no. 1493) showing winged ghosts pouring water into a vat and Sisyphos rolling his stone uphill; and an Attic black-figure *lêkythos* in Palermo (cat. no. 996) showing human figures pouring water into a vat and Oknos with his ass. For representations of the latter two vases, see Keuls (1974, pls. 1 and 2). For the same reason there is no discussion here of Polygnotos' wall-paintings at Delphi.

52 **Hades in Homer.** See *Il.* 5.395; 8.367ff.; 9.158f.; 15.187; 20.61 (Aidoneus); *Od.* 10.534. The significance of the epithet *klytopôlos* ('famous for steeds') is not understood. See *Il.* 5.654; 11.445; 16.625. For discussion, see Farnell (1907, III p. 283).

Hades in Archaic literature. Refs. in *h. Dem.*: 'dark-haired' (347); 'all-receiving' (17, 31, 404 and 430); 'ruling over many' (31 and 376). The god is in fact '*polyonomos*', which may either mean 'having many titles' or 'famous'. For the significance of the proliferation of a deity's titles, see Rohde (1897, 159), Richardson (1974, on 18), Gow (1950, on Theokr. 15.109) and Rose (*OCD* s.v. Hades). The Attic form 'Haides', with aspirate and contraction, first appears in *h. Dem.* 347, though the possibility of corruption in transmission cannot be ruled out. See Richardson (1974, on 347 and pp. 52ff.) for other Atticisms in the poem. Regarding the myth of the abduction of Persephone, as Farnell (1907, III p. 23f.) points out, the connection between the gods of the underworld and those responsible for the earth's fruitfulness is very close. It is manifest not only in the cult of Demeter and Persephone, but also in that of the earth goddess Ge. Ge enjoyed a 'natural affinity' with the powers of death and is prominent in festivals performed on behalf of the dead, such as the Genesia and Anthesteria. Hesiod, who contributes nothing new to the picture of Hades as received from Homer, makes reference to another underworld deity, Zeus Chthonios, to whom, as to Demeter, the husbandman should pray in the springtime in order to ensure a rich harvest (*Erg.* 465ff.). For Hades as *psychopompos*, see Pi. *Ol.* 9.33f.

53 **Hades and Pluto in Classical literature.** With regard to the characterisation 'most hospitable', Hades is generally regarded as accommodating because of the numbers received rather than the warmth of the welcome, though in Aes. *Supp.* the emphasis may well be on the latter. In S. *Ant.* 519 he is described as 'desiring the preservation of the laws', but the context makes it clear that the laws in question are those in which he has a vested interest, namely the right of the dead to proper burial, and not justice in the wider sense. Epithets applied to Hades: 'common to many' (S. *Ajax* 1193); 'where all must sleep' (S. *Ant.* 804 and 811); 'bloody' (Eur. *Alk.* 225). As Pluto, invoked for aid: S. *El.* 110ff.; *Trach.* 1040ff. and 1085. Other refs. to Pluto in tragedy: Aes. *PV* 806; S. *Ant.* 1200; Eur. *Alk.* 360; *HF* 808. Pluto is also mentioned in Hesiod (*Th.* 969), but as the son of Demeter and Iasion. For discussion, see Nilsson (*GGR*³ I pp. 471ff.) and West (1966, on 969). Hades as god of the dead in inscriptions: *Epigr. gr.* 89.4 (Athens). Cf. ib. 26.9. 42.5 and 87.4.

Hades in art. Black-figure lip-cup by Xenokles: see Farnell 1907, III pl. XXXIIb; Vermeule 1979, ch. 1 fig. 26. Vase from Volci: Farnell, op. cit., pl. XXXIIa. *Nekyia* vase in the Metropolitan Museum of New York: Richter and Hall 1936, I p. 169; Jacobsthal 1934-6, pp. 117ff.; Friedländer 1935, cols. 20ff. It is best reproduced in Richter and Hall (II pl. 135). A bearded man leaning on a stick and a youth holding a fillet standing before a pile of branches in the upper register are probably to be identified as the living, performing rites on behalf of the dead, as Richter and Hall suggest on the strength of Ar. *Ekk.* 1030ff.

The cult of Hades. The schol. on Hom. *Il.* 9.158 states that 'in no city is there an altar (*bômos*) to Hades'. Other chthonic deities who did receive a cult include Zeus Chthonios, Zeus Skotias, Eubouleus, Klymenos and Trophonios, who were worshipped in such varied places as Sinope, Byzantium, Corinth, Athens, Sparta, etc. For refs., see Farnell 1907, III pp. 376ff. Strabo (8.3.15) refers to a *temenos* sacred to Hades beside a grove sacred to Demeter in Tryphylia near Olympia. Cult at Elis: Paus. 6.25.2. Inscription from Corinth: *IG* 4.203.20. Ploutoneion near Eleusis: Boersma 1970, cat. no. 62.

54 **Kerberos in literature.** See Hom. *Il.* 8.368 and *Od.* 11.625; Hes. *Th.* 311; S. *OC* 1568ff. and *Trach.* 1098; Eur. *Alk.* 360, *HF* 24 and 611. Mentioned with scepticism: S. *OC* 1568ff.

Kerberos in art. First appearance on a vase: Brommer 1953, Taf. 24b. For examples in Attic art, see Brommer p. 45 with Anhang XI, where 47 black-figure vases and 8 red-figure vases are listed. Red-figure *amphora* attributed to the Andokides Painter: Flacelière

1966, pl. XXI Louvre, cat. no. F204. Sculptural representations: Olympia metope in Brommer, Taf. 1.11; Paus. 3.18.13 ('throne of the Amyklean' in Lakonia); Farnell 1907, III pl. VIIIb.

Hermes Psychopompos in literature. See Hom. *Od.* 24.1ff. (suspected interpolation); *h. Dem.* 377ff.; *h. Her.* 572. In tragedy with epithet *pompaios* (leader): Aes. *Eum.* 91; S. *Ajax* 832 and *OC* 1548. With epithet *chthonios* (of the underworld): Aes. *Ch.* 1 and 727; S. *Ajax* 832; Ar. *Frogs* 1145.

Hermes Psychopompos in art. *Lêkythos* in Jena: Harrison 1900, 101, fig. 1; Vermeule 1979, ch. 1, fig. 19. This problematical scene has been much discussed. Four 'souls' in the form of small winged creatures are represented in all, two fluttering in the upper air, one struggling out of the *pithos*, and a fourth diving headlong back in. Harrison connected it with 'Pithoigia' (Opening of the Storage Jars), the first day of the Anthesteria Festival, but this cannot be proved. Hermes waiting patiently on a rock: Arias, *et al.*, 1962, pl. XLII. Marble *lêkythos* erected to Myrrhine: Johansen (1951, pl. 82); Conze pl. 243. Formerly in private possession, described as 'disappeared' by Johansen, it is now in the Athens Museum (cat. no. 4485). The interpretation has been much disputed, but it seems clear, as Johansen (p. 161) suggests, that Hermes is leading Myrrhine past a group of watching survivors rather than towards them. For further discussion, see above p. 12. Another possible example is listed by Stais (1910, 129 no. 756), but it is not certain that it is a sepulchral monument.

55 **Hermes as assistant in the passage of death.** See S. *Ajax* 83ff., *OC* 1548 and *El.* 110ff.

  Hermes as weigher of souls. See Vermeule 1979, ch. 5, fig. 14 with n. 22.

  Herms. See Farnell 1907, V p. 38; Pfühl 1905, pp. 76ff. and Abb. 13-15.

  Charon in literature. Origins: D.S. 1.92.2 and 1.96.8 Diodorus wrongly asserts that he was called 'Charon' in the Egyptian language. The Egyptian equivalent of Charon, so far as one existed, was Seth, lord of storms. For discussion of the disputed Egyptian origins of Charon, see Vermeule 1979, ch. 2 n. 57. Inscription from Phokis: Peek 1960, no. 41. Epic poem *Minyas*: Paus. 10.28.2; *EGF* p. 215; Huxley 1969, 119. Cf. also Eur. *Alk.* 361 and 438ff.

56 **Charon in art.** In the category of stern Charons I would include *AWL* pl. 50.1, and among kindly Charons *AWL* pls. 23.2; 42.1; 47.2

and 3b. Beazley (*ARV*) lists 50 vases on which Charon appears. There are 8 listed examples by the Sabouroff Painter (*ARV* 846f.) and 15 by artists of the Reed Workshop (*ARV* 1376ff.). Funerary *stêlê* in the Kerameikos: Thönges-Stringaris 1965, Beil. 24.4; Conze 1173/251; Garland 1982b, cat. no. A4g.

Charon in other cultures. For the Etruscan ferryman, see Pallottino 1942, 149 with pl. 83. Virgil's memorable description of Charon (*Aen.* 6.298ff.) 'perhaps suggests something of this grisly Etruscan element', as Austin (1974, ad loc.) notes. In Medieval Greek folksongs he is Charontas, a deadly wrestler (see Levi 1971, I p. 478 n. 170). Belief in a ferryman of the dead can be traced back to the Sumerian myth of the *Birth of the Moon-God Sin*, in which Enlil, banished from Nippur to the underworld for having raped Ninlil, takes the form of various underworld deities, including a ferryman (cf. Kramer 1960, 64 and 1961, 139). Sumerian 'antecedents' for the Greek Hades are in fact striking.

Charon characterised. See Eur. *Alk.* 252ff. and Ar. *Frogs* 183ff.

Thanatos in literature. See Hom. *Il.* 16.671ff.; Hes. *Th.* 211ff. and 764. For refs. in Eur. *Alk.* see especially 49ff. and 261ff. For ancient commentary, see Apollodor. 1.9.10 and Schol. on Ar. *Wasps* 1239. For refs. to Euripides' debt to Phrynichos in ancient commentaries see Serv. on *Aen.* 4.694 and Macr. *Sat.* 5.19.4. Hsch. (1.62) merely notes that Phrynichos wrote an *Alkêstis*. For discussion of these passages, see Dale (1954, xii). The existence of two distinct personalities in the *Alkêstis* of Euripides, 'the one conceived of primarily as King of the Underworld, the other concerned with fetching thither the individual victim', is suggested by the choice of verb at 871 ('Thanatos handed over (*paredôken*) to Hades'), as Dale (1954, ad loc.) notes. Other references to Thanatos in tragedy: S. *OC* 1220; *Ajax* 854f.; *Phil.* 796, cf. Aes. Fr. 255 *TGF*; Eur. Hipp. 1373.

59 **Hypnos and Thanatos in art.** See Vermeule 1979, ch. 5, figs. 2 and 3, with p. 150; Pottier 1883, 30f. *Lêkythos* by the Reed Workshop: *ARV* 1384 no. 17; *AWL* pl. 50.2 and p. 64. Beazley (*ARV*) lists 11 vases on which Hypnos and Thanatos appear, viz. pp. 126, 227, 750, 850, 1228, 1237 (four), 1242 and 1385. For representations, see *AWL* pl. 32.4 and Vermeule 1979, ch. 5 fig. 4. Sculptured drum from Ephesus: Cook 1976, pl. 110 (BM Sculpture 1206).

Thanatos not worshipped. See Eur. *Alk.* 424 (described as *aspondos*) and Ar. *Frogs.* 1392.

60 **Death as the consequence of recklessness.** See Hom. *Od.* 1.7ff.

and 32ff. For *nêpioi*, cf. *Il.* 2.136 and 9.440.

Tantalos, Tityos and Sisyphos. In Homer Tantalos is eternally striving for unattainable food and drink (*Od.* 11.583ff.). In Pindar (*Ol.* 1.57ff.) and Euripides (*Or.* 4ff.), a great stone is suspended above his head, ever threatening to fall. His crime is variously alleged: that he served his son's flesh to the gods, stole their nectar and ambrosia, or revealed their secrets to mortals (Pi. *Ol.* 1.37ff. and 60ff.; Eur. *Or.* 7ff.; D.S. 4.74.2). What is common to all versions is that he had offended grossly the dignity of the gods and abused the privileges which he specifically had been granted. Tityos was the violator of Leto: his vast bulk is spread over acres of land and his liver torn by vultures (Hom. *Od.* 11.576ff.). Sisyphos for various crimes diversely reported has to roll a great stone up a hill from which it constantly rolls back down again (*Od.* 11.593ff.). In addition, Ixion, the first to murder one of his kin, is attached to a revolving wheel (Pi. *P.* 2.21ff.); and Oknos, the hard-working bread-winner of a profligate wife, plaits a cord which a she-ass devours as quickly as it is plaited (Paus. 10.29.1).

Elysion. Elysion is not mentioned in Greek literature again before the Hellenistic period (see A.R. *Argon.* 4.811). Paradise in both Archaic and Classical literature is the Isles of the Blest (see Vermeule 1979, ch. 2 n. 58). The Homeric gods are not only able to transfer humans to Elysion but also to bear them away to their own realms, where they enjoy immortality, cf. *Od.* 5.135f. and 209f. (Kirke offers immortality to Odysseus); 5.333ff. (Leukotheë); 11.601ff. (Herakles); *Il.* 20.232ff. (Ganymede).

61   **The blessed condition of Eleusinian initiates.** Cf. *h.Dem.* 480ff. For discussion, see Rohde 1897, 225ff.; Allen et al., 1936, ad loc. Richardson 1974, ad loc.. Richardson (p. 11) would date the poem to the seventh cent. For other refs., cf. Pi. Fr. 121 *OCT*; Plu. *Mor.* 21f; S. Fr. 753 *TGF*; Ar. *Frogs* 354ff.; Poll. 8.90.

62   **Orphic eschatology.** Abstention from murders: Ar. *Frogs* 1032; cf. Eur. Fr. 472 *TGF*; Thphr. ap. Porph. *Abs.* 2.21. With ref. to Empedokles Fr. 144 *DK*, which speaks of the condition of 'fasting from evil-doing (*kakotês*)', and which is probably inspired by Orphic doctrine, Adkins (1960, 143) claims that 'the form of the phrase, the assimilation of right-doing to abstinence, suggests that abstinence was the most prominent element of such belief'. Detienne (1977, 68ff.) has sought to demonstrate, however, that abstinence should be seen as a way of challenging the official city-state religion and as hence 'a highly subversive act'.

63 **Katharmoi of Empedokles.** See *DK* B117 = *KR* 476; *DK* B115.20ff. Keuls seems to regard all the ordeals of the punished sinners in Hades as 'futility ordeals' intended to effect *katharmos* and hence salvation. She suggests that those who are condemned to undergoing them have 'violated archetypal patterns in life and are punished, or perhaps purified of time, by rites of repetition in the afterlife' (1974, 22). This is too intellectualised. Moreover, the punishments administered to Tityos and Ixion can hardly be classed as 'futility ordeals', as Keuls herself acknowledges (ch. 1 n. 30).
Post mortem judgment in Pindar. Cf. *Ol.* 2.68ff. The syntax is problematical. For ref. to *penthos*, see Fr. 127 *OCT* with Pl. *Meno* 81b. For discussion of the meaning of *hosios*, see Adkins (1960, 132ff.). A description of what is possibly Elysion regarded as the temporary resting-place of the just soul before it has completed its full cycle of lives is provided by Pi. Fr. 114 *OCT*.

64 **Rewards and punishments in Euripides.** Virtue rewarded in this life: *IA* 1034. Death as punishment for the wicked: *HF* 740; cf. *El.* 482ff. and 953ff. Virtue rewarded in the hereafter: *Alk.* 744ff.

66 **Cautious optimism in the afterlife.** In the early dialogues of Plato, Sokrates is equally cautious in his pronouncements about the afterlife. Cf. *Phd.* 63c: 'I am hopeful that there is something for the dead, and, as men of old have declared, that it is something better for the good than for the wicked.' Even more tentative is the conclusion of the *Apology* (42a): 'But now the time has come to leave, I to die and you to live, but which of us goes to a better lot is unknown to anyone except God.'
Theme of family reunion in Hades. Cf. Aes. *Ag.* 1555; S. *Ant.* 898ff.; Eur. *Alk.* 363ff.; S. *OT* 1371ff. For examples in epitaphs, see Welles 1941, 86.

68 **Dexiôsis in Greek art.** For a discussion of the various theories about the meaning of *dexiôsis*, see Johansen 1951, 55ff. Neumann (1965, 58), in his study of the interpretation of various gestures in Greek art sensibly refrains from passing judgment. Aegina *stêlê*: Johansen, fig. no. 23 pl. 11. Johansen (p. 139) points to compositional correspondences between this relief and the famous Chrysapha relief (fig. 3), which shows the living 'worshippers' of the deceased on a much-reduced scale. *Stêlê* of Ampharete: Clairmont 1970, no.23; Johansen, fig. 4; *KB* pl. 31. *Nekyia* vase: Richter and Hall 1936, II pl. 135.
Gaming-boards found in graves. The oldest example is Protoattic and was found at Anagyrous in Attika (see Kallipolites

1963, 123f. and pl. 53). Another set found in Athens is black-figure and dated *c.* 580 (see *KER* VI.2, 394f.; *KB* pl. 12). Herodotus (2.122) reports that the Pharaoh Rhampsinitos 'descended alive into what the Greeks called Hades, and there played dice with Demeter, sometimes winning and sometimes losing'. See Pi. Fr. 114 *OCT* for horses, gymnasia and *pessoi*.

70   **Totenmahl reliefs.** See Thönges-Stringaris 1965, *passim*; *KB* 234; Johansen (p. 163). For the beginning of the series, see Thönges-Stringaris, no. 65, Beil. 7.2. Johansen (p. 163) suspects that some exx. were 'possibly even a little later than the funeral law of Demetrios'. Two such (nos. 69 and 151) are dated by Thönges-Stringaris to *c.* 300. Out of a total 202 listed exx. in Thönges-Stringaris, I counted 35 whose provenance can definitely be assigned to Attika.

    Pomegranates. See Thönges-Stringaris 1965, nos. 78, 84 and 178. Pomegranates had a particular importance for the dead. Clay replicas have been found in the cemetery at Eleusis dating from the Geometric period (Farnell 1907, III p. 226). The queen of the underworld seems to have had a close association with the fruit. It was the eating of 'only a single sweet pomegranate seed' (*h. Dem.* 372) which bound her to Hades for one third of eternity. It is by virtue of this attribute that she is frequently to be identified in sculptural representations (see Cook 1940, III.1 p. 813 n. 5). Porph. *Abst.* 4.16 mentions that pomegranates as food were taboo at the celebration of the Eleusinian Mysteries. The fruit seems to have symbolised not only blood and death, but also fertility and increase. For further discussion see Cook (loc. cit.); Farnell (loc. cit.); Kerenyi 1967, 133ff.; Arthur 1977, 29.

    Eggs. E.g. *AWL.* pl. 19.1 (egg presented at the tomb). For discussion of the symbolism of eggs, see Nilsson 1908, 530ff. For extensive refs., see Boardman 1955, 54 n. 22.

71   **Snakes.** Thönges-Stringaris (p. 56) notes that the snake, which she describes as the 'hero-animal par excellence', does not appear on Attic reliefs at all. The association between snakes and the dead is very close. Plu. (*Kleom.* 39) provides the following biological explanation: 'As rotting oxen breed bees, and horses wasps, and as beetles are produced in asses which are likewise decaying, so human bodies, when the fluids around the marrow collect and coagulate, produce snakes. It was because they observed this process that the men of old associated the snake with heroes'. This is perhaps the reason why modelled snakes appear on the neck, rim and handles of

Geometric vases intended for funerary use. On vases they are represented as inhabiting (or painted upon) graves, either symbolising the dead or else protecting them, cf. Zschietzschmann 1928, pl. 15 (no. 91). A Hellenistic epitaph (Peek 1955, no. 1260) refers to the snake as 'fierce guardian of the tomb'.

72   **Sexual activity of the dead.** Sarcophagus from Volci: Vermeule 1979, ch. 5 fig. 1. For discussion of the poem by Anakreon (*PMG* 395.11f.), see Giangrande 1968, 109ff. According to Giangrande, Anakreon, while using a commonplace opposition (viz. *katabainein/anabainein*), succeeds in transforming it into 'an extremely witty climactic point'. He finds confirmation of his erotic interpretation in the biographical tradition, which represented Anakreon as a man of unfailing sexual powers (cf. Sud. s.v. Anakreon). Relief from Kos: Karusos 1962, Beil. 35. It is perhaps not altogether unrelated that stone objects shaped like giant phalloi sometimes figure as grave-markers in parts of the Greek world. See *KB* 241-4, who dispute the identification.

    References to marriages in Hades. Cf. S. *Ant.* 816; Eur. *Med.* 985; *IA* 461 and 1109; *IT* 369.

74   **Hades as hierarchy.** Cf. Aes. *Pers.* 691; *Ch.* 356ff.; S. *El.* 841. It is not clear in what sense Achilles 'rules over the dead' (Hom. *Od.* 11.483ff.).

    Hades as eternity. Cf. Hom. *Od.* 11.543ff. and 24.20f. for eternal rancour; and *Od.* 11.40f. and Aes. *Eum.* 103 for eternally unhealing wounds.

    Death and the dead do not matter. See Eur. *Tro.* 636 and 1248ff.; *IA* 1251; *Alk.* 381; cf. S. *El.* 244; Eur. *Helen* 1421. Eur. questions the meaning of death in a more philosophical vein in *Polyidos*, Fr. 638 *TGF* ('Who knows if this life be not death, and death be not judged life in the world below?'); and in *Kresphontes*, Fr. 449 *TGF* ('When a man is dead and has found rest from trouble, we should rejoice and carry him from the house with songs of gladness.').

75   **The psychai of the dead transported to the aether.** Epitaph on the dead at Poteidaia: IG I² 945 and Tod 59. Inscription from the Peiraios: *Epigr. gr.* 41. See also Eur. *Supp.* 530ff. and *Epigr. gr.* 90. Lattimore (*TGLE* 32f.) describes the aether as 'in particular the upper air about the stars and planets' which 'was also imagined as the home of the gods and of those whose blessed and indestructible estate makes them virtually the equal of the gods'. Astral transformation: Eur. *Helen* 140; Ar. *Peace* 832ff. For discussion, see

Cumont 1922, 95.
Denial of the existence of Hades. Epigram by Kallimachos:
Pfeiffer 1949-53, *Epigr.* 13.3ff. For discussion of beliefs in the
Hellenistic period, see Rostovtzeff 1938-9, 15. For the Roman period,
see Plu. *Mor.* 1105a; cf. 1104b; Luc. *Luct.* 2. See Cumont 1922.
Papyrus of second cent. A.D.: Page 1941, 416ff. On the date of
composition, Page writes: 'The language and style of the poem
preclude a date of composition much earlier than the date of the
papyrus itself.'
76   **Conflation between Hades and the tomb.** The path to Hades
described as 'mouldy': Hom. *Od.* 24.10 and *Il.* 20.65. See also S. *Ajax*
1167 (*taphon êerôenta*) with Jebb's note. For *êerôenta* ('mouldy'), see
West 1966 on 731. 'Lying in Hades': S. *El.* 463; Eur. *Hek.* 418; *HF*
145. See further below p. 119.

6. THE SPECIAL DEAD

77   **Aôroi.** See Hdt. 2.79.3; Rohde 1897, Appendix 7. Lamented in
tragedy: Eur. *Hek.* 584ff.; *Tro.* 1187ff. Alluded to in epitaphs: *Epigr.
gr.* 12 (Attika); Peek 1955, no. 863 (Athens, mid-fourth cent.);
Epigr.gr. 193 (Thera, second cent.). *Aôrôtatos: Epigr. gr.* 372.32 (Asia
Minor, fourth cent.). Cf. Peek 1955, no. 1697 = Clairmont 1970, no.
62 (Athens, post 350); Clairmont 1970, no. 77 (Cyprus, late fourth
cent.). Philetairos died aged 22: Peek 1955, no. 420 = Clairmont
1970, no. 73 (Athens, mid-fourth cent.).
78   **The elderly.** Chairestrate: Peek 1955, no. 421 and Clairmont
1970, no. 26 and pl. 13 (Peiraios, mid-fourth cent.). Littias:
Clairmont 1970, no. 55 bis (Aegaleo, *c.* 375). See also Peek 1955, no.
930 = Clairmont 1970, no. 58 and pls. 26-7; Peek 1955, no. 1251 =
Clairmont 1970, no. 60 and pl. 21 (n.b. especially the expression '*en
gêrai liparôi*', 'in sleek old age', which also occurs in Hom. *Od.* 11.136;
19.368; Pi. *N.* 7.99. For *tymbogerôn*, see Ar. Fr. 55 D.; *Com. Adesp.*
1172; Thphr. in Phot.; Procop. *Arc.* 6.11. See also the list of
tymbogerontes in Humphreys 1983, 107. The longest-living ancient
Greek known to me was Euphron of Rhamnous, who attained 105
years (cited by Humphreys).
         Child-burials. Pot-inhumations: *KB* 55. Clay tubs utilised:
Kallipolites and Petrakos 1963, 48. Cremation not practised:
Robinson 1942, XI p. 145 (Archaic cemetery at Olynthos);
Karouzou 1947-8, 391 (Classical cemetery near Odhos Panepis-
temiou in Athens). Rudhardt (1963, 13) has drawn attention to the

fact that the apparent ban on cremating the bodies of the infant dead is by no means confined to Classical antiquity, citing Deonna (1955, 232ff.) for evidence of a similar prohibition enforced in India.

80   **Exposure of newborn children.** Bolkestein's assertion (1922, 237) that 'there is no single reason to doubt that the Athenians, with regard to their children, acted and thought in just the same way as other civilised peoples in ordinary circumstances' seems to my mind to beg a number of fundamental questions. Gomme (1933, 80), who is in agreement with Bolkestein's general theory, seems to cast doubt on his claim that the number of children in Athenian families was necessarily small. In Euripides' *Ion*, the Old Man's censure of Kreousa for exposing her child clearly does not indicate that he categorically disapproved of exposure *per se*, but only when resorted to by women who have had illicit sexual relations (925ff.). It seems to me that all that can be concluded safely is that Athenian society was prepared to tolerate frank reference to the subject of exposition. Gomme (1933, 81 n. 2) writes: 'in the ordinary way we should suppose that if abortion could be condemned (cf. the Hippocratic oath), *a fortiori* infanticide would be a crime'. But I am not sure what he means by 'in the ordinary way'. Are we to infer that in exceptional circumstances (viz. of physical and mental incapacity), exceptional measures might have been taken? As Gomme remarks with reference to Lys. Fr. 8, we should like to know more about the *graphê amblêseôs* (criminal prosecution for abortion). For discussion of the Spartan system, see Eyben (1980-81, 23 with n. 66).

82   **Infant-cremations.** See Young 1951, 67ff. The largest of the pyres discovered in the southwest corner of the Agora measures 80cm by 115cm (no. 7), and the smallest 35cm by 65cm. Although the bones are often so minute that they can only be described as 'possibly human' (e.g. nos. 6 and 8), the presence of numerous small funerary vases among the burnt debris 'indicates clearly that they cannot be the remains of simple animal sacrifices' (Rudhardt 1963, 11). It is Young's theory that cremation was practised intramurally for Athenian children at a date when extramural inhumation and cremation was insisted upon for adults that Rudhardt seeks especially to disprove.

Choës. For. refs. see *IG* II² 13139-42; Philostr. *Her.* p. 187.20 *T*. For discussion, see Deubner 1932, 115; van Hoorn 1951, 17; H.R.W. Smith, *CVA* San Fransisco I, p. 48. The *chous* vase was manufactured in two sizes, the larger of which only sometimes carried a scene related to the Anthesteria. Green and Sinclair (1970, 523) comment on the funerary use of the smaller version, that it reflects 'a peculiarly Athenian practice, far more so even than the use of white *lēkythoi*'.

84		**Feeder.** See *KB* 100.

Children's grave-gifts. Pet piglet: Burr 1933, 552f.; *KB* 55. Gold pendant: Agora XIII, 205ff.

Children commemorated on stêlai. Neollarion (after 350): Peek 1955, no. 1499 = Clairmont 1970, no. 17 and pl. 9. Mnesagora and Nikochares (*c.* 420): Clairmont 1970, no. 22 and pl. 11 = Peek 1955, no. 95. Clairmont (84 n. 45) notes that this is possibly the earliest ref. to *daimôn* in epitaphs. The word occurs commonly in a funerary context from the fourth century onwards. Ampharete and her grandchild (*c.* 410): Clairmont 1970, no. 23 and pl. 11 = *KB* pl. 31. Epitaph of Xenokleia (*c.* 360): *IG* II² 12335 (quoted in Humphreys 1983, 108).

87		**Loutrophoroi.** For discussion of marble *loutrophoroi*, see especially Kokula (1974) who maintains that such vases did in fact stand over the graves of the unmarried dead. In her view the two-handled variety stood as a grave-marker for a man and the three-handled type for a woman (182ff.). From surviving exx. of both types, it appears that only one-sixth of the total number was erected in honour of women. It is also striking that the unmarried women are almost invariably represented as being youthful, whereas the men tend to be of maturer years. For *loutrophoroi* in connection with Classical *peribolos* tombs, see Garland 1982b, 400 with n. 20. As Kokula emphasises, such vases were clearly regarded as luxury items.

88		**Hêrôa.** See Bérard 1970, 28ff.; *KB* 298. Situated in the *agora*: Pi. *P.* 5.87 (Battos in Kyrene); Thuk. 1.138.5 (Themistokles in Magnesia). Situated in the *prytaneion*: Hdt. 5.67 (Adrastos and Melanippos in Sikyon). Beside the city-gate: see Lobeck 1829, 281. Within a sanctuary: Pi. *Ol.* 1.93; Paus. 5.13.1 (Pelops at Olympia).

Introduction of hero-worship at Athens. See Alexiou 1974, 19 with ref. to Hdt. 7.6; Rohde 1897, ch. 4. Death of Oedipus. See especially *OC* 1372ff., 1424f. and 1516 (able to foretell the future); 1460, cf. 94 (summoned by a sign); 1542f. (knows the exact spot to die); 1602f. (washed and clothed); 1545 and 1762 (his tomb judged to be *hieros*); 1530ff. (its location to be secret); 1760f. (his spirit not to be invoked).

89		**The war dead at Marathon and Plataia.** See Paus. 1.32.4 and 9.2.5-6; Hdt. 9.85; Thuk. 2.34.5 and 3.58.4; Jacoby 1944b, 40 with n. 11 and p. 47. Though Athens and possibly other cities only exceptionally buried their dead on the battlefield, the facts of war made it impossible to adhere to any system rigidly, see Xen. *Anab.* 6.4.9. See further Jacoby 1944b, 42ff., and Gomme 1956, II p. 94.

90   **Epitaphios logos.** See Thuk. 2.34.6; Plu. *Per.* 28.4; D.H. *Ant. Rom.* 5.17.4; D.S. 11.33; Anaximenes, *FGrH* 72 F 24. For discussion, see Weber 1935, 43ff., and Jacoby 1944b, 39 with notes 8 and 92.

    Dêmosion sêma. See *KB* 108ff.; Stupperich 1977, 26ff.; Garland 1982b, 149.

    Casualty lists. See Bradeen 1964, 1967 and 1969.

92   **Grave monuments erected to the war dead.** Relief in Villa Albani: Clairmont 1970, 43 n. 14. Dexileos relief: Travlos 1971, pl. 411, and Garland 1982b, cat. no. A1a (394/3 B.C.). Relief in Berlin: Clairmont 1970, no. 28 and pl. 14 (420-10 B.C.).

    The dead as agathoi. Cf. *SIG*³ 1225 (Rhodes, third cent. B.C.).

    Disposal of the Homeric dead. For monuments to heroes, see Strabo (*Geog.* 13.1.29ff.). Communal pyres for the ordinary dead: *Il.* 7.331ff. See Page (1959, 315ff.) for discussion of the date of this passage. It is worth pointing out as well that in the *Odyssey* (12.8ff.), there is no thought of transfering the ashes of Elpenor back home from Kirke's island.

93   **Guarding the tomb of the murdered dead.** See Ps.-Dem. 47.69; Poll. 8.65; Harp. s.v. *epenenkein doru*; and possibly Eur. *Tro.* 1147f.

    The anger of the murdered dead. See S. *El.* 442ff. and 482ff.; Aes. *Ch.* 40f. and 278ff.

94   **Maschalismos.** The most thorough discussion of this rite is still to be found in Rohde 1897, Appendix II. The only Classical refs. are Aes. *Ch.* 439 and S. *El.* 445 (with schol. ad loc.). See also Jebb's note on *El.* 445 and Appendix. Later sources all derive from Aristophanes of Byzantium.

    Status of the murdered dead in Hades. See Aes. *Ch.* 354ff. and contrast with S. *El.* 841.

95   **Barathron.** See Plu. *Them.* 22 with Rossiter 1977, 109. For the Kaiades, see Thuk. 1.134.4.

    Anthropological discussions of suicide. See Malinowski 1908, 15; Bushnell 1927, 28; Fenton 1941, 89 and 131; Beattie in Bohannan 1960, 143; La Fontaine in ib., 110f.

96   **Christian attitudes to suicide.** Toynbee (1968, 73) points out: 'At the present day, many ex-Christians, who have abandoned all the rest of the Christian tradition, still retain the Christian feeling that suicide is shocking.' The most famous Christian apology for suicide is John Donne's posthumous work entitled *Biaiothanatos* (1644). Denying that suicide was inevitably sinful, Donne pleaded

for charity and understanding.

Suicide terminology. Words which describe the suicide in Greek include *autocheir* (e.g. S. *Ant.* 1175; Arist. Fr. 502 *T*) and *biaiothanatos* (Vett. Val. 68.7), of which the latter can be also used of a victim of murder. In tragedy the expression *autos pros hautou* ('himself by himself') is regularly used (e.g. S. *Ajax* 906 and *Ant.* 1177). Those who hang themselves are known as *apankomenoi*.

Suicide thoughts in Homer. See *Od* 10.49ff.; *Il.* 3.173; 18.34.

Suicide in tragedy. See S. *Ajax passim*; *Ant. passim* (technically Antigone, Haimon and Eurydike all commit suicide); *Trach.* 719ff.; Eur. *Alk.* 282ff.; *Helen* 135f.; *Herakl.* 500ff.; *Hipp.* 419ff. Suicide pact: Eur. *Helen* 836ff. and 982ff. Suicide wishes: S. *Trach.* 734ff.; Eur. *And.* 804ff. and 846ff.; *Hek.* 1100ff.; *Hipp.* 1410; *Med.* 97, 144f., 227 and 1210. Suicide threat as a form of blackmail: Aes. *Supp.* 154ff.; S. *Phil.* 1207ff; Eur. *Alk.* 897ff.; *Hipp.* 356f.; *IT* 974.

97   **Sokrates on suicide.** Sokrates further elaborates (*Phd.* 62c): 'Perhaps it is not unreasonable to say that a man must not kill himself until god sends some compulsion upon him, as for instance in my own present circumstances.' The peculiarities of Athenian law having made Sokrates a technical suicide by the self-administration of poison, Plato was obliged to avoid an absolute veto on suicide.

99   **Dioblêtoi in mythology.** See Eur. *Alk.* 128ff.; *Supp.* 934ff.; *Bakk.* 244ff.

Gold leaves. The translation of gold leaf A1 as offered is not without difficulties. Zuntz, who argues persuasively against an Orphic origin for the gold leaves, naturally rejects the theory that the deceased is identifying himself with the Titans destroyed by Zeus' thunder. For an account of the excavation of the Timpone Piccolo, see Zuntz (290ff.). Zuntz believes that the earliest tomb (i.e. that which contained A1) was the one found level with the ground, and that the one discovered below ground level was in fact later. There is no surviving description of the third grave.

100   **Deuteropotmoi.** It is perhaps because Alkestis must undergo a similar kind of ritual following her release from the clutches of Thanatos that Admetos has to wait three days before hearing her speak. A curious tale is told by Herodotus (4.14; cf. Pi. Fr. 284 *OCT*) of a poet from Prokonnesos called Aristeas who dropped down dead in a fuller's shop. When the fuller returned with the deceased's relatives, there was no sign of Aristeas anywhere. He turned up later only to disappear once more.

101   **Importance of burial.** Bury (1900, 444) comments on the battle

of Delion: 'There seems little doubt that the conduct of the Boeotians was a greater departure from recognised custom than the conduct of the Athenians.' See Thuk. 4.97. The due of burial was evidently so widely regarded on Greek territory that warring bands of Greek ants, it seems, did not remain unaffected by the sentiment. Plutarch (*Mor.* 967e) quotes a story reported by Kleanthes who allegedly witnessed the return of an ant corpse to the losing ant side in exchange for a grub, which is described as the ransom. 'Some ants,' he says, 'went to an ant-hill, burying the corpse of another ant. Then some others came out of the ant-hill, and, as it were, entered into parley with them. After this they departed. This happened two or three times. Finally the ants living in the ant-hill fetched a grub – the ransom for the corpse, so to speak. The other group picked up the grub, returned the corpse and departed.' This being the practice among the lower order of animals, it should come as no surprise to learn from the second cent. A.D. moralist Aelian (*De nat. animal.* 2.1) that cranes accord the due of burial to their senior member who customarily tours his flock just before it migrates and then drops down dead.

102 **Cenotaphs.** See Hom. *Od.* 1.289ff.; 2.222; 4.584; Thuk. 2.34; Eur. *Helen* 1241ff.; Charito 4.1; *KB* 100 and 257ff.; *AA* 1936, 188. For extensive bibliography, see Vermeule 1979, ch. 1 n. 19.

103 **Ataphoi and apotaphoi.** See Eur. *Hek.* 27ff.; *Tro.* 1081ff.; *Heliod.* 177.15; Luc. *Philops.* 31; Pl. *Ep.* 7.27.11. For the *apotaphos*, the Suda (s.v.), quoting Dinarchos (Fr. 16.5 Bait.-Saup.), gives the definition 'one who has been deprived of his ancestral tombs', whereas Hesychios (s.v.) says they are 'slaves who breakfasted with freemen, and who were not buried with them (i.e. not with slaves)' (emended by Steph.; see Hiller, Syll.³ ad loc.). A third variant is supplied by *Et. Mag.* (s.v.): 'one who is buried separately and in a different place from the grave of the rest of the dead or one who has been deprived of his ancestral tombs.' The British Museum possesses an unusual Rhodian stone *skyphos* (cup) with a relief of ivy leaves below which is inscribed '*apotaphōn taphōn*' in lettering dated to the later Hellenistic period (Fraser 1977, fig. 115a-c). Fraser (p. 69) would translate '"(The boundary) of graves of those buried separately", i.e. the slaves who fell in battle', suggesting the siege of 88 B.C. by Mithradates (Ap. *Mithrad.* 24-7) as an occasion when slaves might have been employed in the service of the city and subsequently honoured with public burial. As Fraser, himself notes, however, 'we should expect an adjective compounded with *apo* to have a privative or

adversative sense'.

7. VISITING THE TOMB

104   **Importance of the cemetery visit.** See Is. 6.65 (visits omitted) and 2.10 (adoption of heir to carry out tomb-cult). Its importance was by no means confined to Attika. Bruck (1926, 177) notes that in Sicily numerous vessels have been found in connection with graves which were evidently used for drink-offerings performed in connection with the cult of the dead. For the *dokimasia*, see Arist. *AP* 55.3 who states that among the questions asked was the following: 'Do you have any *êria* (family tombs)? Where are they?' See also Xen. *Mem.* 2.2.13 and Bonner and Smith 1930, 268.

Women predominate. Not only on vases but also in tragedy women figure most prominently in performing the cult of the tomb, although this is essentially a condition of plot-structure. They include Atossa, Chrysothemis, Elektra, Hermione and Iphigeneia.

Terminology for performing tomb-cult. *Ta nomizomena:* Is. 1.10, 2.10 and 6.65. *Ta nomima:* Thuk. 3.58.4 and Din. 2.8 p.55 *T. Ta hiera patrôa:* Is. 2.46. For *ta nomizomena* used of *prothesis* and funeral, see Is. 4.19, 9.4 and 9.32.

Monthly and annual cemetery visits. Monthly: S. *El.* 277ff. and D.L. 10.18. Annual: D.L. 2.14 and 10.18; Is. 2.46; Pl. *Laws* 4.717e. Explicit references to commemorative rites being held on the birthday of the deceased occur in the case of Epikouros and Antiochos of Commagene (see Humphreys 1980, 101).

106   **Family enclosures.** See Humphreys 1980 and Garland 1982b, *passim*. Humphreys has counted 17 three-generation and 4 four-generation groups. An outstanding exception is the *peribolos* of Meidon of Myrrhinous from which was recovered a *stêlê* recording the names of members of the same family over five generations (Humphreys Table I; Garland cat. no. Q3). As Humphreys points out, Meidon's family was unusual in that it incorporated religious experts. The remarkable continuity which the enclosure demonstrates is therefore best interpreted as self-conscious traditionalism, rather than as evidence of the strength of traditional Athenian piety.

108   **Funerary paintings of the Achilles Painter.** See Furtwängler 1880, 136; Cook 1960, 182; Arias, *et al.*, 1962, 361; *AWL* 41ff.

Baskets. In Homer *kana* are used for distributing bread (*Il.* 9.217 and *Od.* 17.343). Doubtless they remained in domestic service in the historical period. For exx. on *lêkythoi*, see *AWL* pls. 6.1, 18.2, 19.3,

20.1, 20.2, 25.3, 25.4, etc. Instances of their use in a religious but non-funerary context include Ar. *Ach.* 244 and *Peace* 948.
Identification of the deceased on lêkythoi. No firm rules can be established for distinguishing the living from the dead among those figures which stand or sit beside the tomb. Dumont (1874, 56f.) maintained that 'in general' a seated woman at the tomb is the dead. Milchhöfer (1880, 180 n. 3) asserted that it was 'almost a rule' that seated figures and those clothed in white *himatia* are intended to be dead. Pottier (1883, 64f.) more cautiously declared that a seated person 'can sometimes represent the dead, sometimes a survivor'. Kardara (1960, 158) proposed identification on the grounds of the 'pathetic intensity' of expression in the faces of the dead. Finally, Kurtz (*AWL* 223), who pointed out the glaring inconsistencies in the general theory of identifying the seated with the dead, referred to the 'well-established motif of the seated *mourner*'. Since no general interpretation of the role of the seated figure on *lêkythoi* has proved acceptable to the majority of scholars, we are forced to conclude that its meaning depended on the whim of the individual artist, always assuming that he bothered to make a distinction.

Tomb-visits in a heroic context. A red-figure *pelikê* depicts Orestes cutting off a lock of his hair at the tomb of Agamemnon (Cook 1960, pl. 50). It is dated *c.* 380. South Italian vases frequently show gatherings around an elaborate funerary shrine (Cook 1960, 197).

Disappearance of lêkythoi as grave-gifts. Ar. *Ekk.* 994ff., which refers to an old woman painting *lêkythoi* for the dead, suggests that such vases continued to serve as grave-gifts down until the late 390s. (For the date of the play, see Ussher 1973, xxiff.). Kurtz (*AWL* 73), however, suggests that this passage may refer to stone *lêkythoi*.

Foundations. Epikouros: D.L. 10.16ff. Will of Epiktete: *IG* XII 3.330; *DHR* II 1.77ff.; Humphreys 1980, 122 with n. 61. See also Fraser (1953) for a testamentary inscription recording the foundation of a shrine in honour of Artemis (?), Zeus Hikesios and the *theoi patrôoi.*

110 **Terminology for the feast of the dead.** See Artem. *Oneirokr.* 1.4; Plu. *Arist.* 21. The expression *daites ennomoi brotôn* in Aes. *Ch.* 483ff. is especially interesting. *LSJ⁹* render *ennomos* as 'ordained by law', whereas Verrall (1893, ad loc.) connected it with *nemô* and translated 'awarding to you among the rest'. Accordingly Verrall renders 'the feasts of the living will be made so as to include your share', which presupposes that food brought to the tomb was intended for

consumption by the living and dead jointly, which, I suggest below, may have been irregular. I propose instead: 'the feasts will be made so that you (like the other dead) are awarded your portion by the living.' It is noteworthy that in the following line the denial of a share of the feast to a dead man is spoken of as rendering him *atimos* (dishonoured) among his own number. For *enagismata* and *choai* coupled together, see Is. 6.51 and 65; Ar. Fr. 488.12ff. *CAF*.

112   **Ayia Triada sarcophagus.** See Long 1974, pls. 30 and 31. Long (p. 68) suggests that the scene may represent a sacrifice to the afterworld deities, carried out in order to ensure the deceased's safe arrival in their realm.

Odysseus' sacrifice to the dead. See Rohde 1897, 36ff.; Nilsson 1925, 141; Garland 1982a, 74.

Terminology for blood sacrifices. *Haimakouriai*: Pi. *Ol.* 1.90; Plu. *Arist.* 21; Hsch. and *Et Mag.* s.v.; Wyse 1904, 271. *Sphagia entemnein*: Thuk. 5.11 and Plu. *Solon* 9.

Blood sacrifices. Sheep: Hom. *Od.* 11.35f. and Eur. *El.* 92. Ox: Plu. *Solon* 21. Animal bones found in graves: *KB* 66. Sex and colour of victim: Rohde 1897, ch. 5 n. 107; Stengel 1910, 136. As Stengel notes, in the case of sacrifices made to underworld deities, the victim was generally male. Head of victim looking down: Eust. on *Il.* 1.459. Victim skinned: Hom. *Il.* 23.174, cf. 1.459. There is, however, no evidence for this practice which postdates Homer. Time of sacrifice: Stengel 1910, 133f. Although Orestes performs his sacrifice to the dead at night (Eur. *El.* 90ff.), his motive for doing so is to escape detection and therefore cannot be judged typical.

113   **Melitoutta.** There is a ref. in Ar. *Clouds* (507) to *melitoutta* being given to snakes who lived in the cave by those seeking oracular responses from the hero Trophonios. Snakes were commonly identified with the dead and associated with them in worship. See fig. 3. They appear frequently on Totenmahl reliefs. For honey cakes possibly projecting from baskets being brought to the dead, see *AWL* pls. 19.3 and 44.1.

Burning food offerings to the dead. See Phot. and Hsch. s.v. *kauston*. See also the instances collected by Rohde 1897, ch. 5 n. 107.

Terminology for drink offerings. Although *choai* is the word most commonly used for drink-offerings to the dead, other names also occur, such as *loibai* (S. *El.* 52; Eust. on *Od.* 10.518; Hsch. s.v.) and *pelanon* (Aes. *Ch.* 92 and *Pers.* 816). Hsch. defines *loibê* as simply 'an offering of wine'. The scholiast on Aes. *Ch.* 91 says of *pelanon* that it is the name given to anything that is offered in sacrifice. Tucker

(1901, ad loc.) thinks this to be too comprehensive a definition and would explain as 'a thick mess, a cake or clotted liquid'. Whatever the ingredients of the *pelanon*, it was certainly poured (cf. Aes. *Ch.* 92).

114   **Drink offerings to the dead in Minoan and Mycenaean times.** Ayia Triada sarcophagus: Long 1974, pp. 35ff., figs. 17 and 37. Mesara tombs: Branigan 1970, 92ff. Mycenaean tombs: Blegen 1937, 237f.; Travlos and Vermeule 1966, 66f.

Difference between choê and spondê. Eust. on *Od.* 10.518. Lucas (1969, 62) rightly points out that Eustathios' rule is somewhat too rigid, 'since *spondai* were on occasion offered to *nerteroi*, at the taking of oaths, at the libations to heroes and to Zeus Soter, and, more to the point, on such occasions as is described at Eur. *El.* 511' – i.e. where the Old Man pours *spondai* at Agamemnon's tomb. Lucas suggests that the pouring of *spondai* on a grave may have been more informal than the pouring of *choai*, which was possibly restricted to members of the family. For confusion of terminology, see Aes. *Ch.* 149 (*tasd' epispendô choas*). The god Thanatos, personification of Death, is described as *aspondos* (Eur. *Alk.* 424), but possibly the epithet should simply be interpreted as meaning 'implacable, admitting of no truce' (*LSJ⁰*), rather than 'he who does not receive *spondai*'.

Feeding tubes. See *KB* 58; Nock 1932, 332; Dodds 1951, ch. 5 n. 8. Paus. (10.4.10) tells of a Phokian hero whose grave was penetrated by a hole through which the blood of victims was poured. Brouskari (1980) reports the discovery of clay piping possibly intended to facilitate the passage of blood to the dead in a fourth-century *peribolos* which had been erected around earlier graves. Of the 130 or so *periboloi* in my catalogue (Garland 1982b), I know of no other example which was so provided.

Ingredients of choai. Aes. *Pers.* 610ff.: milk, honey, water, wine and oil. Aes. *Ch.* 92: *pelanon*. S. *El.* 894: milk. Eur. *El.* 511: wine. Eur. *Or.* 115f.: honey, milk and wine. Plu. *Arist.* 21: wine and milk. The mixed drink offered to the dead was called *melikraton*. According to Eustathios (on *Od.* 10.519), this consisted of water and honey in Homeric times, but milk and honey thereafter (cf. Eur. *Or.* 115). Stengel (1880, 379) suggests that milk was an essential ingredient of all *choai*, but this cannot be proved.

115   **Vases used at libation ceremonies.** Cf. *AWL* pls. 42.2 and 43.2 (*hydriai*); 27.4 and 28.2 (*oinochoai*); 30.2 and 43.2 (*phialai*). *Lêkythoi*, by far the commonest vase to appear in such scenes, are too

numerous to list. A squat *lêkythos* (pl. 30.1) and *aryballos* (pl. 26.2) are
also represented. Drinking-vessels (pls. 19.1 and 30.1) and a *sakkos* or
wine-strainer (pls. 19.1 and possibly 30.1, 36.1) also appear at the
tomb. For the pouring of libations, see Eur. *Or.* 114ff. and 1187ff. It
goes without saying, however, that vases which appear on *lêkythoi*
whether in the hands of celebrants or placed on the tomb itself, need
not necessarily have been used for administering *choai*, as they can be
explained simply as offerings to the dead, independent of any ritual
significance. To my knowledge, the only vase actually depicted in use
is the *hydria*, which is shown being held by its vertical (i.e. normally
pouring) handle (*AWL* pls. 42.2 and 43.2). Judging from the varied
nature of the liquids themselves, however, it is likely that several
different types of vases were employed.

    Plêmochoê. Cf. *AWL* pls. 18.3, 32:1, 33.2, 35.3, 36.2 and 38.3.
Such so-called *plêmochoai* are a particular feature of the Achilles
Painter's work, often being 'prominently placed in the centre of the
tomb's base' (Kurtz *AWL* 214). The vase gave its name to the last
day of the Eleusinian Mysteries known as *Plêmochoai*, the main
business of which was libations and rites in honour of the dead (cf.
Ath. 11.496 and Hsch. s.v.). For further discussion, see Mylonas
(1962, 279) and Kerenyi (1960, 141). For a different identification of
the *plêmochoê* see Beazley (1946, 12).

    Vases smashed after pouring the choai. As *KB* 215f. note, it is
only rarely that excavators can be certain that vases were
deliberately broken in or near the tomb. Breaking, bending and
burning were the principal methods of killing or cancelling an object
for exclusive use in the spirit world below. See further *KB* (loc. cit.)
and above p. 3.

116   **Decorating the tomb with taeniai.** Wound around the shaft of
the *stêlê*: AWL pls. 19.2, 19.3, 29.3, 32.4, 35.3, 40.3, etc. Hanging
suspended from the top of the *stêlê*: *AWL* pl. 33.2. Decorating the
surface of a burial mound: Smith 1896, pl. 26. Ribbon fillets also
appear on tombstones, either painted on (*AWL* pl. 46.3) or rendered
in relief (*AM* 1970, pl. 45.3). In addition, they are sometimes shown
draped over the corpse at the *prothesis* (Pottier 1883, 67f. and pl. 1).
For a *lêkythos* showing *stêlai* with several *taeniai* see *AWL* pl. 26.2. On
AWL pl. 20.1 a woman brings a basket containing six ribbons to a
stêlê already decorated with two. For the tubular type of fillet, see
AWL pls. 33.2, 33.3, 35.3 and 39.1. As Fairbanks (1914, II p. 232)
points out: 'the decorative *taenia* may have received quite undue

emphasis in *lêkythos* scenes because it so well served the painter's purpose'.

Floral tributes. For refs. in epigrams, see Lattimore *TGLE* 129. Myrtle branches: *AWL* pls. 23.3 and 26.2; Eur. *El.* 324 and 512; Schol.on Pi. *I.* 3.11. Wreath placed on tomb: *AWL* pls. 22.1, 25.1, 29.4 and 36.3. Celery: Plu. *Mor.* 676d; D.L. 8.57; Rohde 1897, ch. 5 n. 40. According to Plu. *Tim.* 26 the fact that celery was chiefly reserved for use as a floral tribute to the dead was the explanation behind the expression 'X needs celery', which was said of a person who was critically ill.

The dead as fertilisers. See Eur. Fr. 757 *TGF*; *Epigr. gr.* 606.4. Humphreys (1983, 159f.) is rightly cautious of the association between death and fertility which she suspects of having been projected onto 'savage' societies by nineteenth-century anthropologists, pursuing 'a train of thought which was already implicit in the anthropologists' own culture'.

118 **Gift of a lock of hair.** See Aes. *Ch.* 6; S. *El.* 52 and 449; Eur. *IT* 172f.; *Or.* 128. Bruck (1926, 144) interpreted the hair-offering by the Achaean army to the corpse of Patroklos before it sets out on its *ekphora* as an 'ersatz human sacrifice'. See Hom. *Il.* 23.135f.

119 **Beliefs about Hades and the grave not mutually exclusive.** Pottier (1883, 84) long ago commented that in spite of all the attempts by poets, philosophers and exponents of the Eleusinian Mysteries to educate the Athenian populace into new beliefs about the afterlife, 'people will always be unwilling to think of the dead as completely rid of all humanity and the needs thereof, and the foundation of their beliefs will always be based on the physical existence of the dead at the bottom of his tomb'. So, too, Nock (1932, 332f.) held that the burial place 'retains its importance, even when it is dogmatically held that the essential element in the man we loved is elsewhere'. Lucian mocked such confused notions by describing the dead in Hades as skeletons piled on top of each other, each allowed to occupy one foot of earth (*D. Mort.* 18.2, 20.2, etc.). For conflation of belief in Greek and Roman epigrams, see Welles 1941, 81f. and 90. For further discussion, see Rohde (1897, ch. 5 n. 136; ch. 14.2 n. 92).

Lyres at the graveside. See Murray and Smith 1896, pl. 13: one lyre rests against the grave, another is being played. *AWL* pls. 18.2 and 31.2: lyre hanging in the background. *AWL* pl. 28.2: lyre resting on top of tomb. Smith 1896, pl. 28: lyre resting against the plinth. *WAL* pl. 61: lyre placed by seated figure.

Bibliography

Page references quoted in the text are to the edition cited in the right-hand column of this bibliography. Since the history of scholarly opinion is itself relevant to this inquiry, the date of publication by which the page reference is proceeded is normally to the first edition of the work.

Adkins 1960   Adkins, A.W.H. *Merit and Responsibility*. Oxford 1960.

Agora XIII   Immerwahr, S.A. *The Athenian Agora* vol. XIII (The Neolithic and Bronze Ages). The American School of Classical Studies at Athens. Princeton, New Jersey 1971.

Ahlberg 1971   Ahlberg, G. *Prothesis and Ekphora in Greek Geometric Art* (Stud. in Medit. Arch. 32). Göteborg 1971.

Alexiou 1974   Alexiou, M. *The Ritual Lament in Greek Tradition*. Cambridge 1974.

Alexiou 1972   Alexiou, S. '*Larnakes kai angeia ek taphou para to Gazi Herakleiou*', *AE* 1972, pp. 86ff.

Allen,*et al.* 1936   Allen, T.W., Halliday, W.R., and Sikes, E.E. *The Homeric Hymns*. Oxford 1936.

Andronikos 1968   Andronikos, M. 'Totenkult' in *Archaeologica Homerica* Band III, Kapitel W. Göttingen 1968.

ANET   *Ancient Near Eastern Texts relating to the Old Testament*. Ed. J.B. Pritchard. 2nd ed. Princeton 1955.

Arias, *et al.* 1962   Arias, P.E., Hirmer, M. and Shefton, B.B. *A History of Greek Vase Painting*. London 1962.

Ariès 1974   Ariès, P. *Western Attitudes to Death from the Middle Ages to the Present*. London and Baltimore 1974.

Arthur 1977   Arthur, M. 'Politics and Pomegranates: an Interpretation of the Homeric Hymn to Demeter', *Arethusa* 10 no.1 (1977), pp. 7ff.

Austin 1977   Austin, R.G. *Virgil Aeneid VI*. Oxford 1977.

ARV   Beazley, J.D. *Attic Red-Figure Vase-Painters*. 3 vols. 2nd ed. Oxford 1963.

AWL   Kurtz, D. *Attic White Lêkythoi: Patterns and Painters*. Oxford 1975.

Barrett 1964   Barrett, W.S. *Euripides' Hippolytos*. Oxford 1964.

Bassett 1933   Bassett, S. 'Achilles' Treatment of Hektor's Body', *TAPhA* 64 (1933), pp. 41ff.

Beattie 1960   Beattie, J.H.M. 'Homicide and Suicide in North Kavirondo', pp. 179ff. in Bohannan 1960.

Beazley 1914   Beazley, J.D. 'Master of the Achilles Amphora in the Vatican', *JHS* 34 (1914), pp. 179ff.

Beazley 1938   Beazley, J.D. 'Attic White Lêkythoi', *The William Henry Charlton Memorial Lecture 1937*. Oxford 1938.

Beazley 1946 Beazley, J.D. 'A Lekythos by the Achilles Painter', *JHS* 66 (1946), p. 11f.
Beazley 1951 Beazley, J.D. *The Development of Attic Black-Figure*. London 1951.
Bérard 1970 Bérard, C. *Eretria. Fouilles et recherches III: l'heróon à la porte de l'ouest*. Berne 1970.
Bickel 1925 Bickel, E. *Homerischer Seelenglaube*. Berlin 1925.
Binford 1972 Binford, L.R. 'Mortuary Practices: their Study and Potential' in *An Archaeological Perspective*, pp. 208ff. New York 1972.
Blegen 1937 Blegen, C.W. *Prosymna. The Helladic Settlement preceding the Argive Heraeum*. Cambridge, Mass. 1937.
Boardman 1955 Boardman, J. 'Painted Funerary Plaques and Some remarks on Prothesis', *ABSA* 50 (1955), pp. 51ff.
Boardman 1977 Boardman, J. 'The Parthenon Frieze – Another View' pp. 39ff. in *Festchrift für Frank Brommer*. Mainz 1977.
Boardman 1980 Boardman, J. 'Posthumous Prospects', a review of *Aspects of Death in Early Greek Art and Poetry*, by E. Vermeule in *The Times Literary Supplement* 25/1/1980, p.97.
Boeckh 1806 Boeckh, A. *In Platonis qui vulgo fertur Minoem*. Halis Saxonum 1806.
Boehme 1929 Boehme, J. *Die Seele und das Ich im homerischen Epos*. Leipzig and Berlin 1929.
Boersma 1970 Boersma, J.S. *Athenian Building Policy from 561/0 to 405/4 B.C.* Groningen 1870.
Bohannan 1960 Ed. P. Bohannan. *African Homicide and Suicide*. Princeton, N.J. 1960.
Bolkestein 1922 Bolkestein, H. 'The Exposure of Children at Athens and the *enchytristriai*', *CP* 17 (1922), pp. 222ff.
Bonner and Smith 1930 Bonner, R.J. and Smith, G. *The Administration of Justice from Homer to Aristotle*. Chicago 1930.
Bosanquet 1896 Bosanquet, R.C. 'On a Group of Early Attic Lêkythoi', *JHS* 16 (1896), pp. 164ff.
Bosanquet 1899 Bosanquet, R.C. 'Some Early Funeral Lêkythoi', *JHS* 19 (1899), pp. 169ff.
Boulter 1963 Boulter, C.G. 'Graves in Lenormant Street, Athens', *Hesperia* 32 (1963), pp. 113ff.
Bousquet 1966 Bousquet, J. 'Le cippe des Labyadcs', *BCH* 90 (1966), pp. 82ff.
Bradeen 1964 Bradeen, D.W. 'Athenian Casualty Lists', *Hesperia* 33 (1964), pp. 16ff.
Bradeen 1967 Bradeen, D.W. 'The Athenian Casualty List of 464 BC', *Hesperia* 36 (1967), pp. 321ff.
Bradeen 1969 Bradeen, D.W. 'The Athenian Casualty Lists', *CQ* 19 (1969), pp. 145ff.
Branigan 1970 Branigan, K. *The Tombs of Mesara*, London 1970.
Brommer 1953 Brommer, F. *Herakles*. Münster and Koln 1953.
Brouskari 1980 Brouskari, M. 'A Dark Age Cemetery in Erechtheion Street, Athens', *ABSA* 75 (1980), pp. 13ff.
Bruck 1926 Bruck, E.F. *Totenteil und Seelgerät im griechischen Recht*. 2nd ed. München 1926.
Brückner 1908 Brückner, A. 'Ausgrabungen an der Hagia Triada', *AM* 33 (1908), pp. 193ff.
Brückner 1909 Brückner, A. *Der Friedhof am Eridanos*. Berlin 1909.
Brückner and Pernice 1893 Brückner, A., and Pernice, E. 'Ein attischer Friedhof',

AM 18 (1893), pp. 73ff.

Buck 1952   Buck, C.D. *The Greek Dialects*. Chicago 1952.

Burkert 1972   Burkert, W. *Homo Necans: Interpretationen altgriechischer Opferriten und Mythen*. Berlin and New York 1972.

Burr 1933   Burr, D. 'A Geometric House and a Proto-Attic Votive Deposit', *Hesperia* 2 (1933), pp. 542ff.

Bury 1900   Bury, J.B. *A History of Greece*. Revised by R. Meiggs. 3rd ed. London 1963.

Bushnell 1927   Bushnell, D.I. 'Burials of the Algonquin, Siouan and Caddoan Tribes West of the Mississippi', *Bureau of Amer. Ethnology* 83 (1927), pp. 27ff.

CAF   Kock, Th. *Comicorum atticorum fragmenta*. 3 vols. Leipzig 1880-88.

Cameron 1932   Cameron, A. 'The Exposure of Children and Greek Ethics', *CR* 46 (1932), pp. 105ff.

Chantraine 1968   Chantraine, P., *Dictionnaire étymologique de la lanque grecque: Histoire des mots*. Paris 1968-80.

Chantraine and Masson 1954   Chantraine, P., and Masson, O. 'Sur quelques termes du vocabulaire religieux des Grecs: la valeur du mot *agos* et de ses dérivés' in *Sprachgeschichte und Wortbedeutung: Festschrift Albert Debrunner*, pp.85ff. Bern 1954.

Clairmont 1970   Clairmont, C. *Gravestone and Epigram*. Mainz 1970.

Clinton 1974   Clinton, K. 'The Sacred Officials of the Eleusinian Mysteries', *TAPhS* (N.S.) 64 part 3 (1974).

Coldsteam 1977   Coldstream, J.N. *Geometric Greece*. London 1977.

Collignon 1879   Collignon, M. 'Note sur les cérémonies funèbres en Attique', *Annales de la Faculté des Lettres de Bordeaux*, 1 (1897), pp. 315ff.

Conze no./pl.   Conze, A. *Die attischen Grabreliefs*. 4 vols. Berlin 1893-1922.

Cook 1940   Cook, A.B. *Zeus: a Study in Ancient Religion*. 3 vols. Cambridge 1940.

Cook 1960   Cook, R.M. *Greek Painted Pottery*. London 1969.

Cook 1976   Cook, B.F. *Greek and Roman Art in the British Museum*. London 1976.

Corbett 1960   Corbett, P.E. 'The Burgon and Blacas Tombs', *JHS* 80 (1960), pp. 52ff.

Couilloud 1974   Couilloud, M.-T. *Les monuments funéraires de Rhénée*. (Delos, Fascicule 30). Paris 1974.

Crusius in *ML*   Crusius, O. *S.v.* 'Keres'.

Cumont 1922   Cumont, F. *After Life in Roman Paganism*. New Haven 1922.

Cunningham 1971   Cunningham, I.C. *Herodas: Mimiambi*. Oxford 1971.

CVA   *Corpus Vasorum Antiquorum*.

Dakaris 1973   Dakaris, S. 'The Oracle of the Dead on the Acheron', pp.139-49 in *Temples and Sanctuaries of Ancient Greece* (ed. E. Melas) London 1973.

Dale 1954   Dale, A.M. *Euripides' Alcestis*. Oxford 1954.

Dale 1967   Dale, A.M. *Euripides' Helen*. Oxford 1967.

Danforth 1982   Danforth, L.M. *The Death Rituals of Rural Greece* (photography by A. Tsiaras). Princeton 1982.

Daux 1958   Daux, G. 'Chronique des fouilles en 1957', *BCH* 82 (1958), p. 681.

Deonna 1955   Deonna, W. 'Cimetières de bébés', *Rev. archéol. de l'est et du centre-est* (Dijon 1955), pp. 232ff.

De Ruyt 1934   De Ruyt, F. *Charun, demon étrusque de la mort*. Rome 1934.

Detienne 1977   Detienne, M. *Dionysos Slain*. Trans. M. and L. Muellner. Eng. ed. London and Baltimore 1979.

Deubner 1932   Deubner, L. *Attische Feste*. Berlin 1932.

Devereux 1961   Devereux, G. 'Mohave Ethnopsychiatry and Suicide', *Bureau of American Ethnology* No. 175 (1961).

DHR   Dareste, R., Haussoullier, B., and Reinach, Th. *Receuil des inscriptions juridiques.* 2 vols. Paris 1898.

Diehl in *PW*   Diehl, E. *S.v.* 'Kommos'.

Diels 1890   Diels, H. *Sibyllinische Blätter.* Berlin 1890.

Dietrich 1965   Dietrich, B. *Death, Fate and the Gods.* London 1965.

DK   Diels, H. and Kranz, W. *Die Fragmente der Vorsokratiker.* 6th ed. 3 vols. Berlin 1951.

Dodds 1951   Dodds, E. *The Greeks and the Irrational.* Berkeley and Los Angeles 1951.

Dodds 1959   Dodds, E. *Plato's Gorgias.* Oxford 1959.

Dohrn 1957   Dohrn, T. *Attische Plastik.* Krefeld 1957.

Douglas 1967   Douglas, J.D. *The Social Meanings of Suicide.* Princeton, New Jersey 1967.

Douglas 1968   Douglas, M. Essay on 'Pollution' reprinted in *Implicit Meanings.* London 1976.

Dow and Travis 1943   Dow, S. and Travis, A.H. 'Demetrios of Phaleron and his Lawgiving', *Hesperia* 12 (1943), pp. 145ff.

DS   Daremberg, C., and Saglio, E. *Dictionnaire des antiquités.* 5 vols. Paris 1877-1919.

Dublin 1963   Dublin, L.I. Suicide: *A Sociological and Statistical Study.* New York 1963.

Dumont 1874   Dumont, A. *Peintures céramiques de la Grèce propre: recherches sur les noms d'artistes lus sur les vases de la Grèce.* Paris 1874.

Eckstein 1958   Eckstein, F. 'Die attischen Grabmalergesetze', *JdI* 73 (1958), pp. 18ff.

EGF   Kinkel, G. *Epicorum Graecorum Fragmenta.* Leipzig 1877.

Eitrem 1909   Eitrem, S. *Hermes und die Toten.* Christiania 1909.

Epigr. gr.   Kaibel, G. *Epigrammata graeca ex lapidibus conlecta.* Berlin 1878.

Eyben 1980-81   Eyben, E. 'Family Planning in Antiquity', *Ancient Society* 11-12 (1980-81), pp. 5-82.

Fairbanks 1914   Fairbanks, A. *Athenian White Lêkythoi.* 2 vols. New York 1914.

Farnell 1907   Farnell, L.R. *The Cults of the Greek States.* 5 vols. Oxford 1907.

Farnell 1921   Farnell, L.R. *Greek Hero Cults and Ideas of Immortality.* Oxford 1921.

Fenton 1941   Fenton, W.N. 'Iroquois Suicides: a Study in the Stability of a Culture Pattern', *Bureau of American Ethnology Bulletin* no. 128 (1941): Anthrop. Papers no. 14, pp. 79ff.

FGrH   Jacoby, F. *Die Fragmente der griechischen Historiker.* Berlin 1923.

FHG   Müller, C. *Fragmenta historicorum graecorum.* 5 vols. Paris 1841-70.

Flacelière 1966   Flacelière, R., and Devambez, P. *Héraclès: images et récits.* Paris 1966.

Fraenkel 1950   Fraenkel, E. *Aeschylus' Agamemnon.* 3 vols. Oxford 1950.

Fraser 1953   Fraser, P.M. 'An Inscription from Cos', *Bull. Soc. Arch. d'Alexandrie* 40 (1953), pp. 35ff.

Fraser 1977   Fraser, P.M. *Rhodian Funerary Monuments.* Oxford 1977.

Freud 1913   Freud, S. *Totem and Taboo: Some Points of Agreement between the Mental Lives of Savages and Neurotics.* Trans. J. Strachey. New ed. Trowbridge and Esher 1960.

Freud 1919   Freud, S. 'The Uncanny', pp. 218ff. in vol.17 of *The Complete Psychological Works of Sigmund Freud.* Trans. J. Strachey, *et al.* London 1955.

Friedländer 1935   Friedländer, P. 'Zur New Yorker Nekyia', *AA* 50 (1935), cols. 20ff.

Friedrich 1956   Friedrich, W.-H. *Verwundung und Tod in der Ilias* = Abh. Göttingen, 3. Folge, vol. 38 (1956).

Freistedt 1928   Freistedt, E. 'Altchristliche Totengedächtnistage', *Liturgiegeschichtliche Quellen und Forschungen* 24 (1928).

Frisk 1960   *Griechisches etymologisches Worterbuch*. Heidelberg 1960.

Fuchs 1961   Fuchs, W. Review of Dohrn, T., *Attische Plastik vom Tode des Phidias bis zum Wirken der grossen Meister des 4 Jh. v. Chr.* (Krefell 1957) in *Gnomon* 33 (1961), pp. 237ff.

Fugier 1963   Fugier, H. *Recherches sur l'expression du sacré dans la langue Latine.* Paris 1963.

Furtwängler 1880   Furtwängler, A. 'Attische Lêkythos', *Arch. Zeit.* 38 (1880), pp. 134ff.

Fustel 1864   Fustel de Coulanges, N. *La cité antique.* Paris 1864.

Ganschinietz in *PW*   Ganschinietz, R. S.v. 'Katabasis'.

Ganszyniec in *PW*   Ganszyniec. S.v. 'Kranz'.

Gardner 1896   Gardner, P. *Sculptured Tombs of Hellas.* New York 1896.

Garland 1981   Garland, R.S.J. 'The Causation of Death in the *Iliad*: a Theological and Biological Investigation', *BICS* 28 (1981), pp. 43-60.

Garland 1982a   Garland, R.S.J. '*Geras Thanontôn*: an Investigation into the Claims of the Homeric Dead', *BICS* 29 (1982), pp. 69-80.

Garland 1982b   Garland, R.S.J. 'A First Catalogue of Attic Peribolos Tombs', *ABSA* 77 (1982), pp. 125-176.

GGR[3]   Nilsson, M.P. *Geschichte der griechischen Religion (Handbuch der Altertums Wissenschaft* V.2.1). 3rd ed. München 1967.

van Gennep 1909   van Gennep, A. *The Rites of Passage.* Trans M. Vizedom and G.L. Caffee. London 1960.

Giangrande 1968   Giangrande, G. 'Sympotic Literature and Epigram' in *Fondation Hardt: Entretiens* XIV *L'épigramme grecque.* Geneva 1968.

Glotz in *DS*   Glotz, G. *S.v.* 'Expositio'.

Gomme 1933   Gomme, A.W. *The Population of Athens in the Fifth and Fourth Centuries B.C.* Oxford 1933.

Gomme 1956, II   Gomme, A.W. *A Historical Commentary on Thucydides.* Vol. II. Oxford 1956.

Gorer 1965   Gorer, G. *Death, Grief and Mourning in Contemporary Britain.* London 1965.

Gow 1950   Gow, A.S.F. *Theocritus: edited with a Translation and Commentary.* 2 vols. Cambridge 1950.

Green and Sinclair 1970   Green, J.R. and Sinclair, R.K. 'Athenians in Eretria', *Historia* 19 (1970), pp. 515-27.

Griffin 1977   Griffin, J. 'The Epic Cycle and the Uniqueness of Homer', *JHS* 97 (1977), pp. 39ff.

Griffin 1980   Griffin, J. *Homer on Life and Death.* Oxford 1980.

Hainsworth 1972   Hainsworth, J. *Tituli ad dialectos graecas illustrandas selecti.* Vol. II (Tituli dorici et ionici). Textus minores 44. Leiden 1972.

Hampe 1960   Hampe, R. *Ein frühattischer Grabfund.* Mainz 1960.

Harrison 1900   Harrison, J. 'Pandora's Box', *JHS* 20 (1900), pp. 99ff.

Harrison 1908   Harrison, J. *Prolegomena to the Study of Greek Religion.* 3rd ed. New York 1955.

Harrison 1913   Harrison, J. *Ancient Art and Ritual.* Bradford-on-Avon 1978.

Harrison 1921   Harrison, J. *Epilegomena to the Study of Greek Religion.* Cambridge 1921.

Headlam and Knox 1922   Headlam, W., and Knox, A.D. *Herondas: the Mimes and Fragments.*Cambridge 1922.

Hertz 1907   Hertz, R. *Death and the Right Hand*. Trans. R. and C. Needham. Aberdeen 1960.
Herzog 1928   Herzog, R. *Heilige Gesetze von Kos*. Berlin 1928.
Homolle 1895   Homolle, Th. 'Règlements de la phratrie des *Labuadai*', *BCH* 19 (1895), pp. 5ff.
van Hoorn 1951   van Hoorn, G. *Choes and Anthesteria*. Leiden 1951.
Humphreys 1978   Humphreys, S.C. *Anthropology and the Greeks*. London 1978.
Humphreys 1980   Humphreys, S.C. 'Family Tombs and Tomb Cult in Ancient Athens – Tradition or Traditionalism?', *JHS* 100 (1980), pp. 96ff.
Humphreys 1982   Humphreys, S.C. *The Anthropology and Archaeology of Death; Transience and Permanence*. Ed. S.C. Humphreys and H. King. London 1982.
Humphreys 1983   Humphreys, S.C. *The Family, Women and Death*. London 1983.
Humphreys and Momigliano 1980   Humphreys, S.C., and Momigliano, A. Foreword to Fustel de Coulanges' *The Ancient City*. Baltimore 1980.
Huntington and Metcalf 1979   Huntington, R. and Metcalf, P. *Celebrations of Death: The Anthropology of Mortuary Ritual*. Cambridge 1979.
Huxley 1969   Huxley, G.L. *Greek Epic Poetry*. London 1969.
IEG   West, M.L. *Iambi et Elegi Graeci ante Alexandrium cantati*. 2 vols. Oxford 1972.
IG   *Inscriptiones Graecae*.
ILS   Dessau, H. *Inscriptiones Latinae Selectae*. 3 vols. Berlin 1892-191.
Inez 1935-36   Inez, M. 'Homeric and Beowulfian Funeral Rites', *CB* 12 (1935-36), pp. 65ff.
Inscr. Cr.   Guarducci, M. *Inscriptiones Creticae*. Rome 1935.
Jacobsthal 1934-36   Jacobsthal, P. 'The Nekyia Krater in New York', *Metropolitan Museum Studies* 5 (1934-36), pp. 117ff.
Jacoby 1944a   Jacoby, F. '*GENESIA*: a forgotten Festival of the Dead', *CQ* 38 (1944), pp. 65ff.
Jacoby 1944b   Jacoby, F. 'Patrios Nomos: State Burial in Athens and the Public Cemetery in the Kerameikos', *JHS* 64 (1944), pp. 37ff.
Jaeger 1936   Jaeger, W. *The Theology of the Early Greek Philosophers*. The Gifford Lectures 1936. Trans. E.S. Robinson. Oxford 1947.
Jebb 1896   Jebb, R.C. *Sophocles' Ajax*. Cambridge 1896.
Jebb 1907   Jebb, R.C. *Sophocles' Electra*. Cambridge 1907.
Jeffery 1961   Jeffery, L.H. *The Local Scripts of Archaic Greece*. Oxford 1961.
Jeffery 1962   Jeffery, L.H. 'The Inscribed Gravestones of Archaic Attica', *ABSA* 57 (1962), pp. 115ff.
Jevons 1895   Jevons, F.B. 'Greek Law and Folk Lore', *CR* 9 (1895), pp. 247ff.
Johansen 1951   Johansen, K.F. *The Attic Grave Reliefs of the Classical Period*. Copenhagen 1951.
Kallipolites 1963   Kallipolites, V. '*Anaskaphê taphôn Anagyrountos*', *AD* 18 (1963) A, pp. 115ff.
Kallipolites and Petrakos 1963   Kallipolites, V. and Petrakos, V. 'Attika and Aigina', *AD* 18 (1963) Chron. B1, pp. 43ff.
Kamerbeek 1974   Kamerbeek, J.C. *Sophocles' Electra*. Leiden 1974.
Kamps 1937   Kamps, W. 'Les origines de la fondation culturelle dans la Grèce ancienne', *Archives d'histoire du droit Oriental* 1 (1937), pp. 145ff.
Karageorghis 1967   Karageorghis, V. *Excavations in the Necropolis of Salamis*. Nicosia 1967.
Kardara 1960   Kardara, C.P. 'Four White Lekythoi in the National Museum of

Athens', *ABSA* 55 (1960), pp. 149ff.

Karouzou 1946   Karouzou, S. 'Choes', *AJA* 50 (1946), pp. 122ff.

Karouzou 1947-48   Karouzou, S. 'Un cimetière de l'epoque classique à Athènes', *BCH* 71-72 (1947-48), pp. 385ff.

Karusos 1962   Karusos, Chr. '*Aspil'en Neoisin*', *AM* 77 (1962), pp. 121ff.

KB   Kurtz, D.C., and Boardman, J. *Greek Burial Customs*. London 1971.

KER VI.I   Kübler, K. *Die Nekropole des Späten 8. bis frühen 6. Jahrhunderts (Kerameikos, Ergebnisse der Ausgrabungen* VI.I). Berlin 1959.

KER VII.II   Kübler, K. *Die Nekropole der Mitte des 6 bis Ende des 5. Jahrhunderts (Kerameikos, Ergebnisse der Ausgrabungen* VII.I). Berlin 1976.

KER IX   Knigge, U. *Der Sudhügel (Kerameikos. Ergebnisse der Ausgrabungen* IX). Berlin 1976.

Kerényi 1967   Kerényi C. *Eleusis: Archetypal Image of Mother and Daughter*. London 1967.

Kern 1922   Kern, O. *Orphicorum Fragmenta*. Berlin 1922.

Keuls 1974   Keuls, E. *The Water Carriers in Hades: a Study of Catharsis through Toil in Classical Antiquity*. Amsterdam 1974.

King 1903   King, J.E. 'Infant Burial', *CR* 17 (1903) pp. 83ff.

Kirchner 1937   Kirchner, J. 'Attische Grabstelen des Dritten und Zweiten Jahrhunderts v. Chr.', *AE* 1937, pp. 338ff.

Kirchner 1939   Kirchner, J. 'Das Gestetz des Demetrios von Phaleron zur Einschränkung des Gräberluxus,' *Die Antike* 15 (1939), pp. 93ff.

Knigge and Willemsen 1964   Knigge, U., and Willemsen, F., 'Zwei spätarchaische Schachtgräber', *AD* 19 Chron. B1 (1964), p. 44.

Knight 1970   Knight, W.J. *Elysion: on Ancient Greek and Roman Beliefs concerning a Life after Death*. London 1970.

Kohler 1876   Kohler, U. 'Ein griechisches Gesetz über Todtenbestattung', *AM* 1 (1876), pp. 139ff.

Kokula 1974   Kokula, G. *Marmorlutrophoren*. Berlin 1974.

KR   Kirk, G.S., and Raven, J.E. *The Presocratic Philosophers*. Cambridge 1957.

Kramer 1960   Kramer S. 'Death and Nether World according to Sumerian Literary Texts', *Iraq* 22 (1960), pp. 59ff.

Kramer 1963   Kramer, S. 'Sumerian Literature and the Literature of the Ancient World', *PAPS* 107 (1963), pp. 485ff.

Kübler 1949   Kübler, K. 'Der attische Grabbau' *MdI* 2 (1949), pp. 7ff.

La Fontaine 1960   La Fontaine, J. 'Homicide and Suicide among the Gisu', pp. 94ff. in Bohannan, 1960.

Lanza 1980   Lanza, D. 'La morte esclusa', *Quaderni di Storia* 11 (1980), pp. 157ff.

Lasch 1900   Lasch. 'Die Verbliebsorte der abgeschiedenen Seele der Selbstmörder', *Globus* 77 (1900), pp. 110ff.

Leaf 1902   Leaf, W. 'Homeric Burial Rites', pp. 618ff. in *A Commentary on the Iliad*. 2nd ed. London 1902.

Lecrivain in *DS*   Lecrivain, C. S.v. 'Funus'.

Levi 1971   Levi, P. *Pausanias' Guide to Greece*. Vol. 1 Harmondsworth 1971.

LGS   Prott, J. de, and Ziehen, L. *Leges Graecorum Sacrae*. Leipzig 1896.

Lobeck 1829   Lobeck, C.A. *Agloaphamus*. Koenigsberg 1829.

Long 1974   Long, C.R. *The Ayia Triadha Sarcophagus*. Göteborg 1974.

LSA   Sokolowski, F. *Lois sacrées de l'Asie Mineure*. Paris 1955.

LSG   Sokolowski, F. *Lois sacrées des cités grecques*. Paris 1969.

LSS Sokolowski, F. *Lois sacrées des cités grecques. Supplement.* Paris 1962.

Lucas 1969 Lucas, D. '*Epispendein nekrôi: Agamemnon* 1393-8', *PCPhS* 15 (1969), pp. 60ff.

MacDowell 1978 MacDowell, D.M. *The Law in Classical Athens.* London 1978.

Malinowski 1908 Malinowski, B. 'Suicide: a Chapter in Comparative Ethics', *Sociological Review* 1 (1908), pp. 14ff.

Macfarlane 1982 Macfarlane, A. 'Death and the demographic transition' in Humphreys 1982.

Macleod 1982 Macleod, C. *Iliad Book XXIV.* Cambridge 1982.

Malten in *PW* Malten, L. S.v. 'Ker'.

MAMA Monumenta Asiae Minoris Antiquae.

Mawet 1975 Mawet, Fr. 'Epigrammes, thrènes et dithyrambes: les lamentations funèbres de l'épopée', pp. 33ff. in *Le monde grec: hommages à Claire Preaux.* Brussels 1975.

Meier and Schömann 1887 Meier, M.H.E., and Schömann, G.F. *Der attische Process.* Revised by J.H. Lipsius. 2 vols. Berlin 1887.

Meuli 1946 Meuli, K. 'Griechische Opferbraüche' in *Phyllobolia für P. von der Mühll.* Basel 1946.

Milchhöfer 1880 Milchhöfer, A. 'Gemahlte Grabstelen', *AM* 5 (1880), pp. 164ff.

ML Roscher, W.H. *Ausführliches Lexicon der griechischen und römischen Mythologie.* 6 vols. Leipzig 1884-1937.

Moulinier 1952 Moulinier, L. *Le pur et l'impur dans la pensée des Grecs d'Homère à Aristotle.* Paris 1952.

Müller-Karpe 1962 Müller-Karpe, H. 'Metallbeigaben der Kerameikos Gräber', *JdI* 77 (1962), pp. 59ff.

Murray and Smith 1896 Murray, A.S., and Smith, A.H. *White Athenian Vases in the British Museum.* London 1896.

Mylonas 1880 Mylonas, K.D. '*Symmikta archaeologika*' *BCH* 4 (1880), pp. 371ff.

Mylonas 1948 Mylonas, G.E. 'Homeric and Mycenaean Burial Customs', *AJA* 52 (1948), pp. 56ff.

Mylonas 1951 Mylonas, G.E. 'The Cult of the Dead in Helladic Times', pp. 64ff. in *Studies Presented to D.M. Robinson.* Vol. 1. USA 1951.

Mylonas 1962 Mylonas, G.E. *Eleusis and the Eleusinian Mysteries.* Princeton 1962.

Mylonas 1963 Mylonas, G.E. 'Burial Customs', pp. 478ff. in *A Companion to Homer.* Ed. by A. Wace and F. Stubbings. London and New York 1963.

Neumann 1965 Neuman, G. *Gesten und Gebärden in der griechischen Kunst.* Berlin 1965.

Nilsson 1908 Nilsson, M.P. 'Das Ei im Totenkult der Alten', *Archiv. f. Religionswissenschaft* 11 (1908), pp. 530ff.

Nilsson 1925 Nilsson, M.P. *A History of Greek Religion.* Oxford 1925.

Nilsson 1927 Nilsson, M.P. *The Minoan-Mycenaean Religion and its Survival in Greek Religion.* 2nd ed. Lund 1950.

Nock 1932 Nock, A.D. 'Cremation and Burial in the Roman Empire', *HTR* 25 (1932), pp. 321ff.

Nock 1944 Nock, A.D. 'The Cult of Heroes', *HTR* 37 (1944), pp. 141ff.

Norwood 1931 Norwood, G. *Greek Comedy.* London 1931.

OCT Oxford Classical Text.

Oliver 1950 Oliver, J.H. *The Athenian Expounders of the Sacred and Ancestral Law.* Baltimore 1950.

Orsi 1906 Orsi, P. 'Gela. Scavi del 1900-1905', *Mon. Ant.* 17 (1906).

Page 1941   Page, D.L. *Select Papyri*, vol. 3 (Loeb Classical Library). London and Cambridge, Mass. 1950.

Page 1959   Page, D.L. *History and the Homeric Iliad*. Berkeley and Los Angeles 1959.

Paribeni 1938   Paribeni, E. 'I Rilievi Chiusini arcaici', *SE* 12 (1938), pp. 57ff.

Pease 1935   Pease, A. *Virgil Aeneid Book IV*. Cambridge, Mass. 1935.

Peek 1955   Peek, W. *Griechische Vers-Inschriften*. Berlin 1955.

Peek 1960   Peek, W. *Griechische Grabgedichte*. Berlin 1960.

Petzl 1969   Petzl, G. *Antike Diskussionen über die beiden Nekyiai Beiträge zur klassischen Philologie*: Heft 29. Meisenheim am Glam 1969.

Pfeiffer 1949-1953   Pfeiffer, R. *Callimachus*. 2 vols. Oxford 1949-1953.

Pfohl 1967   Pfohl, G. *Greek Poems on Stones. Epitaphs from the Seventh to the Fifth Centuries BC. (Textus Minores 36)*. Leiden 1967.

Pfühl and Möbius 1977   Pfühl, E., and Möbius, H. *Die ostgriechischen Grabreliefs*. Mainz 1977.

Pfühl 1905   Pfühl, E. 'Das Beiwerk auf den ostgriechischen Grabreliefs', *JDAI* 20 (1905), pp. 47ff.

Plath 1964   Plath D.W. 'Where the Family of God is the Family: the Role of the Dead in Japanese Households', *American Anthropologist* (N.S.) 67.7 (April 1964), pp. 300ff.

PMG   Page, D.L. *Poetae Melici Graeci*. Oxford 1962.

Popham, Touloupa and Sackett 1982   Popham, M., Touloupa, E., and Sackett, L.H., 'The Hero of Lefkandi' in *Antiquity* vol. 56 no. 218 (Nov. 1982).

Pottier 1883   Pottier, E. *Etude sur les lékythes blancs attiques à répresentations funéraires*. Paris 1883.

Poulson 1905   Poulson, F. *Die Dipylongräber und die Dipylonvasen*. Leipzig 1905.

Preisendanz in *PW*   Preisendanz, K. S.v. 'Nekydaimon'.

PW   Pauly, A., and Wissowa,. G. *Real-Encyclopaedie der classischen Altertums-Wissenschaft*. Stuttgart 1922-.

Raingeard 1935   Raingeard, P. *Hermès Psychagogue. Essai sur les origines du culte d'Hermès*. Paris 1935.

Rayet 1884   Rayet, O. *Monuments de l'art antique*. 2 vols. Paris 1884.

Reiner 1938   Reiner, E. *Die rituelle Totenklage der Griechen*. Tübingen 1938.

Richardson 1974   Richardson, N.J. *The Homeric Hymn to Demeter*. Oxford 1974.

Richter 1945   Richter, G.M.A. 'Peisistratos' Law regarding Tombs', *AJA* 49 (1945), p. 152.

Richter 1961   Richter, G.M.A. *The Archaic Gravestones of Attica*. London 1961.

Richter and Hall 1936   Richter, G.M.A., and Hall, L.F. *Red-Figured Athenian Vases in the Metropolitan Museum*.2 vols. New Haven 1936.

Rivza 1979   Rivza, G. 'Tombes de chevaux', pp. 294-97 in *Acts of the International Archaeological Symposium*: 'The Relations between Cyprus and Crete, c. 2000-500 B.C.'. Nicosia 1979.

Robert 1879   Robert, C. *Thanatos*. Berlin 1879.

Robinson 1942   Robinson, D.M. *Olynthus, vol. XI: Necrolynthia*. Baltimore 1942.

Rohde 1897   Rohde, E. *Psyche: the Cult of Souls and Belief in Immortality among the Greeks*. Trans. W. Hillis. 8th ed. London 1925.

Rose 1948   Rose, H. 'Keres and Lemures', *HTR* 41 (1948), pp. 217ff.

Rossiter 1977   Rossiter, L. *The Blue Guide to Greece*. 3rd ed. London 1977.

Rostovtzeff 1938-9   Rostovtzeff, M. *The Mentality of the Hellenistic World and the After-life*. (Harv. Div. School Bull. 1938-39). Cambridge, Mass. 1939.

Bibliography 181

Roux 1967 Roux, G. 'Les grimaces de Cleisthène', *REG* 80 (1967), pp. 165ff.

Rudhardt 1958 Rudhardt, J. *Notions fondamentales de la pensée religieuse et actes constitutifs du culte dans la Grèce classique.* Geneva 1958.

Rudhardt 1963 Rudhardt, J. 'Sur quelques bûchers d'enfants découverts dans la ville d'Athènes', *MH* 20 (1963), pp. 10ff.

Rüsche 1930 Rüsche, F. *Blut, Leben und Seele.* Paderborn 1930.

von Salis 1957 von Salis, A. 'Antiker Bestattungsbrauch', *MH* 14 (1957), pp. 89ff.

Scharff 1947 Scharff, A. *Das Grab als Wohnhaus in der ägyptischen Frühzeit.* München 1947.

Scherling in *PW* Scherling. *S.v.* 'Tartaros'.

Schliemann 1978 Schliemann, H. *Mycenae: a Narrative of Researches and Discoveries at Mycenae and Tiryns.* London 1878.

Schlörb-Vierneisel 1966 Schlörb-Vierneisel, B. 'Eridanos-Nekropole', *AM* 81 (1966), pp. 4ff.

Schmidt and Trendall 1976 Schmidt, M., and Trendall, A.D. *Eine Gruppe apulischer Grabvasen im Basel.* Basel 1976.

Schnaufer 1970 Schnaufer, A. *Frühgriechischer Totenglaube.* (Spudasmata XX). Hildesheim and New York 1970.

Schuppe in *PW* Schuppe. *S.v.* 'Taenia'.

Schwyzer 1939-50 Schwyzer, E. *Griechische Grammatik.* München 1939-50.

Segal 1971 Segal, C. 'The Theme of the Mutilation of the Corpse', *Mnemosyne Supplement* 17. Leiden 1971.

*SIG*³ Dittenberger, W. *Sylloge Inscriptionum Graecarum.* 4 vols. 3rd. Leipzig 1915-24.

Smith 1898 Smith, A.H. 'Illustrations to Bacchylides', *JHS* 18 (1898), pp. 267ff.

Smith 1896 Smith, C.H. *Catalogue of the Greek and Etruscan Vases in the British Museum.* Vol. 3. London 1896.

Snodgrass 1967 Snodgrass, A.M. *Arms and Armour of the Greeks.* London and Southampton 1967.

Snodgrass 1970 Snodgrass, A.M. Review of Andronikos' *Totenkult* in *Gnomon* 42 (1970), pp. 163ff.

Solmsen 1909 Solmsen, F. *Untersuchungen zur griechischen Laut -und Verslehre.* Strasbourg 1909.

Stais 1895 Stais, V. '*Proistorikoi synoikismoi en Attikê kai Aiginê,*' *AE* 1895, pp. 192ff.

Stais 1910 Stais, V. *Marbres et bronzes du Musée national.* 2nd ed. Athens 1910.

Stanford 1958 Stanford, W.B. *Aristophanes: The Frogs.* London 1958.

Stengel 1880 Stengel, P. 'Totenspenden', *Philologus* 39 (1880), pp. 378ff.

Stengel 1910 Stengel, P. *Opferbräuche der Griechen.* Leipzig and Berlin 1910.

Stephani 1854 Stephani, L. *Der ausruhende Herakles.* Mem. de l'Acad. de St. Petersb., 6, Ser. 8.

Stone 1977 Stone, L. *The Family, Sex and Marriage in England 1500-1800.* Harmondsworth 1977.

Stupperich 1977 Stupperich, R. *Staatbegräbnis und Privatgrabmal im klassischen Athen.* Diss. Münster 1977.

T Teubner edition (Leipzig).

Tab. Defix. Audollent, A. *Defixionum Tabellae.* Frankfurt 1904.

Tainter 1975 Tainter, J.A. 'Social Inference and Mortuary Practices: an Experiment in Numerical Classification', *World Archaeology* 7 no. 1 (1975) pp. 1ff

TGF Nauck, A. *Tragicorum Graec. Fragmenta.* Suppl. B. Snell. 2 vols. Hildesheim 1964.

TGLE   Lattimore, R. *Themes in Greek and Latin Epitaphs.* Illinois 1942.
Thönges-Stringaris 1965   Thönges-Stringaris, R.N. 'Das griechische Totenmahl', AM 80 (1965), 1ff.
Toynbee 1968   Toynbee, A. *Man's Concern with Death.* London 1968.
Travlos 1971   Travlos, J. *A Pictorial History of Athens.* London 1971.
Travlos and Vermeule 1966   Travlos, J. and Vermeule, E.T. 'Mycenaean Tomb beneath the Middle Stoa', *Hesperia* 35 (1966) pp. 55ff.
Tucker 1901   Tucker, T.G. *Aeschylus' Choephori.* Cambridge 1901.
Twele 1975   Twele, J. 'Columellam … aut mensam aut labellum. Archaeological Remarks on Cicero's De legibus 2.66', *The J. Paul Getty MJ* 2 (1975), pp. 93ff.
Tylor 1871   Tylor, E.B. *Primitive Culture: Researches into the Development of Mythology, Philosophy, Religion, Art and Custom.* 2 vols. London 1871.
Ucko 1969   Ucko, P.J. 'Ethnography and Archaeological Interpretation of Funerary Remains', *World Archaeology,* vol. 1 no. 2 (1969), pp. 262ff.
Ussher 1973   Ussher, R.G. *Aristophanes' Eccleziazusae.* Oxford 1973.
Vernant 1974   Vernant, J.-P. *Mythe et société en Grèce ancienne.* Paris 1974.
Vermeule 1979   Vermeule, E. *Aspects of Death in Early Greek Art and Poetry.* Berkeley and London 1979.
Verrall 1893   Verrall, A.W. *The 'Choephori' of Aeschylus.* London and New York 1893.
Wace 1932   Wace, A.J.B. *Chamber Tombs at Mycenae.* Oxford 1932.
Wackernagel 1953   Wackernagel, J. *Kleine Schriften.* 2 vols. Göttingen 1953.
WAL   Riezler, W. *Weissgrundige attische Lekythen.* München 1914.
Weber 1935   Weber, L. *Solon und die Schöpfung der attische Grabrede.* Frankfurt 1935.
Welles 1941   Welles, C.B. 'The Epitaph of Julius Terentius', *HTR* 34 (1941), pp. 79ff.
West 1966   West, M.L. *Hesiod's Theogony.* Oxford 1966.
West 1968   West, M.L.'Two Notes on Delphic Inscriptions', *ZPE* 2 (1968), p. 176.
West 1978   West, M.L. *Hesiod's Works and Days.* Oxford 1978.
Willetts 1967   Willetts, R.F. *The Law Code of Gortyn.* Berlin 1967.
Wright 1886   Wright, J.H. 'Unpublished White Lêkythoi from Attica', *AJA* 2 (1886), pp. 385ff.
Wyse 1904   Wyse, W. *The Speeches of Isaeus.* Cambridge 1904.
Young 1951   Young, R.S. 'Sepulturae intra urbem', *Hesperia* 20 (1951), pp. 67ff.
Zinserling 1965   Zinserling, V. 'Das attische Grabluxusgesetz des frühen 5. Jahrhunderts' in *Wissenschaftliche Zeitschrift der Friedrich-Schiller-Universität Jena, Gesellschafts- und Sprachwissenschaftliche Reihe,* Heft I, Jahrgang 14 (1965), pp. 29ff.
Zschietzschmann 1928   Zschietzschmann, W. 'Die Darstellungen der Prothesis in der griechischen Kunst', *AM* 53 (1928), pp. 17ff.
Zuntz 1971   Zuntz, G. *Persephone.* Oxford 1971.

General index

Absyrtos, 94
Acheron, 49, 51, 55, 72
Acherusian Lake, 50
Achilles, 1, 3, 20f., 26, 29, 34f., 68, 92, 96, 103, 114
Achilles Painter, 108, 116, 166
Adamastos, 52
Adkins, A., 62
Admetos, 8, 14, 67
Aegean islands, 55, 108
Aelian, 102
Aegina, 12, 68
Aeschylus, 24, 51f., 55, 64, 66, 92, 94, 114, 116
Aetolia, 70
Agamemnon, 1, 3, 6, 8, 60, 68, 74
agathoi andres, 92, 163
agôn epitaphios, See Funeral Games
agos, 46, 110
Ahlberg, G., 29
Aiakos, 66
Aides, See Hades
aisa, 84
Aischines, 98, 102
aithêr, 49, 64, 75, 159
Ajax, 1, 4, 8, 14, 16, 53, 55, 59, 74, 92, 96f., 102, 123
alabastra, 36, 68
Alexiou, M., xii
Alkestis, 8, 14, 16, 19, 47, 58, 67, 78, 96, 101
ameilichos, 52
Ampharete, *stêlê* of, fig. 13, 68, 84
Amphiareos, 74
amphidromiai, 81f.
amphorai, fig. 6, 28f., 33, 35f., 51, 54, 78, 144
Anakreon, 72
Anaximenes Rhetor, 90
Andokides Painter, 54
angry dead, 94, 163
anger of survivors, 30, 142f.
anepsiadai, 42
animal remains, 36, 84, 145. See also Horse-burials
annual rites, 104f., 166
Anthesteria, 6, 44, 82, 148
Antigone, 7, 36, 46, 48, 53, 72, 123
Antiphon, 94
aôroi, 77ff., 160
aparchai, 113

Aphrodite, 34
Apollo, 19, 34, 44f., 53f., 58
aponimma, 43, 147
apotaphoi, 103, 165f.
ardanion, 43
Argos, 70
Ariès, P., 17, 19, 118
Aristinos, 101
Aristophanes, 2, 8, 22f., 26, 49f., 56, 62, 75, 113
Aristotle, 10, 18, 81, 98, 113
armour, burial in, 25, 139
Artemidoros, 24, 39, 99, 110
Artemis, 18, 44, 59
Asia Minor, 70, 108
Asklepios, 14
aspondos, 59, 169
ataphoi, See Unburied dead
atasthaliai, 60
Athenaios, 43, 115
Athene, 97
Atossa, 2, 74
auansis, 19
auloi, See Flute-players
autocheires, 96. See also Suicide
Ayia Triada sarcophagus, 112, 114, 168

banquets, funerary, See Death-feast reliefs and *Perideipna*
barathron, 95, 98, 163
barbarian dead, 74
baskets, 108, 116, 166f.
bathing, See Washing
beauties of Hades, 50, 151
beehive burial, 78, fig. 17
beneficent dead, 4
biaiothanatoi, 96. See also Suicide
biers, 24, 26, 28f., 31f., 139
bier-cloths, 24ff., 32, 139
Binford, L., 119
birds, 26, 32, 36, 86, 140, 145
biological theories of death, 18f., 136
blaspheming the dead (forbidden), 8
blessed dead, 8ff., 134
Blest, Isles of the, 61, 63, 156
blood sacrifices, 3f., 33, 36, 112ff., 168
Boardman, J., xii, 27f., 92
Boeotia, 6, 10, 70
Bolkestein, H., 80

Index locorum

(The last number in each case is the page reference in this book)

El. 841, 74
OC 1372ff., 88f.
OC 1389, 51
OC 1548, 55
OC 1586ff., 14
OT 1371ff., 67
Trach. 1040ff., 18
Fr. 753 *TGF*, 61

Strabo
Geog. 10.5.6, 99

Thukydides
2.34, 89f.
2.52, 102
3.104.2, 45
3.58.4, 113

Tyrtaios
Fr. 10 *IEG*, 77

Valerius Maximus
2.6.8, 99

Xenophon
Hell. 1.7.22, 95